Education

State Education for the People in America, Europe, India and Australia

Education

State Education for the People in America, Europe, India and Australia

ISBN/EAN: 9783337314750

Printed in Europe, USA, Canada, Australia, Japan

Cover: Foto ©Andreas Hilbeck / pixelio.de

More available books at **www.hansebooks.com**

STATE EDUCATION

FOR THE PEOPLE

IN

America, Europe, India, and Australia

WITH PAPERS ON

The Education of Women, Technical Instruction, and Payment by Results

SYRACUSE, N. Y.
C. W. BARDEEN, PUBLISHER
1895

Copyright, 1895, by C. W. BARDEEN

CONTENTS

	PAGE
INTRODUCTORY	vii

PART
I.—ANCIENT CIVILISATION AND MODERN EDUCATION—
INDIA. By SIR WILLIAM WILSON HUNTER, K.C.S.I., &c.,
President of the Indian Education Commission . 1

II.—ELEMENTARY EDUCATION IN ENGLAND. By EDWARD M.
HANCE, LL.B., Clerk to the Liverpool School Board 25

III.—STATE EDUCATION IN SCOTLAND . 44

IV.—NATIONAL EDUCATION IN IRELAND 56

V.—THE ENGLISH AND CONTINENTAL SYSTEMS OF ELE-
MENTARY EDUCATION COMPARED . . 74

VI.—WESTERN STATE EDUCATION—THE UNITED STATES
AND ENGLISH SYSTEMS COMPARED. By the Rev. E.
F. M. MACCARTHY, M.A., Head Master of King Edward's Grammar School, Five Ways, Birmingham, and Vice-Chairman of
the Birmingham School Board . . . 82

VII.—NOTES ON EDUCATION IN CANADA AND AUSTRALIA.
SAME AUTHOR . . 105

VIII.—NOTE ON COMMERCIAL EDUCATION . . 112

IX.—THE EDUCATION AND STATUS OF WOMEN. By Mrs.
EMILY CRAWFORD 116

X.—TECHNICAL INSTRUCTION; AND PAYMENT ON RE-
SULTS. By SIR PHILIP MAGNUS . . . 133

XI.—NEW CODE FOR 1890 . . . 146

XII.—EDITORIAL SUMMARY AND CONCLUSION . 155

BIBLIOGRAPHY 163

INDEX 171

STATE EDUCATION FOR THE PEOPLE.

INTRODUCTORY.

No doubt many persons who open these pages will be surprised to find that the first subject of which they treat, is one of the most dry and hackneyed that could have been selected, but a moment's reflection will show that it possesses the most widespread interest, and is of universal application. In its modern forms the question of Education enters into every phase of human intelligence, and into all the conditions of man's welfare and prosperity. It nearly affects religion, war, material industries and commerce, abstract science, and every form and aspect of civilised life.

Theologians are wrangling over " secular " or " denominational," " free " or " assisted " education; military authorities abroad and at home are trying to make every man in the ranks into a General, or at least to teach him to comprehend and use all the improved arms and methods by which he is to accomplish the destruction of his fellow-men; capitalists and artisans are watching with anxiety, and sometimes with jealousy and apprehension, that " technical " instruction which is to revolutionize their industries, and perhaps change their relative spheres of influence; young men of one nationality, aided by superior commercial and linguistic training, and by the modern facilities for locomotion, are pressing hard upon the less highly favoured youths and men of other lands, and are slowly but surely supplanting them in their privileged position. The children of artisans and retail traders, in increasing numbers, are joining the ranks of teachers, investigators, and inventors; even man's helpmate, Woman, is entering the field as a rival of her lord and master, whilst whole peoples who are emerging from barbarism, or beginning to realise the gloom of idolatry and superstition, and more particularly those nations which are tasting the first-fruits of political freedom, are turning their faces towards the light of Western Education for mental guidance and material advancement.

But the vastness and universal application of the subject chosen renders its treatment the more difficult, and all that it will be feasible to attempt here, is to sketch as accurately as possible, though necessarily in a superficial manner, certain representative methods of education as they are practised in different civilised countries.

There is one matter, however, which needs explanation, and that is the overlapping of some of the articles which is the necessary concomitant of their being the productions of several original thinkers writing on closely related subjects. The reader may feel that he has cause to complain of the repetition of facts and opinions, which would not have occurred if the component parts of the work had been the products of a single pen; but it must be borne in mind that this defect is more than counterbalanced by the free play which the independent articles have afforded to the thoughts and utterances of the different writers, and one of the consequences of this latitude will be to make it clear on what phases of the question there is a general concurrence of opinion, and to which, therefore, it is desirable that the reader should direct his special attention.

We propose first to treat of the influence exerted by Western education upon the destiny of nations still living under ancient forms of civilisation, and as a typical illustration we have selected our own great Eastern Dependency, India. Next, we shall deal with the subject as it presents itself in the educational systems of the United Kingdom, and shall then glance at and compare it with those of Continental States, and with the great Republic across the Atlantic. In connection with the latter we believe the reader will find many new and interesting facts not generally known to Englishmen. Two or three subsidiary phases of the question will then be examined, commercial, technical, and female education, and if the forthcoming Education Code has been introduced into Parliament and has assumed a sufficiently definite form, an account of its main features will be appended, and some general conclusions on the whole subject will be summarised for the guidance of our readers. We dare not presume to hope that the opinions expressed in our concluding remarks will meet with general acceptance, for prejudices, habits of thought, and the diversity of economical considerations naturally influence the judgment of readers upon a question so warmly and widely debated as this one; but we have endeavoured to deal with the subject from the broadest and most impartial point of view, and whatever differences of opinion may exist we have no doubt the credit will be conceded to us of wishing to further the cause of Education, and of desiring to facilitate the formation of a correct judgment upon one of the most important questions of this or any other age.

PART I.
ANCIENT CIVILISATION & MODERN EDUCATION.

INDIA.

IN this article I shall endeavour to set forth the effects of a strongly-constructed and vigorously-enforced system of Western instruction upon an Asiatic population. The experiment has been conducted in India over so large an area, an area about equal to Europe less Russia; it has been applied to so many races, geographically neighbours, yet presenting widely-separated stages of human progress; and its action has been noted with such continuity and care, that it affords a unique opportunity for a scientific study of the intellectual, social, and political results. If an accurate record existed of any similar experiment throughout the Roman Empire—although the people who obeyed that Empire did not number one-half the population of the Indian Continent—what a flood of light it would shed on man's history during the transition centuries, when the old world was passing into the new.

India is now going through a quicker and more striking metamorphosis. We sometimes hear its marvellous awakening compared to the renaissance of Europe four hundred years ago. But in India the change is not only taking place on a greater scale; it also goes deeper. It derives its motive power, moreover, not from the individual impulse of isolated men of genius or of cultured popes and princes, but from the mighty centralising force of a Government which, as an engine of human unification, has had nothing to compare with it since the days of Imperial Rome. English Rule in India is, however, calmly carrying out processes of consolidation that never entered the brain of Roman statesman or emperor. While maintaining a policy of cold non-interference towards the rival religions, the domestic institutions, and the local usages of the Indian peoples, it is silently undermining these ancient separatist influences which made for the isolation of races. It has created a new nexus for the active intellectual elements in the population: a nexus which is beginning to be recognised as a bond between man and man and between province and province, apart from the ties of religion, of geographical propinquity, or of caste: a nexus interwoven of three strong cords, a common language, common political aims, and a sense of the power of action in common—the products of a common system of education.

This process of consolidation has, indeed, become so apparent, even to passers-by, that the present danger is rather to over-estimate the extent to which the change has taken place, than to overlook it. Hasty observers frequently fail to allow sufficient weight to two considerations. First, the immense mass that has to be permeated before the whole can be leavened; and second, the constraining influences which have moulded, and are at this moment still further moulding, the exotic system of education into indigenous forms. While, therefore, I endeavour to clearly state the effects of Western instruction systematically applied to the Indian population, I shall not underrate either the inertia of the solid millions with whom it finds itself in impact, or the reacting forces of native customs, native religions, and native modes of life.

The tendency of some writers to underrate these reacting influences operates in a manner which they had not foreseen. The unquestionable progress of India during the past third of a century has been so rapid, as to excite the fears of many sober-minded Englishmen who wish well to the Indian peoples. It seems to such observers that forces have been set in motion in India which are working in a one-sided direction, and without the modifying or controlling influences which in Europe have been found needful to guide these forces to safe results. They therefore look with doubt or suspicion upon the present action of those forces in India, and especially upon their political developments. Exaggeration begets exaggeration, and while the more enthusiastic friends of India over-estimate the actual progress, by underrating the counteracting influences; their English critics over-estimate the dangers of that progress from precisely the same cause.

In place of these opposite and equally one-sided views, I shall endeavour to place before the reader an impartial presentment of the whole of the influences really at work. He will perceive that progress in India is the result, not of any single and overwhelming movement, but of a correlation of forces, whose complexity and variety contain the elements of check and countercheck necessary to the safe and steady advance of races. He will find, in every department of Indian activity, not only the inertia of vast masses, but also the conservative opposition of organised interests and classes. While, therefore, the State system of education started as a foreign system, consciously introduced from without, it has been profoundly modified from the first, and is being still more profoundly modified at the present day by Native requirements, Native conceptions, and the usages of the Native family life. And although the progress of India, under the influence of that system of education, has been rapid beyond precedent, it has been accomplished subject to the free action and reaction of powerful opposing interests, and in the presence of a perpetual inertia which takes the form of deliberate slowness in Indian social reforms, of caution in industrial development, of conservatism in political ideas.

In order to understand the complex forces now at work in India, it will be needful first to summarise the main stages in the construction of the chief engine of modern Indian progress—State Education. Western education in India, as a coherent organised system spread over the whole country, may be taken to date from Sir Stafford Northcote's Despatch of 1854. That Despatch, however, only reared the edifice for which the foundations had been already laid. The encouragement of education has from time immemorial formed one of the recognised functions of government in India. Under the Brahman system this function took the form of royal liberality to high-caste men of learning. The Buddhist reformation placed both education and religion on a more popular basis. The Chinese traveller in the seventh century A.D. found the Buddhist monasteries still at work, and discharging many of the duties of a system of public instruction. After the Muhammadan conquest of India, the Mosques became the centres of educational activity, and were supported by imperial or local grants of land.

The East India Company, in the last century, succeeded to the educational as to the other functions of the Native governments. It maintained existing educational endowments, and in 1781 Warren Hastings established the Calcutta Madrasa, or great Muhammadan college in Bengal. Ten years later the British Government founded and endowed the Sanskrit College at Benares for Hindu philosophy and law. The Permanent Settlement of 1793 recognised in perpetuity the free grants of land enjoyed by the old Hindu and Muhammadan seats of learning scattered throughout the British dominions. Down to 1811 the Court of Directors entertained proposals for the establishment of further institutions on the strictly ancient lines. But the Charter of 1813 gave a new direction to the educational activity of the British Government of India. Hitherto its efforts had been directed to the reproduction of the traditional models bequeathed by the Native rulers. It held that it discharged its duty if it provided the Hindu community with colleges for the study of the Sastras, and the Muhammadans with schools for the study of the Kurán.

Meanwhile the wishes of the Native communities had outstripped the programme of the Government. They were no longer content with the curriculum of their traditional lore, whether Sanskrit or Arabic. They desired that their children should eat of the fruit of the tree of Western knowledge, and learn the English tongue. The Charter of 1813 gave an impulse to these new ambitions by providing that a sum of Rs. 100,000 should be annually expended on education from the Public Revenues. But it was not until ten years later that the Indian Government, under pressure of Parliamentary enquiries, missionary bodies and non-official school-societies, organised measures for giving effect to this provision of the Charter.

For meanwhile non-official agencies of education were springing up in India, and were making their influence felt upon the Government. As far back as 1790 the Society for the Promotion of Christian Knowledge opened a school for Natives in Southern India, a school which still flourishes as St. Peter's College at Tanjore. In the Western Presidency, the Bombay Education Society, supported by voluntary contributions, undertook in 1815 the education of the poor in the Presidency-town and adjoining districts. In Bengal, certain wealthy native citizens of Calcutta, in 1817, opened the Hindu College for the education in English of children of the higher castes. The School Book Society, established in the same year, undertook the preparation of class-books in English and the vernaculars. In 1819, a more ambitious project was started by the Calcutta School Society for establishing schools, both English and vernacular, throughout the country. At length, in 1823, the Indian Government, under the influence of these and other educational movements among the non-official community, organised in Calcutta a Committee of Public Instruction, composed of eminent officials, for the diffusion and control of education.

In this Committee, as indeed throughout India at that time, two educational parties were strongly represented. One party adhered to the ancient lines laid down by the Native Governments and desired that Sanskrit and Arabic learning should form the staples of higher education. The other party believed that the time for that old-world learning had gone by, and that the object of State Education under British rule should be to impart Western knowledge in the English tongue. The more intelligent classes of the Natives took the latter view. The Government officials, true to the traditional models handed down from the Mughal Empire, clung to the former. In 1824 the Committee of Public Instruction founded the Sanskrit College in Calcutta, notwithstanding a powerfully signed memorial of the leading natives, headed by Raja Rammohan Roy, who begged that the institution might be for English and not for Sanskrit teaching. This view gradually spread throughout the intelligent sections of the native community, and at last enabled it to force the hand of Government. The Natives were aided by the missionary bodies and non-official school societies, and before the Committee of Public Instruction had been at work for twelve years, the native view of the extreme importance of English teaching had prevailed. Macaulay's famous Minute in 1835 merely put an end to the deadlock to which the obstinacy of certain of the officials in the Committee had given rise. But before Macaulay set foot in India native opinion had declared so strongly for English teaching, in place of the old traditional learning, that Macaulay's eloquent Minute merely played the part of the shout at which the walls of Jericho fell. The memorial of the Native community in Calcutta in favour of an English rather than a Sanskrit College in 1823 had at length borne its fruits; and it is important to observe that, from the very commencement, State Education in India has been powerfully, although at first slowly, influenced by Native views and Native wishes. From the first, too, there had been a powerful conservative party among the Indians themselves who clung to their traditional past, and a growing party of progress who looked forward to the British future.

The decision, in 1835, in favour of English Teaching, as the medium of Public Instruction in India, was, however, a decision arrived at on a false issue. The true alternative was not as between the classical languages of India, and English, but as between English, the Indian classical languages, and the Indian vernaculars.

RESULTS IN INDIA. 5

This had become apparent to the native leaders and to the missionaries, even before 1835. About that year Mr. Adam drew up his admirable report upon the indigenous village schools of Bengal, and four years later the Governor-General reconsidered and expanded the decision of 1835 upon the broader lines indicated by Mr. Adams' report. In 1839, Lord Auckland laid down the three principles which have since regulated State Education in India. First, that existing institutions for the study of the classical Indian languages and ancient literature of India should be kept up in full efficiency. Second, that English-teaching institutions should be established for education in European literature, philosophy, and science, with English as the medium of instruction. Third, that in the lower schools, the vernaculars of India should be combined with English, and that provision should be made for teaching in both.

On the basis thus laid down in 1839, considerable progress was made during the next fifteen years. But it gradually became apparent that even this broader basis was not a sufficiently solid one for the effective education of India. A necessity for penetrating still deeper made itself felt, and enlightened men in India determined to go to the root of the matter by taking the vernacular schools as the foundation of Public Instruction. Among the foremost of such men, Mr. Thomason will ever be honourably remembered. Lord Dalhousie was so impressed with the useful work done by his vernacular schools in the North-Western Provinces, that, about the year 1852, he urged their extension upon the Home Government. Two years later Sir Stafford Northcote responded by his great Despatch; and the Court of Directors, deliberately accepting education as a State duty in India, laid down with fulness and precision the principles which were to guide the Indian Government in the performance of this task. The Despatch of 1854 still forms the Charter of Education in India. It was reaffirmed in 1859 by the Secretary of State shortly after India had passed to the Crown; and it formed the ground-work of the subsequent developments effected by the Indian Education Commission in 1883.

This Despatch constituted a separate Department of Public Instruction in every province of India. It articulated a regular gradation of institutions, starting from the vernacular schools, and passing through the Anglo-vernacular schools, upwards to the colleges and the universities. At the lower end, it enforced the necessity of increased attention to vernacular teaching as the basis of elementary education. At the upper end it provided for the establishment of universities as the cope-stone of the whole system. The English language was fixed once and for ever as the medium of instruction in the higher branches, and the Indian vernaculars in the lower. English was to be taught wherever there was a demand for it, but it was not to be substituted for the vernaculars in the elementary instruction of the people. While existing institutions for the study of the classical languages of India were to be maintained, an effective machinery was created for bringing useful and practical knowledge within the reach of the masses, by means of a great network of vernacular schools. English became definitely the medium of higher instruction, and the language of the future for the more highly educated sections of the populations.

To Lord Dalhousie belongs the double honour of having urged the importance of vernacular teaching, and of introducing the modern Department of Public Instruction in 1854, which finally accepted vernacular teaching as the basis of State Education in India. The great Pro-Consul regarded the new system with as much pride and enthusiasm as if it had been altogether his own creation. His only fear was that its scope was so extensive that it would be difficult for a time to give it full effect. This anticipation proved correct. The more conspicuous features of the edifice were promptly constructed, and even the Mutiny year, 1857, saw the Acts pass through the Indian Legislature for establishing universities at Calcutta, Bombay and Madras. But, as we shall see, many years elapsed before the solid foundations of the system were finally laid. For underlying the vernacular schools recognised by the Department were the indigenous schools of the people. Splendid as were the results of the Despatch of 1854, those results proved for a time to be one-sided, from three causes which, although not apparent at first, gradually asserted themselves. As regards higher education, the State system tended to centralise intellectual progress at the three Presidency towns, and in the provinces of which they formed the capitals. As regards lower education, it failed to adequately incorporate the ancient and widely diffused agency of the indigenous schools of India. In every grade of education it led the people to trust too much to official action and to Departmental aid, instead of to private effort.

Yet the results were from the outset sufficiently striking. The new Department fairly started in 1855, and during the next fifteen years it was allowed to develope on the lines laid down in 1854 and reasserted in 1859, with little interference from without. In those fifteen years it more than doubled the ascertained school attendance in India: from 923,780 pupils in 1855 to 1,894,823 in 1870.* The increase, however, was not alone one of numbers. The character of the instruction also underwent a significant change. In 1855, the Department found only 88,801 pupils in the secondary schools ; that is to say in the rank of institutions midway between the primary schools and the Arts Colleges. It is the boys in these secondary schools who form the material from which the Arts Colleges and the Indian Universities derive the main body of their students. During the first fifteen years of State education on the lines laid down in 1854, this class of pupils was multiplied four-fold, to 128,708 in 1870.

The rapid increase of the more highly educated youth told at once upon the attendance at the Professional Colleges. The number of young men desiring to enter the learned professions in the modern sense of the word increased three-fold, from the petty number of 912, in 1855, to 2,826 in 1870. The attendance in the Normal Schools and Classes, that is to say, in the institutions for pro-

---

* These numbers represent the attendance in all known institutions, Departmental, Aided, and Extra-Departmental.

fessional training below the grade of the Professional Colleges, had multiplied twenty-seven fold, from 197 in 1855 to 5,368 in 1870. The number of students in the ordinary Arts Colleges increased but slightly during the same period. The three universities did not make much progress until the years following 1860, and their full effects were not developed during the fifteen years at present under review. Broadly speaking, the first fifteen years of State Education in India, upon the lines laid down in 1854, greatly increased the demand for professional training, and created at the same time a greatly increased reserve of educated youth, who were destined to crowd into the Arts Colleges during the subsequent period.

But those fifteen years disclosed another and more striking feature. The Department of Public Instruction, in the first vigour and self-confidence of immaturity, attempted to monopolise the whole area of Indian education. The figures for 1855 show that it started with only 67,569 pupils in every grade of institution, Departmental and Aided, from the colleges down to the primary vernacular schools; and 856,211 in "Extra-Departmental" schools, which, although included in the returns, were outside the sphere of official action. During its first fifteen years, the Department brought members of the "Extra-Departmental" schools under its management. Accordingly, in 1870, the returns show an increase of twelve-fold in the Departmental and Aided schools, while the attendance in Extra-Departmental schools did not increase by one-fourth.

The three immediate effects of State Education in India may therefore be summarised as follows. First, an enormous increase in the number of young men desirous of a professional education, and a rush into the Professional Colleges and Normal Schools. Second, an equally significant increase in the reserve body of boys educated up to the standards which in India lead them to be ambitious of entering the learned professions. Third, great activity by the Department in bringing the Extra-Departmental schools within its system, and thus endeavouring to stereotype Indian education in uniform official moulds.

These results are the obvious conclusions derived from the official returns. But there were other results less obvious, yet of perhaps even greater importance in the development of the Indian peoples. Almost everywhere it was found that the Hindu population seized with avidity on the opportunities afforded by State Education for bettering themselves in life; while the Muhammadan community, excepting in certain localities, failed as a whole to do so. State Education thus put the finishing stroke to the influence of the Muhammadans, as the former ruling race in India. That position they had inherited from the time of the Mughal Empire, and during the first period of the Company's administration they still held an undue proportion of official posts. In the last century, Musalman Collectors gathered the Company's land tax in Bengal. Musalman Faujdárs and Ghátwáls officered its police. A great Musalman Department, with its head-quarters in the Nawáb

Názim's palace at Murshidabad, and a network of Musalman officials over every district in Lower Bengal, administered the criminal law. Musalman jailors kept in ward the prison population of Northern India. Kázís or Muhammadan doctors of law presided in the civil and domestic courts. When the Company first attempted to administer justice by means of trained English officers in its Bengal possessions, the Muhammadan Law Doctors still sat with them, as their authoritative advisers on points of law. The Code of Islám remained for many purposes the law of the land, and the ministerial and subordinate offices of government continued to be the almost hereditary property of the Musalmans.

During the fifty years preceding the organization of State Instruction in 1854, this monopoly had been subjected to serious inroads. The Cornwallis Code, and the construction of a British system of Indian Law, opened the judicial and Revenue Departments in Bengal to Hindus and Musalmans alike. The substitution of the vernacular languages for Persian in the Courts accelerated the change. The Hindus began to pour into every grade of official life; and the State system of education in 1854 completed the revolution. By 1871 there were only 92 Musalmans to 681 Hindus holding gazetted appointments in Lower Bengal—the province which, a hundred years previously, was officered by a few Englishmen, a sprinkling of Hindus, and a multitude of Muhammadans.

A similar change had taken place in the only secular profession which was then considered open to well-born Musalmans, namely the law. Medicine, until the creation of the present system, fell under a different category. The list of Pleaders of the High Court of Calcutta, which I examined in 1869, dated from 1834, and disclosed the following results. Of the surviving Pleaders of 1834, one was an Englishman, one a Hindu, and two were Musalmans. Down to 1838, the Musalmans continued almost as numerous as the Hindus and English put together. Of the Native Pleaders admitted to the High Court between 1845 and 1850 inclusive, the whole survivors in 1869 were Musalmans.

With the organisation of State Education in 1854, and with the educational activity which immediately preceded its introduction, the scene changed. Different tests of fitness were exacted, and a new order of men came to the front. The list showed that out of 240 Native Pleaders admitted from 1852 to 1868, no fewer than 239 were Hindus and only one survivor was a Musalman. Passing to the next grade in the profession, the attorneys, proctors and solicitors of the High Court of Calcutta, on the side of Original Jurisdiction, there were in 1869 twenty-seven Hindus and not one Musalman. Among the rising generation of articled clerks there were twenty-six Hindus and again not one Musalman. Alike therefore in higher official employments, and in the higher practice of the law, the Muhammadans had fallen out of the race in Bengal before the end of the first fifteen years of State Education on the lines laid down in 1854.

But their exclusion was not confined to the more lucrative avocations. It mattered not to what department of the legal profession I turned, the result was the same. In the office of the Registrar of the High Court of Calcutta there were in 1869 seventeen *employés* of sufficient standing to have their names published. Six of them were Englishmen or East Indians, eleven were Hindus, and not one was a Musalman. In the Receiver's Office, four names were given, two Englishmen and two Hindus, but no Musalman. In the office of the Clerk of the Crown and the Taxing Officer were four Englishmen and five Hindus, but no Musalman. In all the nooks and crannies of the law, in the Offices of Account, the Sheriff's Office, Coroner's Office, and Office of Interpreters, twenty names were given, eight Englishmen, eleven Hindus, and one Musalman—the sole representative of the Muhammadan population (numbering 21 millions in the Lower Provinces), and he, a poor *Maula* on six shillings a week. I have confined my scrutiny to the gazetted public appointments in Lower Bengal, and to the legal profession in Calcutta, because it was scarcely a century before that the English received over the government of these provinces, in 1765, from the Muhammadan Nawáb Názim and from a Muhammadan administration. In Bengal Proper, moreover, with Calcutta as its capital, the Muhammadans actually exceed the Hindus in number (1881); and they amount to nearly one half of the Hindu population throughout the whole of the Lower Provinces. I would be careful, however, to guard the reader against generalising from the statistics of individual provinces as to the facts for all India.

Nor do I put forward State Education as the sole factor in producing this disastrous result to the Muhammadans. For a closer scrutiny shows that many other causes co-operated. But the new system of Public Instruction, and the eagerness with which the Hindus availed themselves of it, was the most conspicuous cause, and gave an impulse to other causes which rendered them irresistible. A deep despondency spread among the Muhammadans throughout the Lower Provinces. Their ancient cherished system of religious education, based upon Persian, Arabic, and the Kurán, ceased definitely to enable them to win their way in professional or official life. In some cases, despondency settled into disaffection, and combined with other motives to intensify the general feeling of dislike to our rule, which culminated in the Wahábí State Trials from 1865 to 1870. "I attribute the great hold which Wahábí doctrines have on the mass of the Muhammadan peasantry," wrote the Government officer in charge of the chief Wahábí prosecution, "to our neglect of their education." I do not go so far as this. But it is certain that the Muhammadans in many parts of India became convinced that the new system of Public Instruction, with the new tests of fitness which it created for candidates for public employments and for professional life, was distinctly favourable to the Hindus, and distinctly unfavourable to their own community. "All sorts of employment, great and small," wrote the *Dúrbín*, a Calcutta Persian newspaper, in July 1869, "are being gradually snatched away from the Muhammadans, and bestowed on men of other races, particularly the Hindus."

"Is it any subject for wonder," wrote the Chief Secretary to the Government of India in the Home Department, "that they have held aloof from a system which, however good in itself, made no concession to their prejudices, made in fact no provision for what they esteemed their necessities, and which was in its nature unavoidably antagonistic to their interests, and at variance with all their social traditions? The educated Muhammadan, confident in his old training, sees himself practically excluded from the share of power and of the emoluments of Government which he had hitherto almost monopolized, and sees these and all the other advantages of life pass into the hands of the hated Hindu. Discontent—a feeling if not of actual religious persecution, yet of neglect on account (indirectly) of his religious views—has filled the minds of the better educated. Their fanaticism, for which ample warrant can always be found in the Kurán, has been hotly excited, until at last there is danger that the entire Muhammadan community will rapidly be transformed into a mass of disloyal ignorant fanatics on the one hand, with a small class of men highly educated in a narrow fashion on the other, highly fanatic, and not unwarrantably discontented, exercising an enormous influence over their ignorant fellow-Muhammadans." I do not unreservedly endorse these words: but they show the views of an English official in one of the highest posts, as to the effects of fifteen years of State Education in Bengal.

Those effects were not, however, confined to the depression of the Muhammadans and the exaltation of the Hindus as a whole. It was speedily discovered that two particular races of the Hindus were the chief gainers by the change, one in the South and the other in the North of India. In the South the Maráthás came strongly to the front. This Hindu population, or rather organisation of castes, had been for practical purposes the ruling race from whom the British conquered Western India. The Maráthá Confederacy gave the death-blow to the Mughal Empire before the East India Company came upon the scene as a military power. It was the Maráthás who frustrated the life project of the great Emperor Aurangzeb for the conquest of Southern India. It was they who broke up his armies and insulted his dying distress. During the feeble rule of his successors they spread over the Mughal dominions, and harried its provinces from the Deccan to Lower Bengal. In the end they made themselves masters of the Mughal capital, and it was from the hands of the Marátha conquerors that the British armies rescued the miserable blind old prisoner whom, at the beginning of this century, we saluted as Emperor of Delhi. The Maráthás were essentially a governing race, with a military organisation which taxed the utmost force of the British power to break it, and with talents for administration that quickly reasserted themselves under British rule.

The new system of State Education gave them, in the middle of the present century, a fresh lease of power. The two other races of Southern India, the Tamil and Telugu, although possessed of high qualities, practical and intellectual, did not disclose at first the same plasticity in availing themselves of English Public Instruction.

The Marátha Brahmans after some natural struggle with their hereditary caste feelings, seized upon the new opportunity for engrossing the offices of the subordinate administration. They crowded into the official employments, not only throughout their home-country in Bombay, but spread themselves far and wide, from the districts of Madras, throughout all Western India and the Central Provinces, northwards as far as Sind. In this, as in other developments, the causes had been at work long before the introduction of Public Instruction on the lines of 1854. But the new system gave a fresh impulse to the aptitudes of the Maráthás, and has made them the conspicuous race in the present political movements of Southern India, as they were in its former administration.

In the North of India a very different race rushed into the foreground. The Bengalis had only a history of conquest, and their existence during centuries has been a long and painful struggle against a malarious climate. I speak here of the Bengalis of the Delta, and especially of the districts around Calcutta, for it is to this population that the term is correctly applied. The great provinces of Lower Bengal, with their 66 millions of people, contain as healthy districts and as vigorous populations as can be desired. But the Bengali whom the Englishman in Calcutta, from Macaulay downwards, has seen and described is the Bengali of the Delta. He is the survival of the fittest among a race preyed upon by fen fever and the bacteria which have their home in drying up tropical swamps. The staple food of the Bengali, rice, seems also to develope a less muscular frame than the wheat and millets of the interior provinces. Nevertheless, he is a true survival of the fittest in a long and homicidal struggle between man and nature.

His slender supple body is capable of protracted labour, if not of too severe a nature. His mind is many sided, prehensile of new ideas, yet sobered by a traditional reverence for the past. With a deep-seated love for his own homestead, he has been accustomed by economic necessities to seek subsistence or employment at a distance from his native village. He is not only quick-witted, but he endures the strain of continuous brainwork with a quiet unobtrusive efficiency, which outlasts the more attractive energy of many of the finer physical races of India. To produce the present Bengali of the Delta, millions of families have become extinct in the struggle with the climate; and the survival is eminently equipped with the race qualities which enable Man to contend against unfavourable natural surroundings.

With the establishment of the British ascendancy, the Bengali at length found his chance. Protected from the rough invasion of the peoples of Northern India, and situated in close proximity to the head-quarters of the British Government, the Bengali quickly took the measure of his new rulers, and made himself useful to them. It was he who began the process of ousting the Muhammadans from the administration. It was he who enabled us to carry out our first efforts at judicial and revenue reforms. In all the series of beneficent administrative changes, by which the Lower Provinces with their 66 millions of people have been transferred from a misgoverned corner of the Delhi Empire, into a peaceful and prosperous British country, the Bengali has proved himself the right-hand man of the English Government. When we boast ourselves of the progress of Northern India under British Rule, we ought to remember that the Bengali has been both a principal instrument of that progress, and its most conspicuous product.

Especially was this the case in regard to the measures which Lord Dalhousie took in the middle of the present century with a view to the material development of India. When Lord Dalhousie established the half-ana postage, which is now equivalent to a halfpenny post, for the whole Indian Empire, Bengalis began to spread over Northern India, as the most effective agency for giving effect to the reform. When he started telegraphs, they supplied the material for the sharpest telegraph signallers and clerks. When he laid the foundation of the Indian railway system, the Bengalis filled the railway offices throughout many provinces. All these great schemes were introduced during a short period preceding 1854. The creation of the new system of Public Instruction in that year gave a powerful impetus to the administrative ascendency which the Bengalis were already beginning to acquire in Northern India. The aid which the Government obtained from them for the efficient and economical carrying out of its schemes can scarcely be overrated. But their success made them the most unpopular race in all Northern India. The stalwart peoples of the North-West and the Punjab saw with disgust the old course of invasion reversed, and a host of slender-bodied, quick-witted, soft-mannered men advancing up the Gangetic valley. From Calcutta to Peshawar there was a Bengali faction in every Secretariat. Bengalis sat on half the stools in the telegraph offices, and for a time supplied almost the whole native staff on the railways, above the grade of a navvy or a pointsman.

Fifteen years of State Education on the lines laid down in 1854, had thus led to important results both economic and ethnical in India. The professions were already overcrowded, the candidates for Government Service greatly exceeded the demand, the old ruling race of Muhammadan India believed itself ruined by the new system of Public Instruction, while certain of the Hindu races were unduly engrossing the administration throughout large areas of the country. It became apparent that Western instruction was producing not only a redistribution of employments, but also an upheaval of races. While these were the external results of Education, serious defects made themselves felt within the Department itself. Its foundation in indigenous instruction was still too narrow for the vast superstructure of higher and English education which it raised thereon. It also disclosed a tendency to substitute for the varied popular forms of Indian instruction a single rigid system of its own.

The first great measure which enabled remedies to be provided for these defects, was not an educational measure but a financial one. In 1870 Lord Mayo, under the powerful influence of the Brothers

Strachey, introduced his de-centralisation scheme of Finance. Under this scheme each Province obtained the power to develope its education upon lines suited to its own wants. Among the first Indian administrators who availed themselves of that power was Sir George Campbell, then Lieutenant-Governor of Bengal. He accepted once and for ever the indigenous schools as the basis of the Department of Public Instruction in the Lower Provinces. He determined, while improving that basis to respect its popular character, and to save it from being forced into a Procrustean mould. Under his system the primary schools in the Lieutenant-Governorship of Bengal, recognised by the Department, rose from 68,500 pupils in 1870-71, to 900,000 in 1881-82. While the Department thus rapidly won the confidence of the existing indigenous schools, an outer circle of them sprang up under private Native teachers, in the hope of attaining that moderate degree of efficiency which would entitle them to grants-in-aid.

Other provinces followed in the same judicious lines. The effort to establish Public Instruction upon the actual educational wants of the mass of the people, steadily carried out during the past twenty years, has borne rich results. How important these results have proved, may be judged from the state of a backward province which did not make, or sufficiently persist in, that effort. In 1881 the Education Department in the Punjab spent close on Rs. 1,400,000 in educating 105,000 pupils on its own imported methods. At the same time the indigenous schools in the Punjab, which received neither recognition nor aid from the Department, were educating 135,384 pupils, on their own methods and at their own expense. This, as was well said by a witness before the Indian Education Commission in 1882, "represents the protest of the people against our system of education." It gave emphasis to the doubts which had been raised as to the justice of levying a tax from the peasant cultivators of the Punjab for primary schools, while the Department denied any aid to the indigenous primary schools which gave the kind of education desired by a large mass of the people.

These doubts, and many others which had arisen during the first twenty-five years of State Instruction in India, were laid at rest by the Education Commission of 1882. For if the initial measure which tended to bring State Education into accord with the actual wants of the people was Lord Mayo's Financial Scheme of de-centralisation in 1870, the measure which accomplished the process was Lord Ripon's Education Commission of 1882-83. This body was powerfully constituted of 21 representatives from the various sections of the community, throughout the provinces of India. The Department of Public Instruction, the Missionaries, and Native teaching bodies were ably represented upon it. Its main object was, while accepting the principles laid down in 1854, to ascertain the modifications which experience had disclosed as necessary for the edifice of State Education that had been reared on those principles. It held its central sittings in Calcutta, but also travelled over India, carefully examining 193 witnesses in the various provinces, and receiving 323 Memorials signed by over 233,000 persons. It embodied the results in a report of 639 folio pages, besides copious statistical tables, and formulated its conclusions in 220 distinct Recommendations to the Government. These Recommendations covered the whole area of Native education in India, excepting technical instruction, from the colleges down to the indigenous schools. After an elaborate review of them by the Government of India, they received, with one or two modifications, the sanction of the Secretary of State. They now form the basis on which education rests in India, and on which it probably will continue to rest during many years to come.

The task prescribed by Lord Ripon to the Commission was to extend primary education, especially upon the methods which the people had worked out for themselves. To encourage private enterprise in education, and, whenever expedient, to transfer schools from the Department to Native management. To stimulate female education and to provide means for the instruction of the Muhammadan and other backward races. To examine the machinery and organisation of the Department of Public Instruction and to incorporate into its system the educational activity of the Municipalities, Rural Unions, District Councils, and other public bodies. Above all to provide against the danger of rearing up a too numerous class highly educated upon foreign methods, without a sufficient equipoise of education in the middle and lower classes of the people—in short to make higher and lower instruction advance together at a more equal pace.

Of the social and economic consequences of this great reform, I shall presently speak. They are only gradually disclosing themselves. But the statistical results were immediate, and they have a deep significance. According to the latest Parliamentary Return, the total number of pupils has risen from just over 2 millions in 1880–81, the year preceding the Commission, to $3\frac{1}{2}$ millions in 1888–89, five years after it closed its labours.* This result is sufficiently important, but it fails altogether to disclose the significance of the change. For the object of the Commission was not alone to increase the total of pupils, but to make their education less dependent upon the Government, and in a larger measure the work of the people themselves. I have only the complete Parliamentary Returns down to the year 1887–88. They exhibit the following striking phenomena. While the number of pupils in Government Institutions has only increased from 769,074 in 1880–81 to 971,904 in 1887–88, the number in Aided Institutions has increased from 1,111,843 to 1,708,527; and the number in Private and Unaided Institutions from 314,697 to 800,763. If these be the results of the Education Commission in the green leaf, what will they be in the dry wood?

---

* In this and all subsequent comparisons I follow the returns given in the Blue Book entitled "Statistical Abstract relating to British India," presented to both Houses of Parliament, and dated 12th September, 1889. The total according to my latest information now exceeds $3\frac{1}{2}$ millions. As the Parliamentary Returns do not always coincide with those of the Education Commission, I base my comparisons on the figures supplied by the Parliamentary Returns.

The truth is, that the Recommendations of the Commission are surely and swiftly converting the old Departmental system of Indian Public Instruction into a national system of education for India. The Government in 1882 clearly foresaw that the official resources, both in money and men, were wholly inadequate to the task. It warned the Commission that in providing for the extension of education, "the limitation imposed on the action of Government by financial considerations must always be borne in mind." The Education Commission accordingly called in the people themselves to its aid, with the following remarkable results. While the number of pupils has increased in round figures from 2 to $3\frac{1}{2}$ millions, and while the total expenditure on Indian education has increased in round figures from 10 to 19 millions of rupees, the Government expenditure on education has actually *decreased* by Rs.100,000 from 1880-81 to 1887-88. The people have made good the balance. And they have made it good only to a small extent by Local Rates. The school fees have doubled during the period, while the subscriptions and endowments have increased by over sixty per cent. Under the strong Recommendations of the Commission, moreover, an almost new source of educational income has been developed in the shape of Municipal support. During the same short period the contributions from the Municipalities to schools have increased by more than three-fold. This popular aid has been effective not only in reducing the actual Government Expenditure, but in enforcing a more rigid economy in the cost of Indian education. But at the same time, there was no stint. While the number of pupils has increased in round figures, according to the Parliamentary Returns, from a little over 2 millions, to $3\frac{1}{2}$ millions; the total expenditure on their education has increased from 10 to 19 millions of rupees.

The results have been gained not by a sacrifice of the higher branches of education, and in spite of a vast increase of Educational Institutions of the most expensive class. The number of candidates for the entrance examination, at the Calcutta University has more than doubled, from 2,031 in 1881-82, to 4,305 in 1887-88. The number of such candidates at the Madras University has nearly doubled, from 3,519 to 6,582. Their number at the Bombay University has increased nearly three-fold from 1,260 to 3,012 during the same period.

Judged by the further results of University teaching, the increase is still more striking. The graduates who took their degrees in Law at Calcutta (the great Law University of India), have multiplied by close on seven-fold, from 35 in 1880-81, to 238 in 1887-88. The gentlemen who took their degree in Medicine at Bombay (the great Medical University of India), have increased from 45 in 1880-81, to an average of 120 during the three years ending 1887-88. The gentlemen who passed the B.A. examination at Madras (a chief Arts University in India), have increased by more than three-fold, from 113 in 1880-81, to 437 in 1887-88.

Nor must it be supposed that the standards of the pass-examination in Indian Universities are lower than in England. I have taken some pains to arrive at a just estimate of their comparative difficulty, and obtained the views of one of the most distinguished of the Indian students who have gone through both systems. Mr. Das Gupta, after successful studies at the Calcutta University, came to Oxford and took his B.A. with Honours—a "Second Class" in his eleventh term, the period allowed being sixteen terms. He was awarded an Exhibition from Balliol, and is now reading at that College for Honours in Law. He may therefore be taken as a trustworthy witness, and as certainly not an unfavourable one to the Oxford system.

In an elaborate paper which he has kindly drawn up for me, he analyses the examinations in the two Univerities. He finds that the Entrance Examination at Calcutta corresponds with Responsions at Oxford; the Calcutta First Arts with the Oxford Pass Moderations; and the Calcutta Pass B.A. with the Oxford Pass B.A. He states that both in regard to the books prescribed and the papers set, the Calcutta Entrance Examination is distinctly higher than the Oxford Responsions; and in regard to the books prescribed, higher even than the Pass Moderations at Oxford. As respects the final examination, he shows by comparative tables that the Calcutta Pass B.A. is very much higher than the Oxford Pass B.A. "One might reasonably doubt," he adds "if the Oxford Pass B.A. Standard is any way harder than the Calcutta First Arts Standard." As regards, therefore, the Pass examinations, whose numerical results I have just stated, there can be no question that the enormous increase in the number of graduates of the Indian University, represents a wide-spread and bonâ fide extension in higher education.

That higher education, however, is not the highest. For the modern system of specialising in the English Universities carries their best men much farther than the Indian system does. Mr. Das Gupta, while showing the greater difficulty and wider scope of the Calcutta Pass Examinations, bears testimony to this fact. "When we come to the Honour Schools," he says "we see at once that the Oxford standard is infinitely superior to the Calcutta standard. There can hardly be any comparison between the two. Oxford turns out specialists: Calcutta merely indicates a few lines of study to us to follow up after leaving the University, according to our tastes and predilections."

The reforms in the Indian Education Department, which received their authoritative expression in the Report of the Education Commission, were not, however, confined to the extension of Public Instruction. The Commission endeavoured to grapple with the special difficulties of bringing education within the reach of certain classes of the people. The first of these classes was the female sex. The Commission found that there were certain distinct causes of the backwardness of female education in India. In the first place, the effective desire for education as a means of earning a livelihood, does not exist as regards the female population of India. In the second place, the social customs of India in regard to child-marriage, and the seclusion in which the women of the well-to-do classes spend their married life in most parts of the country, put an end to a girl's school-going in her ninth to eleventh year. In the third place, the supply of female teachers is greatly deficient, and the State system of female education had therefore to be conducted in a large measure by a male staff, a system not in accord with the feelings of the people.

The Commission, having taken evidence on each of these points throughout the various provinces in India, drew up, after anxious consideration, a series of proposals with a view to meeting each class of difficulty. These proposals they formulated into twenty-seven Recommendations to Government, and on those Recommendations female Public Instruction in India now rests. During the six years which have passed since their adoption by the Government, the great impulse given to female education, and the multiplication of the various agencies and methods by which it is conveyed, form one of the most striking features in the social development in India.

The other large classes of the population whom the Commission found in a backward state as regards Public Instruction were the Muhammadans, the aboriginal tribes, and the low castes. For each of these the Commission made special provision, after a searching enquiry into the actual causes which had prevented their acceptance of the State system of education on its previous basis. The Muhammadans in particular formed the subject of a completely exhaustive enquiry. It was found that the backwardness of the Muhammadans in accepting our system of Public Instruction, and their consequent exclusion from public offices, the law, and other employments requiring education, was more or less general: but with two striking exceptions. These exceptions were Oudh and the North-Western Provinces. The Commission having thus differentiated the problem, carefully enquired into the specific causes which had led the Muhammadans to accept our system in certain parts of India and to reject it in others. The result was a series of eighteen Recommendations to Government which went to the root of the matter. The Commission were deliberately convinced that it was better to modify the equitable but hard and fast lines of Indian Public Instruction, rather than to leave so large and important a section of the people outside its scope. For example, however highly it might regard the impartiality of the Public Instruction Department, it deemed it right to modify that impartiality when it found that the Muhammadans, who formed thirty-two per cent of the population in Bengal and Assam, had contributed in 1871 only fourteen per cent. to the school attendance.

The Commission not only recommended that special encouragement should be given to Muhammadan Institutions, but that special provision should be made to meet, what may be called, the Muhammadan religious difficulty. "The one object of a young Hindu," they pointed out "is to obtain an education which will fit him for an official or a professional career. But before the young Muhammadan is allowed to turn his thoughts to secular instruction, he must commonly pass some years in going through a course of sacred learning." "The teaching of the Mosque must precede the lessons of the school." "The Muhammadan boy, therefore, enters school later than the Hindu. In the second place, he very often leaves school at an earlier age," as the Muhammadan parent, being poorer than the Hindu parent in a corresponding social position, " cannot afford to give his son so complete an education."

The Commission, while framing their Recommendations for the Musalmans " not merely with a regard to justice, but with a leaning towards generosity," did not disguise the deteriorating influences of this policy. "Special encouragement to any class," they warned the Muhammadans, "is in itself an evil ; and it will be a sore reproach to the Musalmans if the pride they have shown in other matters does not stir them up to a course of honourable activity ; to a determination that whatever their backwardness in the past, they will not suffer themselves to be out-stripped in the future ; to a conviction that self-help and self-sacrifice are at once nobler principles of conduct and surer paths to worldly success than sectarian reserve, or the hope of exceptional indulgence. We have spoken of the causes ; we here accept the fact that, at all events in many parts of the country, the Musalmans have fallen behind the rest of the population."

The Indian Muhammadans have taken to heart these wise words. Since the enquiries of the Commission they have more generally availed themselves of State Instruction, and they have also endeavoured to meet their special requirements by an increase of institutions of their own. Many of them, however, still hold aloof, alike from Western education and from those political movements among the Natives of India to which Western education gives rise. For example, a certain amount of Muhammadan opposition has appeared to the largest and best known of those movements, namely, the Indian National Congress. But even in such cases when we look carefully into the facts, we find that the Muhammadan opposition is now of a local and partial character. Thus while certain highly respected Muhammadans of the older school, and a section of the Bengal Muhammadans whom the Commission found the most backward in India have held aloof from the Congress, yet the Indian Muhammadans throughout many parts of the country have joined in the movement. The number of Musalman representatives who would have attended the National Indian Congress of 1888, if they had maintained a strict ratio to the total Muhammadan population, should have been 286 to 937 Hindus. The number of Muhammadan delegates who actually attended the Congress was 222. It will be a happy day for India when the disproportion between the Muhammadans who ought to be at school, and those who are actually at school, is reduced to so small a percentage ! At the Bombay Congress, held in a strongly Hindu and non-Muhammadan presidency, the ratio of Musalmans to Hindus was not so equally maintained.

With the further development of education, the aggressive prominence which individual races obtained is beginning to disappear. The non-Marátha provinces of Western India have turned back the tide of Marátha invasion and are filling the local posts in the administration with men born in their own districts and educated in their own schools. The inroads of the Bengali into the North-West and the Punjab have become almost a thing of the past. There is still, I believe, a Bengali clique in several of the capitals of those provinces, but the Local Departments are now for the most part officered by local men. The truth is that the Maráthás and the Bengalis were quick-witted races, who saw their opportunity in the new system of State Education on the lines of 1854, and who made the most of it, while it lasted. By the Maráthás, I here and elsewhere mean chiefly the Marátha Brahmans. They and the Bengalis are still among the foremost races of India in intelligence and education, and they take a leading part in political or social movements, such as the Congress already referred to. But with the development of an autonomous system of education in every separate province, the multiplication of local colleges, and the establishment of new Universities for the North-West and the Punjab, there has been a general levelling up of the other Indian races. The prominence of the Maráthás and the Bengalis is no longer an odious prominence, and their temporary monopoly of official employments has ceased, or is disappearing.

As a matter of fact, the Madras or Tamil races are now taking a foremost place in the political movements of India. At the last Indian National Congress, three schemes of electoral representation were submitted: one from Bengal, one from the Maráthás of Bombay, and one from Madras. It is characteristic of the solidity and tenacity of the Tamil race, that the scheme eventually adopted by the Indian National Congress was the scheme brought forward by the Madras delegates.

The results of the vast extension of education in India permeate every sphere of human activity. In religion, the Indian races are under the cautious forms of a respectful orthodoxy, making one of the greatest new departures which the world has ever witnessed. This new departure is aided by the curious mixture of strength and plasticity in Hinduism. The absence of any fixed canon, like our Christian Bible, enables Hinduism to adjust itself, without any appearance of violent change, to the shifting opinions of each age. To apply the term idolator, in our popular sense of the word, to an educated young Hindu, would now be almost as gross an abuse of the term as to apply it to an enlightened member of the Greek or Roman Church.

The whole body of sacred Sanskrit literature, while venerated as a store-house of philosophy, poetry, and law, is dealt with in the same historical spirit as that in which we regard the Patristic writings or the Talmud. Even the Veda itself has now but few remaining defenders of its claim to literal inspiration among the educated Hindus. Modern Hinduism is a social organisation and a religious confederacy. It allows any number of new sects, theistic or others, to grow up within its own body. It regards with quiet humour the minor sects like the Brahma Samaj, which, in their youthful zeal, may think it needful to separate themselves from the general community. In the course of a few generations it re-absorbs such theistic sects into itself—or into a new development of its old self. The old aggressive use of the term "heathen" in Calcutta or Bombay would now bring an indiscreet Christian within perilous reach of certain clauses of the Indian Penal Code.

The most characteristic feature of Hindu society, next to its religion, is perhaps its almsgiving. Its ancient Scriptures and modern practice agree in according to acts of benevolence a chief function in the scheme of salvation. But between the precepts of the ancient Hindu scriptures and the modern practice, a profound change has been brought about by Western ideas. The Sanskrit sacred writings give special, although not exclusive, value to donations to the priestly class. The young educated Hindu, while not divesting himself of this duty, has accepted more or less fully the doctrines of modern philanthropy. But he maintains that, in so doing, he only makes a reversion to the first principle of Indian Buddhism, namely, "charity to all men." No appeal for a great philanthropic object is now made to the Hindu races without drawing forth a response.

Instead of concentrating their almsgiving upon the Brahmans, they are devoting it to the erection and maintenance of schools, dispensaries, and hospitals, or to a revival of that well-known Hindu form of charity, the construction of tanks and other useful local works. Fifty years ago Lady Dufferin's magnificent project for creating a wide organisation of medical aid for the women of India would have been met with coldness if not with distrust. Nor is it too much to say that the great extension of education recently made in India has been made on Western philanthropic principles, and to a large extent with donations which fifty years ago would have been expended in feeding Brahmans. In this as in every other department of Indian progress, it would be foolish to exaggerate the extent of the change which has yet been effected. But it would be still more foolish to overlook the change which is surely and steadily taking place.

The same may be said of the moral changes at work in Hindu society. The position of widows in India is still a reproach to the country. But the educated Hindus realize that it is a reproach, and there is a widespread movement with a view to its amelioration. The most conspicuous figure in that movement is a Parsi and not a Hindu. And here I take the opportunity of explaining that if I have not mentioned the Parsis as a progressive Indian race, it is only because of the comparative fewness of their numbers, and of the still semi-foreign character in which they are traditionally regarded. But although the most eloquent and ardent advocate for improving the position of Indian women is a Parsi, his most powerful following is among the Hindus themselves. The Hindus, however, realize more clearly the difficulties connected with the question. They perceive that while the law of India, and the usages of Hindu society, maintain the ancient degree of protection given to women, it is almost impossible to combine that ancient protection with the modern ideas of female freedom of action. You cannot give to the same person all the double advantages of a state of pupilage and of a state of independence. This is the problem which the educated Hindus are now endeavouring to solve.

For example, the Hindu widow is regarded as a first charge on the Hindu family. Her maintenance is secured to her from the labour of her husband's male survivors, and every one who has had experience of the working of the Hindu family system, knows how heavy a charge the accumulated female relatives constitute upon the resources of the working males. In Hindu families of a wealthier class, the Hindu law, throughout most parts of India, gives to a widow the usufruct of her husband's whole property, if he leaves no son. But it does so for the special purpose of continuing the religious *persona* of the husband, and to enable her to perform a life-long round of ceremonies for his benefit in the other world. If she marries again she passes out of her late husband's family into the family of her new husband, and she becomes thereby incapable, according to Hindu usage, of performing the very ceremonies for the due performance of which she has succeeded by law to her late husband's property. The British Legislature in India recognised this, and while declaring the Hindu widow free to re-marry, holds that by re-marriage she forfeits her interest in her deceased husband's estate.

The educated Hindus perceive that, in order to obtain the consent of the mass of their countrymen to any large social reform in the position of widows, there must also be a legislative change. I have cited only one aspect of the question. But the same necessity for alterations in the law underlies the other aspects of Indian female life; from the legal age of marriage onward to the abolition and restrictions on re-marriage. The educated Hindus, while aiding by public associations and by eloquent writings in the popular movement, desire that that movement should have its basis in legal reform. I have before me at this moment several such schemes, emanating from Hindus. Thus a distinguished Marátha administrator, the Raja Sir Madava Rao, K.C.S.I., writes to me under date 28th January last, forwarding the last version of the scheme of legislative reform which he has long advocated, " to relieve or mitigate the unhappiness of widows, or rather to reduce the chances of widowhood." In regard to the position of women, Western ideas are bringing about a profound change of opinion among the rising generation of educated Hindus—a change to which their leaders are endeavouring soberly and cautiously to give practical effect.

The same caution marks the progress which the Hindus have made in the industrial life of India. We are all aware that a revolution has been effected in our own days with regard to the food supply of England. But we do not yet realize the full significance of what has taken place. The great food-producing areas of the Western Hemisphere are the Gulf Stream region of Europe and the Monsoon region of Asia. The European region, as has been admirably shown by Mr. Mackinder, the Reader in Geography at Oxford, is the region "blown over by prevalent west winds fed with warmth and moisture from the warm surface waters of the Atlantic. . . . . Historically this is the Roman world," with a modern population of about 300,000,000 inhabitants. The Monsoon region extends over South-Eastern Asia, with 700,000,000 inhabitants, of whom the most important for practical purposes of food production are the 250,000,000 of India.

These two food-producing areas were, down to our times, kept apart by distance and by the difficulties of communication. The Suez Canal and the modern improvements in marine engines have brought them closer into contact, and will probably bring them still more closely. The first races to take advantage of the altered conditions were the peoples of India. Indian commerce, which in its earlier stages consisted of nick-nacks and luxuries, is becoming more and more a wholesale trade in staple agricultural produce. Fifty years ago the total merchandise exported from India averaged, during the five years 1840–44 inclusive, only 14½ millions sterling. The present exports of Indian agricultural staples—grains, seeds, cotton and jute in their various forms, indigo, and tea—alone exceed 53 millions; and India's total exports of merchandise now amount to 83 millions, of which more than 80 millions are strictly Indian produce. These figures are at the conventional rate of exchange.

The truth is, that the Suez Canal has broken down the geographical barrier between the food-producing populations of the Monsoon area and the food-consuming populations of the Gulf Stream area. How rapidly the process is going on may be estimated from a single item, wheat. In 1874–75 the export of wheat from India was one million cwts. The Parliamentary Return for 1886–87 gives the export of Indian wheat at 22¼ million cwts. The trade fluctuates from year to year, but the increase during each period of years is most striking; nor can any man predict the dimensions which it may reach as the Indian railways open out the country. It has been a main factor in reducing by one-half the price of the Englishman's staple food—from over sixty to about thirty shillings a quarter.

This great revolution, while directly the result of cheaper transit, has been aided indirectly, but in an important way, by the intellectual progress of the Indian races. The educated Hindus supply the working staff of English capital in India. Their cheap and effective labour has powerfully assisted the British merchants of Calcutta and Bombay in their competition against German and other foreign firms, who work on somewhat more economical methods than the older English houses. Without a highly skilled Hindu subordinate administration, the Indian railways could not be worked, nor could their accounts be kept, with a profit. From the wayside stationmasters up to the central offices of audit, the English-speaking Hindus supply the mass of the Indian railway *employés*.

For a time the Indian races, with their characteristic caution, confined their commercial attempts to the ordinary operations of trade. They bought and sold produce on their own account, while their cheap labour as clerks or assistants enabled the British merchant to conduct an enormous export business on a low scale of charges. But having thus served their apprenticeship to modern commerce, the Indian races gradually began to take up the work of modern manufacturers. Their old domestic manufactures of the hand-loom had been destroyed by the competition of Manchester manufacturers by means of steam-power. The long drawn-out agony of that period of ruin among the textile workers of India will, I trust, some day be truly told. At the end of it, the Indian commercial class resolved to fight Manchester with her own weapons. Steam-power mills and factories, built with Native capital, worked by Native hands, and controlled by Native firms or by Native Boards of Direction, began to raise their chimneys in Bombay, and along the banks of the Húglí. They are now springing up in many local centres of Native trade. For example, Surat, instead of giving its name only to a class of Indian cotton, is pouring out thousands of bales of Indian piece goods. When a Calcutta company some years ago started a line of river steamers on the Húglí, it was found possible to work them almost entirely by Native masters, Native engineers, and Native pilots.

There is one operation of commerce on which the educated Natives have long looked with envy, but from which with characteristic caution they have hitherto abstained. I refer to the modern system of banking. The Native banking firms still pursue, under certain modifications, their old method of working with their own capital, or with capital obtained in comparatively large sums from their friends and relatives. They are now casting wistful glances at the English and Scotch system of banking, guaranteed by a central body of subscribed capital, but with that capital multiplied by means of small deposits drawn by a network of branches from the agricultural districts. The Government system of Post Office Savings' Banks has acted as an object-lesson to them in this department of finance. That system rapidly expanded during the last five years, for which I possess the Parliamentary returns, from 76,438 depositors and a balance of $6\frac{1}{4}$ million rupees at the end of 1883–84, to 227,865 depositors and 42 millions of rupees at the end of 1887–88.

There seems a possibility that the English system of banking, based upon local branches which draw a multitude of small deposits out of the country, will now attract the attention of Native capitalists. When that time comes the new industrial era in India will enter on a phase of which it is difficult to foresee the result. The great changes which have taken place in the Native methods of commerce, and in the Native methods of manufactures during the present generation, will then find their completion in a change in the Native methods of finance. When it is remembered that during the twenty-one years ending 1888, India has actually swallowed down 1920 millions of rupees worth of gold and silver, it may be imagined what a future is thus opened up. Those 1920 millions are exclusive of 370 million rupees worth of treasure re-exported. The demand for gold and silver as coinage has at the same time been relieved by the growing popularity of Government currency notes. The consumption of bullion for the arts is small in India, except as jewellery for purposes of hoarding.

It would be a difficult and expensive business for the Anglo-Indian financiers to get hold of the accumulated gold and silver in India by means of deposit banking in the rural districts. The multitude of little local branches could be economically worked only by Natives of India, and the risks incident to such a business would at first be greater than in England. But if the hoarded wealth of India can be turned into effective capital for Indian commerce, it will bring about a reduction in Indian rates of interest, and an activity in Indian manufactures and trade, fraught with consequences of magnitude to the whole civilised world.

In this very rapid survey of the effects of Western Education in India, I feel as if I had only touched the fringe of a great subject. Into the political results I am precluded, by want of space, from entering. For to deal fairly and satisfactorily with so vexed a question as the present political movements of the Indian races would demand a detailed treatment forbidden to me here. I may therefore briefly say that those political movements are the legitimate and inevitable result of Western Education in India. The men who conduct them are the men to whom in all other respects, intellectual and moral, we are accustomed to point as the highest products of British rule in India. They are the men who form the natural interpreters of our rule to the masses of the people. To speak of such men, when their activity takes a political direction, as disaffected, would be equally unjust and untrue. For they are the men who, of all our Indian fellow-subjects, realise most clearly that their interests, present and future, are identified with the permanence of British rule.

But brief as this survey has unavoidably been, it suffices to show that the present political movements among the Indian races are only one aspect of a general advance, moral, intellectual, and industrial, that is now going on. The most significant fact connected with the late Indian National Congress at Bombay was not its marvellous assemblage of 1889 representatives from every province of India. It was rather that this great gathering for political purposes was held side by side with a still greater meeting in the same city for ameliorating the condition of Woman in India—the Social Reform Conference attended by 6000 persons, chiefly Hindus. A political movement which is purely political may be wise or unwise, but a political movement which forms part of the general advance of a people to a higher state of society and to a nobler ideal of domestic and individual life, is irresistible. It may be guided, it may be moderated, but it must assuredly be reckoned with.

W. W. HUNTER.

PART II.

ELEMENTARY EDUCATION IN ENGLAND.*

FEW persons even in this country not actually connected, in one way or another, with the work itself have other than very vague ideas as to the system of elementary education which obtains among us. One still frequently hears Board Schools spoken of as if the term were synonymous with "Public Elementary Schools," and as if no such things as Voluntary or Denominational Schools had any existence. Again, it is by no means an uncommon thing to hear even well informed persons express astonishment at learning that the education in Board Schools is not as a rule purely secular. It, therefore, is not altogether out of place that a short account of that system should be included among the contents of even an English Review which aims at dealing comprehensively with the subject of State Education.

Like most of our institutions, our system of elementary education is a growth not a creation. It is the resultant of the action, not always harmonious, of various forces originating in the very depths of our national existence—the outcome of which is a system differing in some of its most prominent features from any which is to be found elsewhere. For a comprehension, therefore, of those peculiar features some knowledge of the history of the system in its gradual development is essential.

Until the commencement of the last century the main, if not the sole, provision for the education, elementary as well as higher, of the people in England and Wales was to be found in the so-called "Grammar Schools" which were scattered, in greater or less numbers, over nearly the whole of the country. These were for the most part free, and as in Scotland were attended without distinction of class by the children of the surrounding district. The noble dream of the Reformers in the 16th century, realized to a great extent in the kingdom north of the Tweed, that each parish should have its school and each school its direct connection with one of the Seminaries of higher learning, was in this country almost entirely brought to nought by the rapacity of the courtiers of Henry VIII. Still, the many schools which in different localities still commemorate the short reign of Edward VI. not only indicated the aspirations of the Reformers, but set an example which in happier days was largely followed by private benefactors, until by the middle of the next century few parts of the country were without some educational provision of this kind. Though open to all, however, the advantages of these schools were in fact confined almost exclusively in country places to the children of the yeomen and the

* Vide also Part XI. New Code for 1890.—ED.

inferior gentry, and when these classes were, by the rise of commercial centres, attracted in increasing numbers from the country into the towns, the great majority of the Grammar Schools fell into decay.

The crowding of the population into the towns, and the consequent need of additional provision in those places for their education, was one of the causes which led to the formation, in 1698, of the now venerable Society for Promoting Christian Knowledge. Beginning in that year with four schools in London and Westminster, the operations of the Society extended so rapidly that before twenty years had elapsed more than 1,000 schools, of which nearly 120 were in London or its immediate neighbourhood, had been called into existence in different parts of this country and the sister island. These schools were entirely free, and in most cases provided the children with clothing in addition to education, and not infrequently with board and lodging also. In several respects this early effort anticipated what we are accustomed to think special features of our present system, and, in one instance at least—that of manual and industrial training—was somewhat in advance of that system. Security for efficiency was taken by means of regular inspection and periodical examination; the necessities of industry were reconciled with those of education by means of a half-time system; and the special needs of those whose earlier education had been neglected were partially met by evening classes. After the first enthusiasm had expended itself, however, the system gradually languished until the educational revival which took place at the close of last century through the exertions of Lancaster and Bell, when it practically merged into that of the National Society.

The work of Joseph Lancaster commenced in 1798, and resulted after ten years in the foundation of "The Royal Lancasterian Institution"—a body which in 1814 changed its name into that of "The British and Foreign School Society." The "National Society" was founded in 1811—partly, it would seem, as a protest against the undenominational character of the schools established by the Lancasterian Society—for promoting the education of children in the principles of the Church of England. Until 1833 these societies, in worthy rivalry, were between them instrumental almost exclusively in promoting, entirely unaided by the State, the supply of whatever provision was made for the elementary education of the children of this country. Differing mainly in the arrangements they made for religious instruction, the two societies agreed very largely in the principles upon which they carried on their work. Both devoted themselves principally to the encouragement of local efforts for the establishment and maintenance of schools; both conducted model schools in London, in connection with which they carried on a system of training for teachers; both adopted the plan of instruction known as the "monitorial system," under which the teacher was dependent almost entirely upon the elder scholars for whatever assistance was needed in carrying on the instruction; both originally carried on their schools as free schools, and both gradually introduced the system of requiring small weekly payments from the parents, as a means of obtaining additional income and as a security for regularity of attendance. The National Society, though the younger of the two, was soon enabled by its superior wealth to far outstrip the rival society in the extent of its operations and in the number of its affiliated schools.

The year 1833 is memorable in the history of education in this country as that in which, for the first time, aid was afforded by the State to elementary education. The amount voted by Parliament was only £20,000; but this modest sum marked the commencement of a new era in which practical effect has been increasingly given to the principle—enunciated for the first time publicly in this country in 1816, in one of the reports of the Committee of the House of Commons, of which Mr. Brougham was Chairman—that "the education of the people is a matter in which the State has a vital concern."

The disbursement of this small grant was confided to the Treasury, by whom, in obedience to the Act under which it was made, it was distributed solely " in aid of private subscriptions for the erection of schools for the education of children of the poorer classes in Great Britain." Under the terms of the Treasury Minute adopted on the 30th August, 1833, assistance was given only in cases where a report either from the National Society or the British and Foreign School Society satisfied the Treasury that the application was one deserving of attention, and that there was a reasonable prospect of the school being permanently supported. In 1835, a special grant of £10,000 was made by Parliament towards the erection of Normal and Model Schools, but the Treasury appears to have experienced so much difficulty in determining how best to apply this sum that it remained in their hands still unappropriated in 1839.

In 1839, two further important steps were taken; the grant, increased to £30,000, was no longer limited exclusively to the erection of schools, but was made generally for the promotion of public education; and a separate Committee of the Privy Council was appointed "to superintend the application of any sums voted by Parliament" for that purpose. This Committee met for the first time on the 1st June, 1839, when they adopted a report, confirmed by Order in Council two days later, by which they recommended that the £10,000 voted by Parliament in 1835 towards the establishment of Normal Schools should be divided equally between the National Society and the British and Foreign School Society, and that the annual Parliamentary grants should continue to be chiefly applied in aid of subscriptions for building schools connected with those societies. Power, however, was reserved to devote part of the fund to the support, in particular cases, of schools similarly connected; to the aid, in exceptional cases, of other schools; to the conduct of enquiries as to the state of education in England and Wales; and to carrying out a system of Inspection of all schools aided by the State. It was further recommended that submission to such inspection should in future be made a condition of any aid granted either towards the establishment or support of normal or other schools.

This claim of a right of inspection, which appears to us not merely a natural corollary to the grant of pecuniary assistance, but almost an inherent duty on the part of the State, gave rise at the time to a great deal of difficulty on all sides, and particularly with the supporters of the British and Foreign School Society. With regard to schools in connection with the National Society or the Church of England, the difficulty was speedily solved by an arrangement that the Inspectors for such schools should be appointed, and continue in office, only with the concurrence of the Archbishop of Canterbury or York, as the case might be; that the instructions to such inspectors, with regard to religious teaching, should be framed by the Archbishops; and that copies of the Inspectors' reports should be sent to them and to the Bishops of the respective dioceses. Similar arrangements were about the same time made in respect of schools connected with the Church of Scotland—the Committee of Council undertaking to consult the Education Committee of the General Assembly with respect to the selection of the inspectors of such schools. In reference to the British Schools, however, the controversy lasted for some years, being settled in the end by the Committee of Council making a similar concession in this as in the other cases, and agreeing that the Inspectors should not be appointed without the entire concurrence of the Society. Even this arrangement was not arrived at without entailing the secession of a considerable number of the Society's supporters, who formed themselves into a new organization for the promotion of schools which should be entirely free from support or control by the Government.

The next important step in the progress of our educational system was made in 1846, when what is known as the Pupil-Teacher system was introduced in place of the monitorial; both the payment of the pupil-teachers themselves and the remuneration of the Head teachers for instructing them being directly undertaken by the State. Exhibitions of £20 or £25 were also provided to enable the more promising pupil-teachers, on the completion of their apprenticeship, to enter a normal school; and payments of £20 at the end of the first, £25 at the end of the second, and £30 at the end of the third year of instruction, were offered to the managers of such school for each student satisfactorily trained by them for three years. At the same time, as a further inducement for teachers to undergo a course of training, a special payment, varying from £15 to £30 a year in the case of a schoolmaster, and of two-thirds of those amounts in the case of a schoolmistress, was promised to each teacher who, after one, two, or three years' training, accepted appointment to a school under inspection. Power was also taken for the Committee of Council to grant a pension to any teacher who, after fifteen years' service, should be rendered incapable by age or infirmity of continuing to teach a school efficiently. These regulations practically transformed the teachers into paid servants of the State.

The rule limiting aid almost exclusively to schools connected with either the National or the British and Foreign School Society was repealed in 1847; and, on the 28th June and 18th December of that year respectively, minutes were passed admitting to the benefits of Government aid schools connected with either the Wesleyan Association, or the Roman Catholic Poor School Committee.

In 1853, capitation grants were introduced tentatively, in agricultural districts and unincorporated towns of less than 5,000 inhabitants. The amount varied from 4s. to 6s. per head in the case of boys', and from 3s. to 5s. in the case of girls' schools, according to the relative smallness of the schools; and the grant was subject to certain conditions as to income, attendance, and results—of which, probably, those most deserving of attention at the present time were the requirements that each scholar should pay a fee of not less than 1d. per week, and that three-fourths at least of the children should pass certain prescribed examinations. The restriction of these grants to agricultural districts and small towns was removed in January, 1856, and from that time the Capitation Grant became a distinct feature, of universal application, in the Government's scheme of assistance to elementary schools.

In 1856, a Vice-President of the Committee of Council on Education was appointed, who should be directly responsible to the House of Commons for the distribution of the sums voted by them for the promotion of education.

The appointment, in 1858, of a Royal Commission (usually known as the Duke of Newcastle's Commission) to enquire into the state of popular education in the country, marks the close of what may be called the period of tentative development in the relations of the State to education—a period which had lasted for just one quarter of a century, and during which the annual Parliamentary vote had grown in amount from £20,000 to little less than £700,000.

The report of that Commission, presented early in 1861, contained many important recommendations, to scarcely any of which has effect been given to the present day. They would, to some extent, have approximated our educational system to that which had then been recently introduced into the Province of Upper Canada, and upon which many educational reformers still look as a model for imitation. The report suggested the universal creation of County and Borough Boards of Education, to whom the duty of examining the schools in their respective districts should be delegated, and who should be required to supplement the Parliamentary grant by payments from the local rates. On the other hand, it recommended that the State should cease to make payments to individual teachers, dealing exclusively in future with the managers of schools, and that to secure the more uniform distribution of the teaching given in schools, each child should be individually examined, and " the prospects and position of the teacher" made "dependent, to a considerable extent, on the results of this examination."

In the following year, Mr. Lowe, then Vice-President of the Committee of Council, introduced what is known as the " Revised Code " for regulating the future distribution of the Parliamentary grant—a document professedly based upon the recommendations of the Royal Commission, but which in fact did little more than adopt, in a crude and most objectionable form, the single recommendation of the Commissioners for "individual examination" and "payment by results." On the principle of "payment by results" much difference of opinion still exists, but of the method by which it was sought to apply that principle in the "Revised Code" there is, among educationalists, practical unanimity of condemnation.

The withdrawal from them, without any form of compensation, of the direct payments, and particularly of the prospects of superannuation, previously guaranteed them, has always been denounced by the teachers affected, as a distinct breach of faith on the part of the Government—a breach of faith which has ever since led teachers to adopt an attitude of suspicion towards the central authorities.

The principles introduced by the Revised Code, into the system upon which the Parliamentary Grant is distributed, remain in force to the present day, though the details of their application have been very much modified, and its area greatly extended during the interval. It is, however, by no means improbable that before these lines appear in print, proposals will have been made by the Government which, without absolutely abandoning those principles, will so far modify their application as to permit the restoration of the better features of the earlier system, while excluding the evils by which they were then attended.

The subsequent history of the subject is too recent, and too much within the memory of the general public, to need more than such a passing reference as will recall to mind its most prominent incidents. In 1870 was passed the first of the Education Acts. It had for its object to secure that there should be in "every school district a sufficient amount of accommodation in public elementary schools" for "all the children resident in such district"; incidentally it provided for the formation under certain circumstances of School Boards, and permitted such boards when formed to make school attendance compulsory in their respective districts. The Act passed in 1876 placed for the first time on the Statute book a declaration that it is "the duty of the parent of every child to cause such child to receive efficient elementary instruction in reading, writing, and arithmetic," and provided certain penalties for non-fulfilment of this duty—creating, for districts not under School Boards, a new class of authorities, called School Attendance Committees, for its enforcement. Besides these two main enactments, Acts of minor importance were passed in 1878 and 1880.

Within the last few years two important Royal Commissions have examined and reported on various aspects of the educational system, making numerous recommendations which still await the necessary steps being taken for carrying them into effect. The first was the Royal Commission on Technical Instruction appointed in 1881; the second, that nominated in January, 1886, to enquire into the working of the Education Acts. Whenever practical operation is given to the suggestions of these Commissions, elementary education in this country will enter on an entirely new era, and one fraught with momentous effects on the well being of the nation.

The distinctive features which the course of its development, as traced in the foregoing sketch, has impressed upon our English system of elementary education—those in which it differs from the corresponding systems of every other country—may be said to be :—

(1.) Its dual system of management, under which two-thirds of the provision for elementary education is in the hands of private managers;

(2.) The arrangements by which a system that, so far as the State is concerned, is professedly an entirely secular one, is in reality of a pronouncedly religious, and in the great majority of cases of a distinctly denominational character;

(3.) The fact that the supervision of the central authority is based, not upon any inherent right in the State to regulate the education of its future citizens, but upon the share which it bears in the cost of the education provided; and

(4.) The system by which the amount of the central authority's contribution towards the maintenance of a school is regulated—a system popularly known by the name of " payment by results."

Other conspicuous features of the system, but in which it is not so markedly contrasted with those of other nations are :—

The methods adopted for the selection and training of teachers;
The contribution by the parents in the form of school fees; and
The arrangements for enforcing school attendance, and for dealing with the children of vicious or criminal parents.

From the brief outline of the history of the system which has just been given it will be seen that, following the example of the two societies which acted as pioneers in the work, the Government of this country has throughout limited its action almost exclusively to fostering local effort. In the course pursued for this purpose it deliberately relied—so long as it could do so entirely—upon the zeal and enthusiasm of the various religious bodies; and it was only when these proved unequal to the enormous task of providing and maintaining school accommodation for the whole of the child population of the kingdom that resort was had to any other form of local effort. The object and effect of the Government's action was very accurately described by Sir J. Kay-Shuttleworth (a former Secretary of the Education Department), in his " Memorandum on Public Education " drawn up in 1868. He says " The intention of the Minutes of 1846 was to give an impulse to the growth and improvement of the system founded by the religious communities; " and he states that the steps adopted with that object " drew every religious communion, except the Congregational dissenters and bodies allied with them, into co-operation with the Government, and created a vast denominational system, which firmly established popular education on a religious basis." So far, at one time, was this reliance upon the religious denominations carried, that in 1853 the Committee of Council refused an application for aid to a secular school on the ground " that educational grants had not hitherto been applicable to schools exclusively secular "—adding " that they believed that such a decision was in accordance with the views of the great majority of the promoters of education; " " under these circumstances," they concluded, " they had no intention of rescinding the rule on which they had hitherto acted." Although the rule here mentioned was at a later period somewhat relaxed, it was still true in 1870 that almost the whole of the schools in receipt of Government assistance were directly connected with one or other of the various religious denominations in the country, and, subject to inspection by the officers of the Department, were managed exclusively by private persons belonging to those denominations.

The Act of 1870, though it brought into existence local bodies charged with the duty of supplying whatever deficiencies might be found to exist in the school accommodation of their respective districts, was instrumental in greatly increasing the number of schools under private and denominational management. On the one hand, while withdrawing for the future all parliamentary grants "in aid of building, enlarging, improving, or fitting up any elementary school," it permitted such grants to be made in respect of any application received before the close of the year in which it was passed ; and, on the other, it provided that, before any district should be called upon to provide Board School accommodation, a period not exceeding six months should be allowed for the deficiency in accommodation to be provided by voluntary means. No less than 3,111 applications for building grants were lodged within the prescribed period, in about half of which number the erection of the building was subsequently carried out with the aid of a grant. Since that time, 4,800 new or enlarged buildings have without Government assistance been added to the number of voluntary schools, in many, if not in most of which cases the direct object of the provision has been to prevent the necessity arising for the formation of a School Board. In 1870, the officers of the Department inspected 8,281 schools, all under private management, with accommodation for 1,878,584 children. In 1888, they visited 14,659 schools of this kind, with accommodation for 3,547,073 children. It is estimated by the Education Department that these additions from voluntary sources to the educational provision of the country have entailed upon their promoters an expenditure, on buildings alone, since 1870, of nearly £7,500,000.

But in one respect a complete revolution in the action of the Department was brought about by the Act of 1870. While permission was continued to private managers to supply what religious teaching they pleased in the schools under their control, and option was given to the public bodies created under that Act to afford religious instruction of an undenominational character, the direct connection of the State with such instruction, whether denominational or undenominational in its character, was absolutely severed. H.M. inspectors were prohibited from examining the scholars in other than secular subjects, and no portion of the grant was to be given, either directly or indirectly, on account of any religious instruction given in the school; nor was the Department's recognition of a school to be in any way affected by its supplying or failing to supply instruction in religious subjects.

At the time when the Act of 1870 was passed, there were very few of the large towns in which the educational zeal of the religious bodies had been able to keep pace with the rapid growth of the population; while even in country places the number of parishes adequately supplied with school accommodation bore a comparatively small proportion to the whole number. Taking the kingdom as a whole, provision did not exist for the needs of much more than one-third of the entire population, and the system on which even this provision had been made, had the additional drawback that it left districts untouched precisely in proportion to their poverty or lack of enterprise. Inadequate and unsatisfactory though these results may appear, they were the outcome of sustained educational efforts during nearly three-quarters of a century, and of the voluntary expenditure of several millions of money—not to mention the ever-increasing contributions by the State during about half that period. It was clear, therefore, that if the accommodation was ever to overtake the educational needs of the country, and especially if education was to penetrate into the poorest and most backward districts, the system which had previously existed must at least be supplemented from some other quarter. The Act of 1870 accordingly introduced a machinery by which either at the request of the locality, or in the event of sufficient school provision not being supplied by other means to the satisfaction of the Education Department, a School Board might be called into existence in any district, whose duty it would be to supply the deficiency of accommodation at the cost of the local rates. The new Act was at once voluntarily adopted by all but one of the boroughs with a population of 50,000 or more, by a majority of the smaller boroughs, and by a considerable number of parishes. Before three years were expired nearly half the population in England and Wales had, mainly by this means, been brought under the influence of School Boards. The subsequent extension of the system has not been equally rapid nor so generally voluntary; but, at the present time, the districts under School Boards comprise nearly two-thirds of the total population of the kingdom.

The share, however, of the school accommodation of the country which it has fallen to School Boards to provide has not been by any means equally large. The total number of schools which they have either erected or taken over is, according to the latest returns of the Education Department, 4,562, with accommodation for 1,809,481 children, and provided at a cost of some £20,000,000.

It will thus be seen that the provision for elementary education in this country is supplied by 19,221 schools, with a total accommodation for 5,356,554 children—of which rather more than one third is supplied by Board, and the remainder by voluntary schools. The former are as a rule larger and more costly than the latter—their average size being for 397 children as compared with 242, the average of the voluntary schools. The difference in size, and partially in cost, is to be explained by the fact that a larger proportion of the Board than of the voluntary schools are to be found in the great centres of population. Of the voluntary schools, nearly five-sixths in number (11,825), with five-sevenths of the accommodation, are connected with the Church of England. The remaining 2,834 include 909 Roman Catholic and 553 Wesleyan Schools, while 1,372 are British or undenominational.

All these are what are called "public elementary schools"; that is to say, schools which, whether or not primarily intended for children belonging to a particular religious body, are open to children of all denominations, and in which the religious opinions of the minority are safeguarded by a "Conscience Clause." Section 7 of the Act of 1870 provides that, for a school to be a Public Elementary School and qualified to participate in the Government grant, "it shall not be required as a condition of any child being admitted into or continuing in the school that he shall attend or abstain from attending any Sunday School or any place of public worship," and that "any scholar may be withdrawn by his parent from" any religious "observance or instruction" practised or given in the school "without forfeiting any of the other benefits of the school,"—with several minor provisions having the same object in view. In a Board School, it is further provided, by section 14, that "no religious catechism or religious formulary which is distinctive of any particular denomination shall be taught;" subject, however, to this restriction, it is left to the discretion of the School Board to give or withhold religious instruction, and to regulate the amount and character of the instruction if given. In the arrangements which have been adopted by School Boards in the exercise of this discretion there is almost infinite variety—extending from the mere reading of a chapter of Scripture without note or comment to the giving of systematic instruction in Scripture in accordance with a definite syllabus, which includes the learning of the Lord's Prayer, the Ten Commandments, and, in some cases, the Apostles' Creed. How far the Board Schools, as a whole, are from being justly open to the charge of giving a "Godless" education may be gathered from the following extract from the Report of the late Royal Commission on Education (page 113), viz.:—"We find that out of 2,225 School Boards, representing the judgment of more than sixteen millions of our population, only seven in England and 50 in Wales, according to the Parliamentary Returns of 1879, 1884, and 1886, have dispensed entirely with Religious Teaching or Observances. Most of the School Boards of large towns, following the example of London, have adopted careful schemes for Religious Instruction. Of the large School Boards, one alone dispenses with reading the Bible, and one other alone dispenses with prayers and hymns, while those small Boards which shut out direct religious teaching from their day schools are, in the most part, in Wales, where the Sunday-School system powerfully affects the whole population." The charge, groundless though it is, is a somewhat double-edged weapon; for it is an imputation not so much upon the School Board system as upon the religious character of the constituencies who elect, and whose opinions are represented by, the Boards, and therefore inferentially upon the religious teachers who are very largely responsible for the views of the community on religious matters. In this respect there can be little ultimate difference between voluntary and Board Schools; since the security for the religious character of both alike rests, in the last resort, on a common basis, viz.: the religious convictions of the nation. On this point the following remark of a clergyman, who is at once a prominent educationalist and a sincere friend of voluntary schools, is worthy of the most careful consideration by those who advocate a religious basis for elementary education. He says: "English parents will not readily be induced to permit the elimination of religion from the curriculum taught to their children. If England should be secularized, nothing could then stop the secularization of English schools. But the schools will not be secularized so long as the nation continues to be religious."

In all these schools, Board and voluntary alike, the actual management and the financial responsibility rests with the locality. The managers or the School Board appoint and pay the teachers, maintain the fabric, and supply the books, apparatus, and all other articles necessary for the efficiency of the school. The action of the Government is limited almost exclusively to ascertaining, by means of their staff of Inspectors, that the statutory regulations are complied with, and the conditions, as to efficiency, staff, sanitary arrangements, &c., required to qualify for a grant, duly fulfilled. Failure in these respects may be punished by the reduction, or withholding, of the grant, or in the case of a Board School may, if serious, be visited by a declaration that the Board is in "default," whereupon the Board may itself be superseded for the remainder of its three years' term by another appointed by the Education Department.

The aggregate cost of carrying on these schools amounted during the last year to £7,165,612, or slightly less than £2 for each child in average attendance—of which sum rather more than three-quarters was paid for the salaries of teachers. The cost in Board Schools amounted to £2 4s. 7½d. per child, and in voluntary to £1 16s. 4d. —the former paying 6s. 5¼d. per child more for teachers than the latter. The £4,075,430 of expenditure on voluntary schools was met (nearly) by a grant of £1,874,315 from the Government (equal to 17s. 1¾d. per head on the average attendance), £1,240,287 from school fees, £162,180 income from endowments, and £745,340 from voluntary contributions. The £3,090,182 expended on Board Schools was slightly more than covered by income, derived as follows:—£1,195,070 from Government grants (equal to 18s. 1½d. per head on the average attendance), £621,416 from school fees, £3,902 from endowments or voluntary contributions, and £1,231,787 from the local rates. In the case of the latter schools, a further sum of £968,145 was paid during the year for the sinking fund on the cost of erection.

The conditions which regulate the amount of the Government grant to individual schools, are contained in a document entitled the "New Code," which is laid annually before Parliament, with such alterations as may from time to time be considered desirable. Though considerable changes have been introduced in late years, these conditions are still based on the principle of "payment by results," introduced by Mr. Lowe in 1862. They necessarily differ somewhat in their application to Infants' Schools and schools for older scholars. To the former, the grants are all calculated on the average attendance, and consist, (i.) of a fixed grant of 9s. per head; (ii.) of a "Merit" grant of 2s., 4s., or 6s. according as the Inspector reports the school to be "fair," "good," or "excellent"; (iii.) of 1s. if needlework be satisfactorily taught; and (iv.) of 1s. (or 6d.) if the children are taught to sing by note (or by ear); the maximum receivable by a purely Infants' School is, therefore, 17s. per head. The grants payable to schools for older scholars consist, (i.) of a fixed grant of 4s. 6d. per head; (ii.) of a merit grant of 1s., 2s. or 3s. according as the school is rated "fair," "good," or "excellent"; (iii.) of 1s. (or 6d.) if the children are taught to sing by notes (or by ear); (iv.) of 1d. for every unit of the percentage which the number of "passes" on an examination of each individual child in reading, writing and arithmetic, bears to the whole number of the children whose names have been on the rolls of the school for the twenty-two weeks immediately preceding the close of the month before that in which the examination is held; (v.) of 2s. (or 1s.) for each of two (if so many are taken) of the subjects, English, Geography, Elementary Science, History, and (for girls) Needlework, if the Inspector's report on the examination of the children by classes is good or fair; (vi.) of 1s. if the girls are satisfactorily taught needlework, but not presented for the last-mentioned grant for that subject: —these six items are calculated upon the average attendance—and (vii.) of 4s. per head per subject for each of the elder girls who has received a prescribed amount of instruction in Practical Cookery, and for each child who passes in not more than two "specific" subjects, *i.e.*, subjects other than those previously mentioned—provided that such child has also been presented for examination in one of the highest three grades (or standards) into which the elementary subjects are divided. The maximum grant obtainable under these rules for any boy is £1 8s. 10d., and for any girl £1 9s. 10d.—the average actually earned being about 18s. A further grant is made of £2, or £3, for each of a limited number of pupil-teachers who passes fairly, or well, in the annual examinations for such teachers held by H.M. Inspectors. The total amount of grant, which can be paid to any particular school, is subject to the further condition, that it shall not exceed 17s. 6d. per head on the average attendance, except to the same extent that the income of the school from other sources also exceeds that amount; this restriction is popularly known by the name of "the 17s. 6d. limit."

Both the principle of "payment by results," and "the 17s. 6d. limit" have been the subjects of strenuous and prolonged controversy. With regard to the former it is contended that it is essential Parliament should have sufficient security that the purposes for which it votes the public money are in fact attained, and that where so large a proportion of the schools aided are under the sole control of private and irresponsible persons, the only adequate guarantee possible is supplied by the searching examinations of H.M. Inspectors. It is also urged that the abrogation of the system would lead to a revival of the evil, previously obtaining, of the elder and brighter scholars receiving an undue amount of attention, and of the younger and more backward being comparatively neglected. It is likewise maintained by some prominent educationalists that the system, in some form, affords the only security for the adequate remuneration of the more deserving teachers ; for if the ready means now afforded, of approximately estimating the relative ability of different teachers, were removed, the representatives of the ratepayers at least would have much difficulty in justifying the payment to one teacher of more than to another, with the inevitable result that salaries would tend more and more to sink to a dead level. In support of this view it is pointed out that already the salaries of teachers in England have risen to a level higher on the average than that obtaining in any other large country, and that this rise shows no signs of ceasing. In 1851 it was calculated that the average salary of certificated masters—taking head and assistant teachers together—was only £65 ; in 1868 it was £91 ; in 1877, £115 ; and in 1888, £120 ; while between the last-mentioned dates the percentage of the total number receiving salaries of £200 a year or more, rose from 5·6 to 12·75, and the actual number receiving £300 a year or more, increased fivefold. In the State of New York, notwithstanding the relatively much higher cost of living, the average income of schoolmasters is given at 409·27 dollars or a fraction over £85 a year.

On the other hand, the evils of the system are very widely and very strongly urged. In the first place, when the Government pay so much per subject, it is necessary for them to place some limit upon the number of subjects taken, and this necessarily leads to the curriculum in the schools being unduly meagre ; it is difficult to say whether a knowledge of History or of Geography is the more important to the future citizens and rulers of a world-wide empire, yet both cannot be taken—nor either, except to the exclusion of Elementary Science, than which perhaps no subject, except drawing, forms a more important part in the education of a great industrial people. Again the endeavour to bring up all children to the same level regardless of the diversity in their natural abilities, leads to the over-pressure of the dull, and to the neglect, and consequent discouragement of the clever. A system, moreover, under which the exclusion of a few backward children would directly increase the teacher's emoluments, as well as diminish his trouble, offers an almost irresistible temptation to the adoption of that course ; while nothing more directly tends to induce, one might almost say to manufacture, truancy, than this discouragement, on the one hand, of the backward, and, on the other hand, of the brilliant children. The necessity of making each child "pass" leads inevitably to "cram" being substituted for teaching ; with the result that a very large portion of the "knowledge" paid for by the State is forgotten almost immediately it has served the purpose of getting the child through the examination. After weighing carefully, as they say, all the evidence laid before them tending to show the evils which arise from the present method of payment by results, the late Royal Commission on Education expressed the conviction " that the distribution of the Parliamentary grant cannot be wholly freed from its present dependence on the results of examination without the risk of incurring graver evils than those which it is sought to cure." Nevertheless, they added that they were "unanimously of opinion that the present system of 'payment by results' is carried too far, and is too rigidly applied, and that it ought to be modified and relaxed in the interests equally of the scholars, of the teachers, and of education itself." It is more than probable that effect will, to a large extent, be given to these opinions of the Commissioners in the forthcoming revised edition of the New Code.

"The 17s. 6d. limit" was imposed for the purpose, which its supporters contend it has fulfilled, of inducing greater liberality on the part of voluntary subscribers, and it is urged that any relaxation of this rule would be immediately followed by a falling off in receipts from private sources. On the other hand, it has certainly had the effect of inducing managers, very often much against their will, to raise their fees to the utmost obtainable, and thus of increasing the burden which the education of their children entails upon the poor. The income derived by voluntary schools from this source was 8s. 7¼d. in 1868, and in 1888, 11s. 0¾d., an increase of 28·5 per cent. The principal objection, however, that is raised to the limitation is, that its effect is almost exclusively confined to schools, which, though situated in poor neighbourhoods, are carried on with thorough efficiency; that its effect on such schools is in direct proportion to their efficiency; and that it cripples the education of the poor by discouraging the managers and teachers undertaking subjects the grants for which would be earned only to be withheld under this provision. For its ostensible purpose, moreover, the limitation is not particularly successful; for the school in which only low fees can be charged frequently suffers deduction under this clause, notwithstanding that the managers have raised considerable sums from voluntary sources, while a school with high fees will receive its grant in full, though the managers may contribute little or nothing to its maintenance. The Commissioners accordingly recommend that the limitation be repealed.

Among the conditions upon which a school is permitted to receive a Government grant, one of the principal is that the head teacher shall hold a certificate from the Education Department, and that there shall be staff of teachers recognized by that Department, bearing a definite proportion to the attendance. The recognized teachers consist of three main divisions, Certificated, Assistant, and Pupil-Teachers. As the latter form the main source from which the other classes are recruited, it may be well to deal with them first. Pupil-teachers are young persons of not less than fourteen years of age, who, after passing an entrance examination, are apprenticed for a term of four, three, or two years, according to their age and attainments. During their apprenticeship they are to be employed in school work for not more than twenty-five hours per week, and in return for their services are entitled to receive, in addition to a small stipend, instruction for not less than five hours per week from a certificated teacher or teachers. At the end of each year of their term they are examined by H.M. Inspectors, whose adverse report may lead to a prolongation of their apprenticeship. On the satisfactory completion of their term they are entitled to recognition as Assistant Teachers. As to the value of this system, which was originally adopted from Holland, there exists among educationalists much difference of opinion. On the one hand, it is contended that "the time occupied in teaching destroys the pupil-teacher's intellectual freshness and energy, so that both teaching and learning suffer," and that as a source for the supply of the future teachers of the country "it is at once the cheapest and the worst possible." On the other hand, experienced Principals of Training Colleges speak most highly of the advantages of the system in preparing young persons to be teachers; for "the power which is acquired between the ages of fourteen and eighteen can scarcely ever be acquired to perfection afterwards," and they find that there is "the greatest difference between students who have been pupil-teachers and those who have not, in their ability to handle a class, in their power of discipline, and in their capacity to deal with all the little difficulties of school work." The truth appears to lie in the combination of the two views; the system is an admirable one for developing the power to teach, but, as at present usually carried out, scarcely affords the young teachers sufficient opportunities of self-culture. To remedy the latter evil is the special object of the "centre-system" of teaching which has recently been adopted, with most encouraging results, by several of the larger School Boards. Under that system the pupil-teachers are generally relieved, especially during the earlier years of apprenticeship, of some of the teaching previously required; and, instead of receiving their own instruction exclusively in their schools, are (in some places in addition, in others in substitution) gathered together into classes for collective instruction. Imperfect, and capable of improvement, though the system may be, probably its strongest defence lies in the fact that it does furnish the country with an adequate supply of teachers, while it is more than probable that, under the special economic conditions of this country, any other system would fail to do so—at least in the case of male teachers. This latter consideration prevailed with the Commissioners, and led them to express the opinion that, "with modifications, tending to the improvement of their education, the apprenticeship of pupil teachers ought to be upheld."

In the July of each year the Government hold an examination—attended chiefly by young persons who have just completed, or are in the last year of, an apprenticeship, but which is open to any person who "will be more than 18 years of age on the 1st January next following the date of the examination "—on the results of which "Queen's Scholarships," entitling the holders to two years' residence and training at the expense of the Government in a Training College, are distributed to the number of some 700 for males and 900 for females each year. Persons who pass this examination, but are for any reason unable to take up Queen's Scholarships, are recognized as Assistant Teachers, even though they may not have been pupil-teachers.

For the training of the holders of Queen's Scholarships there are in all 43 colleges—17 for masters only, 25 for mistresses only, and 1 for both masters and mistresses. Of these, 13 for masters and 17 for mistresses are connected with the Church of England; 1 for masters and 2 for mistresses are Roman Catholic ; and 1 for masters and 1 for mistresses are Wesleyan ; while 2 for masters and 6 for mistresses are undenominational. All alike are exclusively residential at present; but strong representations were laid before the Royal Commission as to the desirability of the establishment of Day Training Colleges, especially in connection with some of the numerous University Colleges which have been founded of late years in the large centres of population; and it is not improbable that effect will shortly be given to these representations. The couse of training in the present colleges extends over two years, at the end of each of which the students are examined by H.M. Inspectors ; those who are successful in the 2nd year's examination receiving 2nd class certificates, and those successful in the 1st year's examination, 3rd class. The former, which alone entitle the holders to train pupil-teachers, are raised to the 1st class after ten years successful service. These examinations, and the dependent certificates, are also open to persons serving as assistant teachers in elementary schools, provided they are not less 21 years of age.

For several years past some effort has been made to attract to the elementary schools, as teachers, persons who have had the benefit of university or other higher training ; but the requirement that they should serve for twelve months under a certificated teacher, and should afterwards obtain certificates themselves only by undergoing the usual examination, has hitherto practically deterred university graduates from offering themselves for the work. The demand, however, which exists, and which is yearly increasing, for the services of teachers with higher attainments than those that the possession of a certificate necessarily implies, is inducing considerable numbers of certificated masters to qualify themselves for the degrees of universities, like London and Dublin, which do not insist upon residence. And there can be little doubt that, if sufficient encouragement is given by the Department to local university colleges, the opportunities of higher culture afforded by these institutions, will be gladly embraced by a considerable number of those who are seeking to enter the ranks of elementary teachers.

Except in country districts with a sparse population the English schools are usually divided into three separate departments, for boys, girls, and infants respectively, each under its own head teacher. In some of the larger districts, however, where schools of more than ordinary size are possible, it is not uncommon for there to be a fourth department, intermediate between that for infants and those for older children, and confined to children in the lower standards. These are usually mixed schools ; as from considerations of economy are the majority of schools in rural districts. In some districts—especially in the north of England—schools of the Scotch type have been introduced. These are large institutions, containing sometimes 1,000 or more children, in which the sexes are mixed throughout, and in which the whole school is placed under one head.

It is claimed for these latter schools, that the unity of purpose running throughout them economizes the teaching power and renders it more efficient; that the massing of the children in such large numbers permits of a finer graduation according to ability; and that the mixing of the sexes has moral advantages of much value, and facilitates considerably the maintenance of discipline. From these various circumstances mixed schools seem to be growing somewhat in favour, and now include in number fully 64 per cent. of the separate departments in public elementary schools for children above the age of infants. Twenty years ago the corresponding percentage was 55.

Until the year 1871 attendance at schools was entirely voluntary, except in the case of children employed in Factories and Workshops, and of children committed to Industrial Schools and Reformatories or detained in Workhouse Schools.

A series of enactments, commencing with the Factory Act of 1833 and terminating with the Factory and Workshop Act, 1870, had been passed for regulating, among other things, the employment of women and children in factories and workshops. These required as a condition of the employment of children under thirteen years of age in any of the regulated industries, that the children should attend school either half each day or on alternate days. These enactments were extended by later legislation, and were finally consolidated by the Factory and Workshop Act of 1878, which now regulates the matter.

Another series of statutes, commencing with the Reformatory Schools Act of 1854 and consolidated by the Reformatory and Industrial Schools Acts of 1866—the provisions of which, somewhat extended by subsequent legislation, are still in force—had provided for the commitment of children who had fallen into crime or were living under certain specified conditions likely to lead them to do so, to schools in which they would not only be fed, clothed, and educated, but receive industrial training of such a nature as to prepare them to earn their own living honestly after the expiration of their term.

By the Act of 1870, which did not come into practical operation until the following year, an optional power was given to School Boards to make bye-laws requiring the attendance at school of children of "not less than five nor more than thirteen years" of age. In 1876 this power was extended to a new set of authorities, called into existence under the name of School Attendance Committees, for districts not under School Boards; and at the same time a new method of procedure was provided, and applied to children up to fourteen years of age, for dealing with cases of habitual neglect, or with children in evil surroundings or not under proper control, and a system of indirect compulsion was introduced, by the prohibition of the employment of children who had not attained a given standard of education, or, as an alternative, fulfilled certain requirements as to school attendance. By the Act of 1880, the making of bye-laws ceased to be an optional matter with School Boards or School Attendance Committees, who were universally required to adopt and enforce such regulations; and at the same time indirect compulsion was made more stringent by abolishing the alternative qualification for employment by school attendance. The combined effect of the various enactments above referred to—Factory Acts, Reformatory and Industrial Schools Acts, and Elementary Education Acts—is a somewhat complicated system of direct and indirect compulsion, which may, however, with sufficient accuracy be summarized as follows:—

1. The parent of any child between the ages of five and thirteen years who has not passed the Exemption Standard fixed by the local Bye-laws—generally the fifth or sixth standard—may be fined a sum not exceeding (with costs) 5s. if the child does not attend school regularly; as may also, under similar circumstances, the parent of a child between thirteen and fourteen years of age who has not passed the Fourth Standard.
2. A child under fourteen whose education is habitually neglected —generally the child of drunken or dissolute parents—may be committed to a Day Industrial School.
3. A child under fourteen who is beyond the control of his parents may be sent to a Truants' School.
4. The child under fourteen of criminal or grossly immoral parents may be committed to a Certified Industrial School— as may also a child of the like age who is a vagrant or the companion of criminals, or a child under twelve who has fallen into crime.
5. A child over twelve who has committed actual crime may be sent to a Reformatory.
6. The employer (and the parent) of any child under thirteen years of age (or under fourteen, unless he has passed a prescribed standard) in any regulated industry may be fined an amount, not exceeding from £2 to £5, according to the particular circumstances (or in the case of the parent, not exceeding £1), if the child does not attend school half time.
7. The employer in any other manner of a child who has not passed the Exemption Standard corresponding to his age may be fined any amount up to £2.

Day Industrial and Truants' Schools are institutions called into existence by the Act of 1876. The former are, as their name implies, day schools; and the children committed to them are fed as well as taught, and are to some extent trained in industrial work. Failure to attend is punishable by commitment to a Certified Industrial School, and the parent or any other person who may prevent the child attending is liable to any penalty not exceeding £5. The cost of carrying on a school of this kind is ordinarily about 3s. a head per week, of which sum 1s. is defrayed by a grant from the Treasury, and the remaining 2s. is nominally assessed upon the parents, but under existing arrangements can be collected only to a very limited extent. The term of commitment is usually for three years, but children may at any time after one month be licensed on condition of regular attendance at an ordinary school. Day Industrial Schools are under the inspection of the Home Office.

The Truants' School is a modified form of Certified Industrial School, in which children are detained under rigid discipline, but usually for very short terms. They are also subsidized by the Treasury, and inspected by the Home Office. The term of commitment is usually until fourteen or sixteen years of age, but licences conditional upon attendance at an ordinary school, and revocable at any time in case of non-compliance, are generally granted after the expiration of about six weeks or two months of the term.

The whole of the existing arrangements, however, with regard to Reformatory, Industrial, Truants' and Day Industrial Schools will probably before long undergo entire revision, in accordance with the recommendations of a Royal Commission, which enquired into the subject some few years since. Bills for this purpose have been introduced into Parliament for the last two or three sessions by the Government, but have failed to pass owing to the pressure of other business.

The foregoing sketch of the history and present condition of the English system of elementary education is necessarily very incomplete; some important matters, such, for instance, as the methods of instruction pursued, are altogether omitted, while others are passed over with but brief allusion. It is hoped, however, that the sketch, imperfect though it is, may serve its purpose in removing some of the misapprehensions on the subject which are widely prevalent.

The system itself is at the present moment in a transitional condition, and will probably within the next few years be largely transformed. The abolition of school fees—already to a great extent effected in Scotland—which in principle appears to have received the acceptance of both of our great political parties, cannot fail, if carried out, to profoundly modify existing arrangements. The demand for technical instruction, though not directly affecting elementary schools to any great extent, may indirectly produce material changes in their constitution, and especially in their ordinary curriculum. The hitherto almost exclusively literary character of their instruction will probably, in face of this demand, give place to training of a more practical nature, and the bias given by the education be rather towards the higher forms of manual work than to the career of a clerk. The growing perception that a child's education cannot, in any rank of life, be considered complete when he is thirteen or fourteen years of age, and that, if not kept up, a vast amount of the knowledge upon which the nation is expending so lavishly its time and money, is entirely forgotten, is bringing to the front the question of providing evening continuation schools. Already the attention of Parliament has on several occasions been drawn to this subject, though as yet without effect; and there can be little doubt that even without legislative assistance, the action of the Education Department, and the initiative of local bodies, will be sufficient to carry largely into effect the important and unanimous recommendations on this subject of the recent Royal Commission.

EDWARD M. HANCE.

PART III.

STATE EDUCATION IN SCOTLAND.

In England, a national system of Education is, comparatively speaking, a thing of yesterday. Until the Act of 1870 was passed by Mr. Forster, there was nothing but a casual provision for any educational supply throughout the country. In some districts, indeed, the liberality of the "pious founder" had established the means of education: but the extent to which these means were used, and the degree of efficiency in which they were maintained, was left to the accident of local energy. And for the rest, the education of the people was left altogether to the voluntary efforts of public-spirited men, aided by the charity of those who chose to contribute to their work. Not until 1870 was there any guarantee that the work of charity should, if need be, be supplemented by statutory means. Not until the Acts of 1876 and 1880 were passed, was there a statutory authority in every parish, armed with the power of enforcing compulsory attendance at school. And even the Acts which found a place upon the Statute Book between 1870 and 1880, related only to Elementary Education. The State has as yet assumed no responsibility in the sphere of Secondary Education, so essential to place the coping-stone upon any complete system. Encouragement has, indeed, been given by the grants from the Science and Art Department, towards one very important branch of such Education: but the State encourages only—it does not initiate or organize. Secondary Education is still mainly dependent upon endowments. These Endowments have, it is true, been re-arranged, and in large measure adapted to modern needs, by means of the Endowed Schools Acts. But such re-arrangement has proceeded upon no very certain or definite plan: and, as a consequence, jealousies have been engendered, bitter political feeling has been aroused, and serious checks have been placed in the way of the work, from the fact of the nation having no very certain or clear idea as to the relation of the Secondary to the Elementary Schools, as to the real interest which the poorer classes have in higher education, and as to the functions which higher schools have to fulfil in any national system worth of the name. As it is, the re-organization of these schools has not proceeded far enough. The schemes which have been passed provide for no inspection of the schools, and leave them exposed to the danger of inefficiency and gradual decay, to which so many amongst them have already, in so many instances, succumbed.

But in Scotland the work of National Education has a far longer history, and has been far more drastic in its operation. The national instinct was the first prompter in the movement. For a nation, fairly populous in proportion to its territory, with few resources of internal wealth to enable it to compete with its richer neighbours; but at the same time, energetic, ambitious, and full of expedient, Education offered the surest leverage by which to force its way to the front. It is to the credit of her leaders, for centuries past, that they recognized this need, and endeavoured to provide for it. The earliest schools were naturally those connected with the religious houses. But even before the Reformation, other educational provision had sprung up to share the field with these. The leading towns had their Grammar or Latin Schools, with elementary schools below them. As early as the days of James IV., before the close of the 15th century, there was a statute requiring all freeholders of substance to send their heirs to school, and to keep them there until they had "perfect Latin"—Latin being then the common language of all civilised Europe, and the only means by which young Scotchmen could successfully push their way to high employment abroad. After the Reformation, the Educational movement acquired a new impetus. The Reformed Church in 1560 prescribed a plan, which had almost as much force as statutory authority, according to which every town "of reputation" was to have a "Latin School"; while the "upland" or country parishes were to have, each, a teacher of the first rudiments. Nor were the upper and lower ends of the ladder neglected. In the chief towns there were to be colleges for "logic, rhetoric, and the tongues": while assistance was to be given to the poor to send their children to school.

The "Book of Policy" in which the Church laid down this scheme, had an authority, as we have said, little less than statutory. But the disturbed state of the country, and the narrowness of available resources, often led to the scheme being more honoured in the breach than in the observance. No assessment was as yet imposed for the purposes of education; nor was such an assessment established until the Privy Council in 1616 laid a tax upon the land, to provide a school in each Parish. The decree did not receive statutory authority until 1633, when Episcopacy was dominant under the influence of Laud: but the power of assessing, which was placed mainly in the hands of the Bishop, was probably but little exercised in practice during the stormy interval which followed. Finally in 1696, after the Revolution, a period of educational activity set in, reaching from the Universities, which were made the subject of a thorough and searching examination by a Commission, down to the Parish Schools, which were at last given a secure and permanent existence. The settlement of these schools did not come one moment too soon for the urgent necessities of the nation. Had Scotland, disturbed and torn by nearly two centuries of unceasing religious and political struggle, during which the early promise of her literature had been well-nigh crushed out of life, begun the critical epoch of the eighteenth century without an organized system of national education, she would have been ill-fitted to take her place in that partnership for which the Union paved the way, and still more ill-fitted to reap the rich harvest of prosperity which the development of commerce yielded, and which only the vigour, enterprise, and sound equipment of her sons enabled her so richly to share. As it was, the Parish School soon became the most characteristic trait of Scottish life: a nursery of sound though simple training, in which all classes of the Scottish people found new encouragement to a common sympathy, that mingling of class with class which is an absolute necessity in a poor but courageous nation, and which became so typical of the "kindly" Scot.

The Act of 1696 imposed upon the heritors, or landowners, of each parish the duty, at their own cost, of providing a school-house, and of paying a salary to the teacher. It provided, what previous Acts had failed to provide, a means of preventing indifference or neglect: because the Presbytery of the bounds was empowered, in case of failure on the part of the heritors, to erect the school, and maintain the teacher, at the cost of the defaulting heritors. It is not too much to say that this Statute opened a new era in the lowlands of Scotland, and first pointed out the road by which those sons of Scotland who had previously sought service in the armies of any contending powers in Europe, began to spread their influence over the civilized world by the peaceful methods of enterprise and commerce. It was long, of course, before the influence of the Act could extend to the remote valleys and mountains of the Highlands: but it spread as the rule of law prevailed, and insufficient as the provision often was, it still formed the charter of Scottish education, by which each Scottish boy could claim as a right the education fitted to give him a start in the world.

The maintenance of the teacher was, naturally, in so poor a country, calculated upon a scale incredibly small, even allowing for the great difference in the value of money. It was not until 1803, that the salary was fixed at a sum varying from £15 to £20 a year, with a house and garden. But small as were his resources, the teacher was a freeholder, who, once appointed, could not be dismissed, except by a process strictly laid down by statute. He was poor, but he was also independent: and the advantages of his position were enhanced by the fact that he could count the highest as well as the humblest in the parish amongst his pupils, and was generally able to send, yearly, a quota of scholars to the University who might, in future years, reflect some glory upon their former Dominie.

As time went on, however, the destitution of the Highland districts became more appalling. There the Act was practically a dead letter. Through wide regions in Invernesshire and Argyllshire, where parishes stretched for thirty or forty miles, there was no school within the reach of some 95 out of every 100 children. In 1824, the attention of the Church was especially directed to this, partly by the Commission of Inquiry set on foot by Lord Brougham. The Church made vigorous efforts to grapple with the evil; but it was obliged to admit that charitable and voluntary effort was overpowered;

that the existing statutes were insufficient to overtake the needs of these vast stretching parishes; and that larger resources must be provided if the evil was to be met and overcome. The last statute, dealing with the old Parish Schools, was passed in 1861. It considerably curtailed the old privileges of the Church; restricted the formularies to which the adhesion of the teacher was required; and substituted the Universities for the Presbyteries in the examination of teachers. The salaries of the teachers were at the same time increased; and on the whole, while wide gaps in the national system still remained, the Parish Schools had been strengthened, enriched, and liberalized before the Commission of Inquiry of 1864, which was the prelude to the Education Act of 1872. Not only was there a strict conscience clause, but that conscience clause was operative in practice. Roman Catholics as well as Presbyterians were educated at the Parish Schools; and in 1829 the General Assembly of the Church had expressly enjoined that no instruction should be pressed on the children of Roman Catholics to which their parents or the priest objected. We have seen how, so long ago as the 15th century, provision was to be made for assisting the poor in obtaining education. In practice this still prevailed. Fees were charged as a rule; but their amount varied by usage according to the means of the parent; and in the case of the poor they were not exacted at all.

Already, as in England, so in Scotland, the State had stepped in, as a source of assistance and encouragement. In England that assistance—first granted towards buildings in 1832, developing in 1839 into a system of inspection, and in 1846 into grants for maintenance according to certain defined principles—was an encouragement offered to purely voluntary effort, unprescribed by the Statute Book. In Scotland—while it followed, as to dates and objects, exactly the same course—we must not forget that it was merely a contribution from the national exchequer towards schools which, in by far the greater number of cases, were the direct creation of statute law. It is thus necessary to remember that the financial assistance granted by Parliament rested upon a very different principle in England and in Scotland. But in both countries, the Committee of Privy Council, or the Education Department, as it soon afterwards was called, exercised exactly the same control and authority. It merely laid down the conditions of grant, and by means of its Inspectors ascertained that these conditions were fulfilled. It did not belong to the Department to enforce the Statutes to which the Scottish Parish Schools owed their existence, any more than it fell to it to compel the establishment of National Schools by voluntary effort in England.

We have thus brought down the history of the Scottish Parish Schools to the eve of recent legislation. But this does not exhaust the whole sphere of the national system. We have seen how early efforts had been made to establish Secondary or Grammar Schools. These had gradually taken shape; and not the least important part of the Scottish Educational provision was that afforded by the Burgh Schools. These Burgh Schools were part and parcel of the national system, and were by no means dependent upon charity or endowments. They derived a certain income from the Common Good, or public funds of the Burgh, and their maintenance was a duty laid upon the Town Council. In principle this was tantamount to their being rate-supported Schools; and although the available funds were often scanty, the part they played in the education of the country was no insignificant one. In a country so poor as Scotland it was impossible that lavish endowments should be spent upon grammar schools, or that a long period in the lives of Scottish youth, who had their way to push in the world, should be consumed in higher education. But within their own sphere these schools were vigorously and energetically conducted. Their fees were reduced by prudent management to the narrowest possible limits. Their staff, though scantily paid, consisted of the picked men of an active and an independent profession. The widespread interest in education, and the management of a public body, were guarantees against their sinking into the state of inefficiency so common in English Grammar Schools. The constant stream of pupils passing from the Burgh Schools to the Universities, served to keep up a high ideal of scholarship. As a consequence, when the Assistant Commissioners appointed by the Schools Inquiry Commission of 1864, accustomed to the slipshod methods and listless inefficiency of the English Grammar Schools, visited Scotland, they were struck by the healthy vigour which pervaded in the Burgh Schools, and saw in them a type which they would gladly have seen more widely spread amongst the richly-endowed Grammar Schools of England, managed by close bodies of trustees, and invigorated by no general educational interest such as prevailed amongst the middle class of Scotland.

These various parts of the national system provided in Scotland that "ladder" which it has been the ambition of educational reformers to repeat all over the kingdom. In the Parish Schools all classes mixed together. This bridged over many a social gulf: and in their picked scholars, who were beyond the reach of the Burgh Schools in the larger towns, the Parish Schools kept in touch with the Universities and with higher education. In the towns, again, all parents who had any ambition for their sons, found at their hands the Burgh Schools, sustained by some contribution from public funds, and providing, at moderate cost, an education fully adequate to the preparation of students for the Universities.

What, then, were the faults which the Commission of Inquiry of 1864 proved to exist in the Scottish national system? In the first place, the Parish Schools, however good in themselves, were unequal to overtake the task imposed upon them by an increasing population. In the Highlands they left wide tracts of country unprovided, and in the towns, a single Parish School was quite insufficient to meet the requirements of crowded areas. Voluntary effort doubtless did much; but not only was it casual in its operation, it was also incapable of rapid and certain development. The Burgh Schools found themselves more and more crippled by want of funds, which left the salaries of the staff insufficient to attract to the profession men of vigour and capacity. The weakness of the Burgh Schools, again, told upon the Universities, which, in the absence of any complete system of secondary education were forced to take upon themselves the education of the tyro, and to receive pupils at an age when they would have worked to more purpose under the strict supervision of a schoolmaster than in the more independent sphere of a professor's lecture-room. The very excellence of the Scottish teachers often led them, inevitably, into a habit of attending most to the picked company of higher scholars, and neglecting the rank and file of their pupils from whom they could not hope to acquire credit in the higher walks of life.

The conviction of these defects gradually gained ground, and prompted the desire to complete, upon an adequate and worthy scale, the national system of which the foundations were so satisfactorily laid. Several attempts at legislation were made before success was attained. But there was one element which made success more easy in Scotland than in England. In Scotland the denominational difficulty presented itself mainly as one of management and not of system. The rivalry between the sects had led to the establishment of Schools which were necessary to maintain their influence, but which gave an education which even in its religious features was practically identical. Such rivalry was certain to continue so long as the Established branch of the Presbyterian Church retained its supremacy in the Parish Schools; and therefore, however liberal and successful its government had been, it was inevitable that such supremacy should cease, seeing that there was something very nearly approaching unanimity amongst Scottish parents as to religious teaching, and the distinction between Schools was maintained only as a badge of sectarianism.

It was in 1872 that Lord Young, then Lord Advocate, succeeded in placing upon the Statute Book the Scotch Education Act, which revolutionised the system. In many of its features that Act presented a striking contrast to the English Education Act which had preceded it. It was not merely an Elementary Education Act: but was intended to provide education "for the whole people of Scotland." Its object was not merely to establish local authorities in places where further provision was required: it established, on the contrary, a School Board in every parish, and placed that Board at once in the management of the Parish Schools, and, in the towns, of the Burgh Schools. In the English Act, building grants were allowed to voluntary managers in order to enable them to supply deficiencies, and thus ward off the intrusion of statutory authorities. In the Scottish Act, such building grants to voluntary managers were to cease, and instead, School Boards were allowed assistance from the exchequer in providing Schools to supply the deficiencies which they found. In the English Act, Voluntary Schools were allowed full liberty of religious teaching, subject to the Conscience Clause, but School Boards were allowed to teach religion only under strict limitations as to formulæ and creeds. In the Scottish Act, a conscience clause was the only restriction upon equal liberty for all; and each locality was left to regulate the religious instruction of its schools, through its own elected representatives. Although no grant was offered to the higher schools, yet these being placed under the management of the School Boards, were continued as part of the national system, and by subsequent statutes were given increased assistance from the rates. Lastly, compulsion was introduced into England only by a gradual process: in Scotland the duty of giving education to his children was imposed as a necessary duty upon every parent by the Education Act of 1872, and an authority was at once brought into existence in every parish for enforcing these compulsory clauses of the Act. A certain uniform standard of exemption from school attendance was imposed by one stroke over the whole of Scotland. Changes of detail had subsequently to be introduced, and the meshes of the net had to be made smaller: but since 1872 it has never been possible to find in Scotland what is still to be found in England, a variation in the standard of exemption as fixed by the bye-laws of two neighbouring parishes.

Upon this solid legislative foundation, the new relations between the Education Department—now, so far as Scotland was concerned, a Scotch Education Department—and the School Boards or other managers of Schools, were based. We have now to see what these relations were, and what are the lines which have been followed by the Central and Local authorities in the development of the national system.

In the first place, with regard to the Imperial grant. The effect of the Act of 1872 was to increase enormously the cost of the system: and the Imperial Exchequer had to take its share of this increase. But more strict conditions of efficiency had to be attached to the larger grant. Local authorities now existed to whom, and not to the teachers, the Department had to look as responsible for the efficiency of schools. With these authorities it rested to make such terms as they pleased with their teachers, and, if they thought it well, to bear casual fluctuations in the grant; but it was necessary to satisfy Parliament that the money it granted was not ill-spent; and at the outset it was therefore considered necessary to impose the strict system of payment by results, which had been introduced by Mr. Lowe's Revised Code of 1862. The Scotch Code, indeed, from the first, recognised something beyond the elementary subjects, and admitted higher education in the ordinary schools as something deserving of a grant. But a severe test had to be imposed in order to check that tendency to neglect the backward scholars, which the previous system, with all its undoubted advantages, certainly was apt to encourage. For fourteen years that system was continued practically without a change. Only in 1886 was it deemed safe to relax the severity, or rather the minuteness, of the test: and in that year, a class examination, with a uniform payment on graduated scales, was substituted for individual examination in the two lower standards. The experiment has been so far successful that the Department has now, in its Code for 1890, just issued, extended that system to the whole school. Individual examination, it is stated, may still be resorted to, as a check upon doubtful efficiency; but otherwise individual examination is no necessary part of the Scottish system, and it will not determine the amount of the Parliamentary subsidy. A similar change was attempted last year for England; but the question was surrounded by too many stormy subjects of debate, in the relations of the Board and the Voluntary Schools, and the attempted change was necessarily postponed. In Scotland, that freedom of organization which has been so long demanded is now conceded, and the rigour of a minute system which, it was asserted, tended to check the best efforts of school and teacher, has been abandoned; and it now rests with the local authorities to show that their own zeal for education is sufficient to dispel all danger of inefficiency as the result of the relaxation. During the seventeen years which have elapsed since the Act was passed, the Parliamentary grant has increased from £140,000 to about £600,000 a year; so that the responsibility thus imposed, first upon the local authorities, and finally upon the Central Department, is no light or nominal one.

During the same period, the contribution from rates has grown until it reaches £247,000 a year, besides the annual obligations which are incurred in loans for the erection of schools. Besides this contribution from the rates to Elementary Schools, there is an annual contribution to the Burgh Schools (in addition to the Endowments derived from the Common Good) of £9,196. This contribution is not met, like the rest of the income derived from rates, by a grant from the Department, because the principle of grants to Higher Schools has not yet been recognised. But if the Department does not allow grants to Higher Schools, it gives, at least, a guarantee, by inspection, of their efficiency. The Education Act of 1878, which gave School Boards enlarged powers of aiding the Burgh Schools, also provided for the inspection of Higher Schools by the Department: and this function was largely extended, in 1882, by the Educational Endowments Act, which required that each scheme should provide for the periodical inspection of Endowed Schools by the Department. The organization of this system of inspection, long a crying want in Scotland, was only completed after the lapse of some years: and it was not until 1886 that the Department was enabled to enter thoroughly upon the work. In that year, however, the system was put in operation. There are now three classes of Higher Schools which are inspected by the Department; the Burgh Schools, towards the cost of which a contribution is made by the Treasury; the Endowed Schools, which are required by their schemes to defray the cost from their endowments; and Private Schools, which, if they apply for inspection, must meet the cost themselves. The system has been completed by the institution of a Leaving Certificate Examination which stamps the standard attained by scholars leaving these Higher Schools, and which is accepted in lieu of various professional examinations, and by the Universities, both of England and Scotland, as exempting from certain preliminary tests. The system has not yet had full time to show its fruits; but the statement issued by the Department shows that while 972 candidates presented themselves at the first examination, the number at the second examination (in 1889) was 2,066.

STATE EDUCATION.

The result so far as the Higher Schools are concerned has been to check their threatened extinction, and to enable them to hold their own in the hope that, some day, a subsidy from the State may enable them to compete on a more secure basis with their better endowed elementary rivals. No result could be more untoward for Scotland than the extinction of her Higher Schools, and the insufficient equipment which her sons would then have for the struggle for existence, which is ever growing in intensity and for which every surrounding nation is preparing with ever-increasing ardour.

In connection with this, it is necessary briefly to refer to two closely related subjects, which are of great importance for the future of higher education in Scotland. The first of these is the re-organization of her endowments under the Educational Endowments Act of 1882. The Commission charged with that work has now come to a conclusion, after seven years of very arduous work. Their course has not always been a smooth one, and they have met at times with a keen, and sometimes a virulent, opposition. The suspicion has been aroused that endowments left for the poor are being diverted to the well-to-do; and such a suspicion, once aroused, is naturally not soon lulled to sleep. It has been kept on the alert by the dislike of avowed reactionaries to change of any sort, and by what is little more than a sentimental regard for those older Hospitals, or institutions, in which the beneficiaries were boarded as well as educated, which have been repeatedly condemned by the verdict of successive Commissions of Inquiry. It is inevitable that the disturbance of charitable funds, however great the evils which these funds have brought in their train, must sometimes involve hardship, and always provoke a certain amount of opposition. But we say unhesitatingly that the opposition has been for the most part undiscriminating and unwise. No Commission could have carried out its work with a more anxious wish to deal leniently with existing interests, and above all to preserve the advantages secured to the poor. But they were bound to deal firmly. Until not only political economy, but the hard facts on which political economy is founded, are banished to Saturn, the evils of indiscriminate doles will inevitably appear. To give by charitable endowment advantages which are secured to the people by statute, as a right, is not to benefit the poor, but to benefit those upon whom the statute has placed a burden which the endowment, so administered, enables them to avoid. To have preserved the Hospitals would have been to perpetuate a system alien to Scottish habit, and condemned by all who studied their effect, as stunting and weakening the faculties of their pupils. And, lastly, to assume that all help to higher education is help withdrawn from the poor, is to be false to all the best traditions of Scotland, to all that intellectual ambition which has been the chief characteristic of her sons, and to discourage that mingling of class with class which has been the best sign of her schools. But to give the opportunity of prolonging his education unduly to a boy selected only on the ground of poverty and not on that of merit, is to inflict upon that boy the irreparable hardship of wasting some precious years of his life in work for which he is unfitted. By all means take every security that the poorest shall have his merits recognized, and that no one shall lose an opportunity by which he might in any way profit, or miss the chance of developing any faculty he possesses. But discriminate in your selection, or you will inevitably take from the boy the healthy stimulus of exertion, and will earn for yourself later the well-deserved blame of having hindered, instead of helped him, in his start in life. Stone by stone the edifice of elementary education has been raised, and step by step the roads towards its portals have been smoothed, until at last even the small toll previously levied at its entrance by way of fees, has been removed. It is now for the nation to build up that separate, but sister, edifice of higher education. No sacrifice is too great to accomplish the work. But it would be the most fatal error to allow the idea to gain credence that this sister edifice is for a class apart, that the nation as a whole has no interest in it, and that to use endowments, either to strengthen its foundations, or to gather aspirants to share its advantages, is in any way to rob the poor.

The Commission may safely allow the results of their work to answer eventually the charges brought against them. In regard to several of the largest endowments, indeed, their action was anticipated by previous reform. The uniquivocal success of such institutions as Watson's College in Edinburgh, Hutchesons' Schools in Glasgow, Gordon's College in Aberdeen, will surely impress the people with the wisdom of the plan on which they have been reorganized. These models have been followed by the recent Commission; and the result of their labours is seen not only in the great reorganized institutions bearing the name of George Heriot in Edinburgh, but also in numerous lesser schools which the reformed application of endowments has enabled them to establish in various parts of Scotland.

Another sphere of higher education has quite recently been submitted to the action of an Executive Commission—that of the Universities. The Scottish Universities present neither in their foundation nor in their history, any very close analogy with the Universities of England. They were not a gradual aggregation of colleges owing their origin to private beneficence and gradually forming the aggregate of a University. The three pre-Reformation Universities of St. Andrews, Glasgow, and Aberdeen, were founded by Bulls of the Pope: the last, that of Edinburgh, was founded by the initiation of the Town Council, and under the patronage of the Crown. Such elements of collegiate foundations as once existed in St. Andrews and Aberdeen have almost disappeared. Throughout their history, all the Universities have been constantly subject to the active exercise of public authority; they were early deprived of the main part of their original property, and have since subsisted partly on annually voted grants by Parliament, and partly on the fees of students, which a practical monopoly of professional education secured to them. But this monopoly was preserved only by the fact of their conforming themselves very strictly to the requirements of the nation. In the widest sense they were national institutions, with small fees, and easily accessible to the poorest. The curriculum which they afforded and the standard of attainment at which they aimed, were both suited to a poor nation, to which a prolonged preliminary training was impossible; and their intimate connection with the schools of the country kept their range of instruction strictly upon the lines which were adapted to the requirements of the Scottish people, which before the development of Scottish commerce, rendered a professional career the object of chief ambition to the most promising Scottish youth. Popular as they were, therefore, the Scottish Universities were limited in the range of studies which they offered. The Church, Medicine, and the Law, were the spheres which the talented Scotch boy sought to enter; and a single course of studies, comprising Classics, Mathematics, and Mental Philosophy, was held to be the course most fitted as a preliminary to all these professions. Of late years the social conditions of the country have been changed. Commerce, Colonial enterprise, and the practical application of mechanical science, now offer tempting careers. The professions no longer present the one goal of ambition; and if, therefore, the Universities are to hold their place as popular and national institutions, they must offer courses of training fitted for these new careers, as the old course was fitted for the three learned professions. So to adapt them is the work that lies before the Commission which is now entering on its labours, and to this the efforts of the Commission must be chiefly directed. No mistake will be more fatal than to attempt a reconstruction of the Universities according to any preconceived ideal or any foreign model. They are the product of Scottish history, and the result of Scottish requirements. These requirements have changed and have multiplied, and the range of the Universities must accordingly be widened. But they must remain as they have been, popular institutions, less occupied with minute scholarship or research than with practical educational needs. The Scottish youth will not be likely to spend a larger part of their lives at the Universities in the future than in the past. The expenses of a University education must not be increased. But on their old lines they must meet the new requirements of the day. As they do so, they will not interfere with, but will enormously increase, the functions of the Secondary Schools. Already the School Boards are doing much in the way of developing these schools: and by means of reformed endowments, their equipments are being increased, and a modern and technical side is being added to the old classical and mathematical course. A new impulse will be given to all this when the Universities introduce a wider choice of studies; and when, by their means, new aims are definitely set before the Schools, the latter will be able to press with greater force their claims to more liberal local and Imperial assistance. The whole range of Scottish Education presents a sufficient number of flaws and gaps; but in its forward progress it has these advantages on its side—a sound tradition, a long growth, a foundation in the history of the country; popular sympathy and interest, and a determination to adapt all its resources energetically to meet new requirements. It has at least avoided one educational danger—that of apathy and stagnation.

We have left to the last any reference to the most recent and momentous change which Scottish Education has undergone. Free Education, or such "assistance" to Education as might at least escape the evident anomaly of forcing a man to pay for what he is forced by statute to supply to his child, has long been a question of academical discussion. No one denies that it presents certain unfavourable aspects, and that the diminution in parental responsibility may involve, at first, some diminution in parental ambition or interest. But such a result must surely be short lived. The compulsory law can be enforced with far greater strictness when the doors of the school are opened free of charge; and compulsion in one generation produces in the next an anxiety to partake of benefits which are realized more distinctly in proportion as they are widely spread. And even those who gave greatest weight to the possible drawbacks were forced to recognise that the change was inevitable. It was left to Scotland to end the academical discussion by a quick practical advance. In 1888 the Chancellor of the Exchequer assigned to local authorities the product of certain taxes, chiefly that of the Probate Duties. When the English Local Government Act was passed the County Councils received their share as a subsidy to local rates. This boon Scotland denied herself; and instead she insisted on devoting a sum, which will amount to about a quarter of a million annually, to the relief of fees. The resolution being taken, the means and plan, according to which it might be carried out, were quickly devised. An arrangement by which the sum should be distributed amongst all State-aided schools, on condition of their relieving fees up to a certain standard, was devised. Into the details and intricacies of this scheme it is unnecessary to enter here; but it is enough to say that from the 1st of October, 1889, the compulsory standards (up to and including the fifth) are entirely free in 3041 out of 3126 Scottish Schools, and in 774 of them the boon of free education is extended even further. The change was easily accomplished; and throughout the whole of Scotland, in spite of varying conditions, and apparently insuperable difficulties, the practical good sense of the nation has enabled it to effect what is little less than a revolution with scarcely any perceptible friction, and with an expedition that was marvellous.

In England, this stage of education has not yet been reached, and many of her leading minds are now agitated with the question whether she will soon follow where Scotland has led the way. The principle was decided by the debate of the 21st February in the British Parliament, and it is to be hoped that no difficulties will stand in the way of carrying into practice in England what has been found beneficial elsewhere. For Scotland, it is only necessary to add that it will be for her to complete the national system by an extension of Secondary Education on a scale which will give her an educational lead amongst the nations, and secure for her more firmly that rich inheritance which it is her business to preserve and develope.

PART IV.

NATIONAL EDUCATION IN IRELAND.

SECTION 1.—*Historical.*

FOR a due elucidation of the subject of National Education in Ireland, it is necessary to look back to the time of Henry VIII., when for political purposes, rather than for any real interest in the intellectual progress of the people, the Act 28 Henry VIII., c. 15, was passed in the Irish Parliament enacting : " That the said English tongue, habit and order, may be from henceforth (and without ceasing or returning at any time to Irish habit or language), used by all men " . . . Every priest was to learn the English tongue, and to cause his people "to bid their beads in English." The next educational law was the 12th Elizabeth, establishing, in 1570, the Protestant Diocesan Schools, one in each diocese, which nominally continued until the disestablishment of the Irish Church in 1869. The 7th William III., c. 4, 1695, was the next important provision in respect to Irish education. It enacted that Irish Roman Catholics should not go for the education denied to them at home to foreign countries.

The Protestant Charter Schools were established in 1753. The Charter recites : " That in many parts of this Kingdom there were great tracts of land almost entirely inhabited by Papists ; that the generality of the Popish natives were kept by their Clergy in gross ignorance, and bred up in great disaffection to the Government ; that the creating Protestant Charter Schools in these places would be absolutely necessary for their conversion and civilization." These schools received during their existence under parliamentary support £1,105,869.* Until 1803 they received no pupils except Roman Catholics. The hollowness of the administration of them is exposed by the great philanthropist Howard : " The children were sickly, pale, and such miserable objects, that they were a disgrace to all society."

Whilst this course of paternal legislation was proceeding, no thought was given to the substance of education itself, to books for the young, the training of teachers, the erection of school-houses, or any of the thousand needs of popular instruction.† The motto

---

* Royal Commission, 1868–70. Rep. p. 492.
† Address of Sir Patrick Keenan, K.C.M.G., C.B., to Social Science Congress, Dublin, 1881.

might have been inscribed on all, "The zeal of mine house hath eaten me up!" The Irish people were not, however, destitute of love of learning, as we find testified by Dr. O'Donovan and other Irish scholars, including Mr. Eugene O'Curry in his evidence in 1849 before the Parliamentary Committee on Public Libraries. Their ancient laws afford evidence of their civilization from a remote past, and German philologists have shown the importance of the Irish language. The first real attempt to remedy the evils of the old system of educational legislation for Ireland was in 1805, when a Commission was appointed to report on schools of public or charitable foundation in Ireland. This Commission made several reports, and testified to the general desire of the people for education. In 1811, a society was founded in Ireland, popularly known as the "Kildare Place Society," comprising both Roman Catholics and Protestants, for the encouragement of schools in which the reading of the Holy Scriptures, without note or comment, would form part of the daily curriculum. The Society obtained grants from Parliament, commencing with £6,980 in the year 1814, and subsequently rising to about £30,000 a year, and continuing for several years at that rate. At first the Society made somewhat fair progress, but the requirement as to Scripture reading for all the pupils eventually proved fatal to its success. Opposition was excited amongst the Roman Catholics, the teachers of the Society's Training College and Schools were denounced, the pupils fell away; at length the Duke of Leinster, and other distinguished Protestants as well as Catholics, resigned connexion with the Society, and soon afterwards, in 1831, the Parliamentary Grants ceased.

We have, however, here to observe the fact, that a real effort was made in Ireland towards establishing popular education some years before England first attempted anything resembling a Governmental system, which was not until 1839. The failure of Kildare Place Society brings us to the birth of the present system of National Education.

SECTION 2.—*The National System and its results.*

Of all the agencies brought into existence in the present century for redeeming past misgovernment in Ireland, perhaps the most pervading and effective is the System of National Education, instituted in October 1831, in a letter from Mr. Stanley (afterwards Lord Derby) to the Duke of Leinster, when Lord Grey was Premier, Lord Anglesea was Lord Lieutenant of Ireland, and Mr. Stanley himself the Chief Secretary. The letter describes the new system as one for combined moral and literary and separate religious instruction; the books used are to be under the sanction of the Board; and the Board are to permit and encourage the Clergy to give religious instruction to the children of their respective persuasions.

The constitution of the Board itself should give a security to the Country, "that whilst the interests of religion are not overlooked, the most scrupulous care should be taken not to interfere with the peculiar tenets of any description of Christian pupils."

The National System was thus a compromise, whereby the special interests of the denominations as regards religious teaching were to be harmonized with the general demand for safe and efficient literary and moral education. To administer this system a Board was appointed of eminent individuals,—independent, and representative of the various sections of the Community.

The original Board constituted by the Government to undertake this great work comprised seven members, of whom two were Archbishops, one Protestant, Dr. Whately, the other Catholic, Dr. Murray. In 1838 three additional members were appointed; in 1839 two more; and so on until we find in 1852 that there were fifteen members, of whom six were Roman Catholics. In 1845 the Board was incorporated by Royal Charter; and in 1861 a Supplemental Charter was granted under which ten members must be Roman Catholics and ten Protestants. The only paid member of the Board is the Resident Commissioner, who is the centre and Chief of the general administration.

The inauguration of the National System was hailed with satisfaction by the great body of the Catholic Clergy and Laity. It was bitterly opposed by the Clergy of the Established Church, who resented the violation of the exclusive right that had been claimed by their predecessors, and that they themselves had inherited, of educating the entire Community. The Presbyterians shared with them a common apprehension as to the enormous power, under the system, that would be given to the Catholic Clergy, and they too showed great hostility. There was, moreover, in the Catholic Church itself, no inconsiderable section, headed by Archbishop MacHale, who would not touch the compromise, holding fast to the venerable maxim: "The Jews have no dealings with the Samaritans!" The fact stands out clear, however, in the history of the system, that—as made from the standpoint of the Commonwealth—it was a sincere endeavour to meet the demands of the Catholics of Ireland. The plan was cautiously accepted by Mr. O'Connell in Parliament. The Roman Catholic Bishops, in 1826, whilst proposing safeguards, passed, *inter alia*, the following Resolution:—"That the admission of Protestants and Roman Catholics into the same Schools for the purpose of Literary instruction may, under existing circumstances, be allowed, provided sufficient care be taken to protect the religion of the children, and to furnish them with adequate means of instruction;" * and Bishop Doyle, the vehement denouncer of the Kildare Place Society, and demander of Catholic Schools, was quite prepared to accept the principle of the system: "I cannot refrain from expressing the ardent desire I feel of having the children of all Irishmen without distinction united in Schools and in every relation of life;" moreover, this prelate issued a Circular Letter to his Clergy in December, 1831, recommending them to adopt the National System (Rept. Commrs. N.E. 1839).

The Royal Commissioners of 1868–70, recording the general

* Royal Commission, 1868–70, p. 122.

sentiment of Roman Catholics at the inauguration, state (Report, p. 70) : "In general they received the new system willingly."

The beginnings were very humble, and gave but faint forecast of the future developments. In 1834, the Schools numbered 739, and were attended by 107,042 children. The salaries of the Teachers from Imperial funds were £12 for Masters and £8 for Mistresses. The population of Ireland at the time was 8,000,000. The Commission looked forward to an ultimate development, when the Schools would number 5,000, and the annual expenditure by the State on National Education would rise to £200,000. The event compares favourably with this moderate anticipation.

In the year 1840 occurred what is historically known as the junction of the Presbyterians with the Board, when the Commissioners first definitely recognised the distinction between Vested and Non-Vested Schools; in the former of which, built by aid from the State, the Pastors or others, approved by the parents, have the right of access at convenient times to impart religious instruction to the pupils of their own creed; whilst in the case of the Non-Vested Schools, Managers are not required to give such access. This concession in no way infringed the great principle of the Conscience Clause, which must be as rigorously enforced in Non-Vested as in Vested Schools. The Conscience Clause itself has always had for its object the protection of the conscience of every child, but it underwent various modifications of form, until it assumed its present scope, namely, that when the religion of a child is once entered on the School Register, the teacher, if of a different religious persuasion, must not permit the child—unless under the written authority of the parent on a certificate duly witnessed—to remain in attendance whilst religious instruction is proceeding.

The Conscience Clause is, of course, mainly in full efficiency in those Schools which have a mixed attendance, that is, 48 per cent. of all the Schools of the country, most of the minorities in the mixed schools consisting only of a few pupils.

The following evidence before the Lords Committee of 1854, given by a distinguished Roman Catholic divine, Very Rev. Dean Meyler, who was also a Commissioner of National Education, throws a very gratifying light on the system in its early years :

"The Pope, although in the beginning he had entertained a very different opinion, at length called upon the Bishops to thank the Government for giving so much of its wealth to the poor children of their country ; 'Let it go on,' he said, 'but be cautious against the use of improper books.'"

Thenceforward the National System advanced by leaps and bounds. Nothing could arrest the tide of progress; not even the temporary difficulties that arose in the course of time, mainly, it must be confessed, through influences from the Protestant side, to warp the system, if possible, from its direct aim of excluding the possibility of proselytism. The Schools rapidly multiplied, and children gathered to them by hundreds of thousands, and a Social and Political Revolution was advancing. General intelligence was already producing fruit in popular literature and the omnipresent newspaper. The peasant in his thatched cabin beheld in the magic broadsheet a new world. Political life was opening to his view. From the nursery of the humble National School he had come at length to realise that "knowledge is power." Different, indeed, was his position from that of his progenitors in the olden time, when—

"Still crouching 'neath the sheltering hedge or stretched on mountain fern,
The teacher and his pupils met feloniously to learn!"

SECTION 3.—*Difficulties regarding Building Grants and School Books.*

The difficulties just referred to, that beset the Board at intervals of its earlier history were few, but some were serious. Space would not permit to revert at any length to old controversies; but there were two matters of such importance that they must be noticed. The first had relation to building grants, and the second to books. Before the Charter of 1845 was granted, under which the Commissioners in their corporate capacity could have schools vested in themselves and hold lands, the Schools built by aid from the State had to be vested in trustees for educational purposes; but this arrangement, after the grant of the Charter, was discontinued. This step led to suspicion on the part of the Roman Catholic Prelates as to possible ulterior objects, and in 1850 was denounced by the Synod of Roman Catholic Bishops which was held at Thurles.

As regards the other difficulty, certain books written by Archbishop Whately on the "Truths" and the "Evidences" of Christianity were, for a time, allowed to be used in the National Schools during the combined instruction of the pupils. The Commissioners in 1853 decreed their banishment. A veritable "Battle of the Books" ensued. The Archbishop committed official suicide by resigning his commission in protest against the Board's action. Great excitement was created amongst Protestants almost in every part of the Empire that culminated in the appointment, in 1854, of an unusually strong Committee of the House of Lords. The Committee, however, failed to make a Report on the evidence taken, and its enquiries practically ended in a vindication of the Board, and in the permanent exclusion of the books as unsuited for common use in the National Schools.

The difficulty in the former case was not got over until 1861, when the Board reverted to the original arrangement as to building grants, giving henceforth to Managers the option of having the Schools vested in trustees, or vested in the Commissioners in their corporate capacity. As the result of this remedial action, we find there are now

Schools Vested in Trustees . . . 1,961 } Total 2,933
,, Vested in the Commissioners . 972 }

The activity in respect to School buildings in Ireland may be judged

from the following figures taken from the last Report of the Commissioners:
Building grants made within the last seven years:—

To Roman Catholic Managers	£172,630
To Managers of the late Established Church	6,847
To Presbyterian Managers	10,980
Total (7 years)	£190,457

It would appear that the work of building Schools might proceed even more briskly, but for the difficulty often experienced in obtaining sites.* In view of the abolition long since of grants to build in England, we must say that Ireland is especially privileged in having such aid still offered to the Managers of her National Schools.

Besides the 2,933 Vested Schools there are 5,643 Non-Vested Schools.

SECTION 4.—*School Management and Inspection.*

Managership of Schools under the Irish National System is unique in character. It is local government by one man, and, as a rule, that man the Priest, the Parson, or the Presbyterian Minister. The Manager is, in point of fact, supreme. He holds the appointment and dismissal of the Teachers; the arrangement of the Time Table of daily School business is under his control; the determination of religious instruction is his vital concern;—all these functions, however, for their due exercise, coming under the purview of the Inspector of Schools. It is scarcely necessary to observe that the vast bulk of the Schools are under the management of the Clergy.

In the year 1881 (the latest returns we have been able to obtain) the distribution of the Schools as to management was as follows:—

1,481 Roman Catholic Managers govern 5,128 National Schools.
786 Church of Ireland ,, 1,365 ,, ,,
536 Presbyterian ,, 814 ,, ,,
90 Other denominations ,, 124 ,, ,,

Of course, the Schools under the Roman Catholic Managers are, generally, larger than those under Protestants, as may be judged from the total number of pupils of the respective denominations on the rolls of National Schools:—

Roman Catholic pupils . . 826,181, or 77·9 per cent.
Church of Ireland pupils . . 109,687, or 10·3 ,,
Presbyterian pupils . . 111·072, or 10·5 ,,
Other denomination pupils . 13,955, or 1·3 ,,

* Act 44 & 45 Vic. c. 65, 1881, was introduced to enable limited owners to grant sites for National Schools in Ireland. Mr. Campbell-Bannerman more recently, when Chief Secretary, proposed a Bill for the compulsory acquisition of sites for such purpose, but it fell through.

We cannot dismiss this subject without reference to an important consideration. Whilst the power of the Local Manager is practically absolute—subject to the Conscience Clause—a power certainly far beyond what any other country in the world that has a public system of education recognizes, a power, moreover, so great that we have seen Archbishop Walsh not long since intervening to check it by means of episcopal authority in respect to the dismissal of teachers, yet we find that the Managers are responsible for only one-fifth part of the burden of maintaining the Schools:—

INCOME IN 1888.

From Government Grants to the Schools . £737,123
    (Rate per pupil . . £1 10s. 2¾d.)
From Local Sources £194,984
    (Rate per pupil . . £0 7s. 11¾d.)

The duties of a School Manager are no sinecure. He has to check and certify the School returns, and afford to the Commissioners his guarantee for the correctness of these accounts as well as for the conduct of the Teachers, and the observance of the Rules of the Board. On the whole, the Managerial office in Ireland presents an interesting instance of denominational mediation between a mixed Board and a mixed Community, for the common good.

In immediate connexion with the duties of Managers, we have to glance at the kindred topic of inspection.

It is the practice of the Board—we think it a wise one—to subject all candidates for the office of Inspector to Examination in an extensive and appropriate programme, by the Civil Service Commissioners. This programme is the "scientific frontier" against all attempts at jobbery; and, especially in earlier years, when many oblique influences tried to beset the administration in this respect, the arrangement to shut the door against them was highly prudent.

Further, with a view to commanding the public confidence in the fair play of the administration, the Board appoint one-half of the Inspection Corps Protestant and the other half Catholic. Their Inspectors, however, have no responsibility as regards the efficiency, &c., of religious instruction in the National Schools, the Managers looking zealously to that department. The Inspectors' function being secular, there is freedom from cross-sectional business, such as is involved in denominational inspection, and there is corresponding economy of time and cost.

SECTION 5.—*School-Teachers and Maintenance.*

On the 31st December, 1888, there were 7,921 Principal Teachers and 3,166 Assistant Teachers, all of whom were Certificated, in employment in the National Schools.

The pay of National Teachers comprises Class Salaries (fixed); Results-fees payable on ascertained proficiency of pupils at the annual Results examination of the schools; and local emoluments, such as school pence of pupils, subscriptions, and (in a few Poor-Law Unions) contributions from the rates.

The last Report of the Commissioners gives the following particulars under these heads for the Principal Teachers.

AVERAGE INCOME OF PRINCIPAL TEACHERS.

Class of Teacher.	Number of Teachers included in Return.	FROM PARLIAMENTARY GRANT IN AID.						FROM LOCAL SOURCES.								
		Class Salary and Good Service Salary.			Results-fees, Gratuities, &c., from Board.			Results-fees from Rates.			Local Contributions, including School pence of Pupils.			Total.		
		£	s.	d.	£	s.	d.	£	s.	d.	£	s.	d.	£	s.	d.
Males :—																
I^1. . .	224	70	9	3¼	32	9	0¼	4	2	3¼	43	10	6¾	150	11	1½
I^2. . . .	474	53	15	8	25	1	0¼	1	17	1¾	22	19	2	103	13	0
II. . . .	1,954	44	6	11	21	10	8¼	1	9	2	16	11	2¾	83	18	0¾
III. . . .	1,474	35	1	0	16	18	5	0	19	3	12	7	7	65	6	3
Total . .	4,126	...			...			...			...			...		
Average for all classes . .	...	43	10	7	20	17	8	1	9	5¼	17	15	3	83	2	11
Females :—																
I^1 division .	150	57	14	10	28	3	3	2	9	10	23	4	10	111	12	9
I^2 division .	353	43	12	7	23	13	11¾	1	15	6¾	18	7	1	87	9	2½
II. . . .	1,268	34	15	1½	19	16	11	1	8	4½	13	6	5½	69	6	10½
III. . . .	976	27	10	3¾	16	12	5	1	0	3¼	10	19	0½	56	2	0½
Total . .	2,747	...			...			...			...			...		
Average for all classes . .	...	34	11	7	19	12	11	1	7	7¼	13	13	4¾	69	5	6

Although we are far from saying that the condition of the Irish Teachers is entirely satisfactory, or indeed anything like it, yet we observe that in the table there is no indication of the cases where the incomes of husbands and wives as teachers are combined. We have reason to believe that there are large numbers of instances of such educational partnership in the carrying on of Schools, to the family benefit.

This table, however, when compared with the incomes of the English Teachers, shows rather hard lines of provision for the Irish Staff, but also shows that the deficiency is entirely in the local aid. In 1875, Sir Michael Hicks-Beach tried to remedy this defect by bringing in a Bill authorizing Boards of Guardians to contribute out of the rates towards augmenting the Results-fees. This Act, however, has failed to realize the hopes of the Government, the contributions last year from a few Unions amounting to only £17,683; whereas, had all the Unions availed themselves of the power conferred on them by the Act, the amount would have been £101,000.

STATE EDUCATION.

In 1885, Mr. Campbell-Bannermann, with the approval of the Commissioners, brought in a Bill to secure the contributions by making the rating compulsory, but the Bill never reached a second reading.

Loans Acts were passed by the Legislature in 1875 and 1879 to enable Managers of Schools to provide Residences for their Teachers. An Act passed in August 1879 that appropriated the sum of £1,300,000 of the Surplus of the Irish Church Fund towards the establishment of a Pensions' Fund for the Teachers. One-fourth of the entire annual premiums is contributed by the Teachers themselves, the remaining three-fourths being met by the interest on the appropriated sum. The teachers complain that the calculations of the scheme have been made on the hypothesis of lives approaching the longevity enjoyed by Methuselah—an hypothesis which, relieved of its exaggerated form of the description, is, we should think, susceptible of some actuarial improvement in favour of the Teachers' Pension prospects.

As regards that part of the Teachers' income that concerns results-fees, it is so important, not only as a means for increasing their remuneration, but also as an instrumentality of educational efficiency, that it deserves more than a passing notice. Soon after Mr. Lowe (now Lord Sherbrook) metamorphosed the system of Parliamentary grants for elementary education in England, by a system of payments for results, instead of personal salaries to the Teachers, Mr. Fortescue (now Lord Carlingford), Chief Secretary for Ireland, suggested to the Board of National Education in Ireland a trial of the new system on a partial scale. This was in 1866. The Commissioners approved of Lord Carlingford's suggestion, but owing to a change of Government, the proposal fell for the moment into abeyance. In the meantime, some of the leading Educational officers of the Board were engaged in a consideration of the whole question, and the examinations of some of the National Schools were conducted experimentally as to its effect educationally, and its bearings upon the payments of the National Teachers. Early in 1868, Mr. Keenan (now The Right Honourable Sir Patrick Keenan) formulated the results of all those experiments and considerations in a scheme which, in the course of his evidence, he submitted to the Royal Commission which was then under the Presidency of Lord Powis, inquiring into the Irish National System.*

The English system was held to be faulty in three most important respects :—

> (1) It abolished the personality of the teacher in his relation with the Education Department, by the cancelling of all personal grants of salary ; (2) It limited the grants to a School to the precarious issues of the examination for results ; (3) The fee for a Pass in Reading, Writing, and Arithmetic was an all-round one—the same for every subject and every class.

Sir Patrick Keenan's plan was to maintain the individuality of the Teacher, to continue the old system of personal salary to him,

---

* Rep. Royal Commission, 1868–70—Evidence, vol. iii., p. 89.

and to award him, as a bonus or supplementary grant, fees for ascertained results. This principle was adopted by Lord Powis' Commission. Further, Sir Patrick's plan, instead of the uniform fee, as in England, for every subject and every class, graduated the fee according to the importance of the subject and the class of the child. A pupil, for instance, in the first, or lowest class, could earn for its teacher a certain amount of results-fees, whilst a pupil in the sixth class might earn more than double that amount. The great advantage of this system was that it equilibrated the reward of labour, and held out very cogent inducements to the teachers to qualify their pupils for promotion from class to class.

The Commissioners, in their investigations as to the best form in which a system of payment by results might be administered, had under serious investigation various other Suggestions and Schemes; but, in 1871, the system which we have described was partially, and in 1872 was fully, applied in the examination of the scholars and the payment of the Teachers.

Although introduced after so many years of close investigation and experiment, the Commissioners, feeling that in the light of experience, the system as a mode of examination, and as governing the course of instruction in their Schools, was susceptible of development, have every year since 1871 held a Conference of their Head Inspectors to consider its operations and to extend its efficiency. Scarcely a year has since then passed without some new development—either in detail as to the incidents of examination or the matter of instruction—as the outcome of the Conferences of their Head Inspectors.

But the ears of the Commissioners were also open from year to year to the representations of the Teachers; for, as a rule, at their annual Congress a Deputation of them waited upon the Resident Commissioner, and at his ready bidding unfolded their views and suggestions as to the "results" programme, and the general procedure of the examinations. These representations were in due course presented to the Head Inspectors for deliberation; and finally, if approved, reached the Board to be fiated for incorporation in their Code.

SECTION 6.—*Reforms and extensions of the Educational system.*

A narrative of these changes would engage us in such an historical account of Irish Primary Education as would outstrip the bounds we have in view in writing this article; but as a sample we would point out the division of the Fifth and Sixth classes (the highest), each division occupying the course of a year, thus extending the period of a child's instruction, beyond the mere infant stage, from six to eight years, each year carrying its own results-fees for proficiency in the subjects of the school programme.

We cannot, however, fail to notice, as bearing upon the utilitarian aspect of Irish National Education, that one of the developments of the "results" programme is to make agricultural instruction obligatory for boys, and carrying a substantial and additional results-fee for proficiency in all rural schools, in the fourth, and in each division of the fifth and sixth classes. Nor again can we fail to glance at the recent rule* which, whilst declaring that the literary education of girls who have passed the two stages of the Fifth class is substantially adequate, lays down that the remainder of their school-life should be mainly devoted to Industrial training,—such training carrying with it results-fees to the Teachers equivalent to those paid on the old literary programme.

But it must be added that the Results system, whilst encouraging, by the award of fees, proficiency in Reading, Spelling, Writing, Arithmetic, Grammar, Geography, Book-keeping, Needlework (for Girls), Agriculture, and Vocal Music in the Ordinary Programme, has developed, in a course of Extra branches carrying results-fees, a curriculum which embraces Drawing, Geometry, Algebra, Mensuration, Trigonometry, Handicraft (for Boys), Sewing-Machine, Domestic Economy, Cookery, Dairying, Management of Poultry (for Girls), Hygiene, the Physical Sciences, Navigation, Classics, French, German, Irish, and even Instrumental Music.

But this does not represent all that the Commissioners have from time to time been attempting to accomplish in the perfecting of their scheme, as it is well known that "My Lords" of the Treasury unfortunately stand in front in many important questions to resist some of their most interesting proposals; for we learn from Sir Patrick Keenan's evidence before Lord Cross's Royal Commission of 1887 (Q. 53,290—2) that their educational policy in regard to Programmes of certain Extra Branches as well as the adoption of Kindergarten, has been called in question by the Treasury. The following is his statement in reference to a new Programme in Geometry:—

"We sent the Programme to the Treasury with an intimation that it would involve some extra expenditure, and the decision of the Treasury was, that the old programme was good enough for the needs of the country."

The Results system, however, which in the year 1871 was inaugurated under very humble auspices, has thus by gradual developments been brought to attain dimensions which we apprehend are not discernible in any other system of public instruction in the world.

To record what the Commissioners may very naturally regard as triumphs of their system, in simplest fashion, we must content ourselves by noting what has been done for the "three Rs," or Keys of Knowledge, as they are often designated. The percentages of pupils who passed were:—

Year.	Reading.	Writing.	Arithmetic.
1870	70·5	57·7	54·4
1888	94·1	95·9	82.3

* Commissioners' N. E. Report, 1888, p. 21.

THE IRISH SYSTEM.

The results-system in Ireland has contributed largely to improved attendance of pupils, the average daily attendance having risen from 355,821 in 1872 to 493,883 in 1888, and the total number examined for results-fees from 315,646 in the former to 565,468 in the latter year. The system has had its effect on the homes of the children in awakening an increased interest in the school arrangements of their children on the part of the parents, and in quickening the emulation of the scholars themselves in a manner unknown previously.

The Scale of Results-Fees, last year, is as follows :—

SCALE OF RESULTS-FEES.

Ordinary and Optional Branches.

Subjects.	Infants.	First.	Second.	Third.	Fourth.	Fifth Class, 1st Stage.	Fifth Class, 2nd Stage.	Sixth Class, 1st and 2nd Examinations.
	s. d.	s. d.	s. d.	s. d.	s. d.	s. d.	s. d.	s. d.
Infants' Course	3 0	...	...	...	...	...	...	...
Reading .	...	2 0	2 0	2 6	2 6	2 6	2 6	2 6
Spelling .	...	1 0	1 0	1 0	1 0	1 0	1 0	1 0
Writing .	...	1 0	1 0	1 6	1 6	1 6	1 6	2 0
Arithmetic .	...	1 0	2 0	2 6	2 6	2 6	2 6	3 0
Grammar	...	...	...	1 0	1 6	1 6	1 6	1 6
Geography .	...	...	...	1 0	1 0	1 6	1 6	1 6
Book-keeping (optional)	...	...	...	...	...	2 6	2 6	3 0
Needlework (girls) . .	...	...	0 6	1 0	2 0	2 6	2 6	3 0
Agriculture .	...	...	...	...	4 0	5 0	5 0	5 0
Vocal music (optional) .	...	...	1 6	2 6	2 6	2 6	2 6	3 0

Extra Branches-Fees for Passes.

Drawing.	Six examinations according to class.	Third Class.	Fourth Class.	Fifth Class, 1st Stage.	Fifth Class, 2nd Stage.	Sixth Class, 1st and 2nd Examinations.
		s. d.	s. d.	s. d.	s. d.	s. d.
		2 6	2 6	2 6	2 6	3 0

For pupils of 5th and 6th classes :		Each series of examinations may commence in the 1st or 2nd stage of 5th class, or in the 1st or 2nd year of 6th class, and whenever commenced may be completed, except in the case of Navigation, which can be commenced only in 6th class. In thoroughly organized infants' schools or departments, 4s. per infants' pass is payable; and if Kindergarten be efficiently practised, 2s. additional to the ordinary fees per pupil in Infants' 1st, 2nd, and 3rd classes.
Girls reading-book and domestic economy (combined) . .	Two exams. 3s. each	
Greek . . .	Three ,, 10s. each	
Latin . . .	Three ,, 10s. each	
Irish	Three ,, 10s. each	
French . . .	Three ,, 5s. each	
Other extra branches approved by Commissioners (set forth page 66, *supra*)	Number of exams.as per code } 5s. each	

Originally the grants from public funds to National Schools bore only a small proportion to the total cost of maintenance, and the early reports of the Board frequently assert that the salaries payable were only supplemental to local payments.* The Grants have, however, steadily increased from the first modest salaries of £12 a year to Masters, and £8 to Mistresses, to the present scale, which, irrespective of Results-Fees, rises according to class from £35 the lowest, to £70 the highest rate for Masters, and from £27 10s. the lowest, to £58 the highest rate for Mistresses, with £35 to Male and £27 to Female Assistants. The total Salaries from the Board in 1888—9 reached £427,069, whilst the Results-Fees from the Board amounted to £202,266, a supplemental income of nearly one-half the class salaries. In addition, the sum of £10,524 was paid to the Teachers for special instruction of their Monitors, and the sum of £52,931 went to the Monitors themselves in small salaries.

The following figures show the development, since the year 1840, in the number of Schools, number of Scholars, and the Parliamentary Grant:—

Year.	Population.	National Schools.	Total No. of Pupils on the Rolls of the National Schools.	Total Parliamentary Grant (including buildings).
1840–1	8,196,597	1,978	232,560	£ 50,000
1860–1	5,798,967	5,632	804,000	294,041
1889–90	4,750,722	8,196	1,060,895	953,675

SECTION 7.—*Training of Teachers.*

The training of Teachers for the National Schools was long the subject of angry controversy, and even still disputes are not altogether ended. The Commissioners opened their own College for Masters in 1833 on the mixed principle of Catholics and Protestants being educated and domiciled together in the same institution. At first it was impracticable to do more than merely give the outline of a training course to the Teachers, who were admitted for brief courses of from three to five months. In the year 1840, the Training College for Mistresses was opened on the same principle. Each College was largely frequented by both Catholics and Protestants, until, in 1850, the Synod of Thurles denounced the system of mixed training, and demanded separate grants for Denominational Training Colleges. The numbers of the R. C. Students gradually diminished from being in a proportion of four to one to only about one half, and the training of the Catholic Teachers became thereby a matter of serious concern.

The Commissioners had already, so far back as 1834, tried the stipendiary monitorial system in Dublin—a time long antecedent to

* Commissioners of N. E. Reports, 1846, 1847, *et seq.*

the introduction of pupil-teachers in England by Sir Jas. K. Shuttleworth—and in 1845 they extended it throughout the country. This system they gradually improved and enlarged until it became an important nursery for teacherships. Again, in 1856, they appointed a staff of " Organizers of Schools," consisting of twelve Masters and three Mistresses, all of them persons of the highest qualifications and wide experience, to travel about the country and show the Teachers how schools should be conducted on the most approved methods. Much was done by these means to maintain the standard of education amongst the Roman Catholic Teachers.

In 1866, the Commissioners proposed measures to Mr. Chichester Fortescue, and in 1874 to Sir Michael Hicks Beach, when Chief Secretaries for Ireland, with the object of meeting the views of the Roman Catholic Ecclesiastical Authorities; but nothing definite was accomplished, owing to difficulties arising from the Protestant opposition.

In 1881, however, the first step towards denominational training was taken in connexion with an application from the Protestant Authorities themselves—the Synod of the Church of Ireland—to have the Queen's Scholars of the Marlborough Street College, who were members of the Church of Ireland, domiciled in their own denominational institution in Kildare Place, whilst receiving their professional training and instruction in Marlborough Street.

A very short experience of this experiment led, in 1883, to a proposal by Lord Spencer, then Lord Lieutenant, to extend the English System pure and simple to Ireland,—a proposal which, with the sanction of the Government, was adopted by the Commissioners, *mutatis mutandis*, with a view of securing certain privileges not enjoyed under the system in England to which the Roman Catholic authorities attached the greatest possible weight. Of these the main points were, provisions, (*a*) to allow of the continued award of the Teachers' Salaries on condition of their paying substitutes during their residence in the Training Colleges ; and (*b*) to enable each of the Irish Training Colleges to be managed by an individual, instead of by a Committee as is the requirement in England.

The Commissioners' College still continues ; but inasmuch as it is wholly supported from the Public funds, and the Queen's Scholars are admitted free,* whilst the Denominational Colleges can only claim (as recommended by the Powis' Commission) 75 per cent., as in England, of their total certified expenditure, a not unreasonable cry has been raised by both Protestant and Catholic authorities either to level up or level down.

There are three Denominational Training Colleges, two under the Roman Catholic, and one under the Protestant Archbishop of Dublin, as the Managers, respectively, with a total number of 398 Queen's Scholars in residence last year. In the Marlborough Street Mixed Training College the number was 199. Even with these Colleges, and their substantial muster of Students, it is evident that many years must pass before the great arrears in training represented by

---

* The Powis Commissioners, however, recommended that a fixed payment from private sources should be required from each scholar.

the 7,234 Teachers still untrained out of the total staff of 11,087 will be cleared off. A proposal has been made to fall back upon the original plan of short courses of a few months for Teachers advanced in age who could not be expected to attend for a full period of one or two years. The proposal, which under all the circumstances appears to be excellent, awaits only, it is rumoured, the sanction of Government, as the Board of National Education a few years ago expressed approval of it.

SECTION 8.—*School Books: Model and Agricultural Schools.*

The review of the Irish system requires a reference to the mode of supply of books, &c., to the schools. The Commissioners, although having only a veto against the use of improper books, and having long ago thrown open their copyright, yet have a virtual monopoly of the school supply, owing to cheapness, good quality, and prompt delivery. The demands are, in the total, of course enormous, and the Commissioners have consequently opportunity of obtaining the books and other requisites on the most favourable terms. Originally, suitable books were not in existence, and the Commissioners were accordingly under the necessity of themselves producing them. Their books soon gained such repute as to be in demand in Great Britain and in the Colonies, to which the Commissioners sold annually large quantities. This practice awakened the hostility of the London publishers, who, in 1849 and subsequently, appealed to Government to restrain the Commissioners. The Board's action was, however, defended by Lord John Russell, then Prime Minister. But since that period matters have changed. The Commissioners' sales of their own publications, and of books produced by private authors for their purposes, have been restricted to the National Schools, and are sold (carriage free) at cost price. The receipts for their sales amount annually to about £30,000, but this is an enormous saving on the ordinary shop prices,—a saving which goes to the benefit of the pupils, inasmuch as Teachers are strictly prohibited from making any advance on the prices as published in the Commissioners' School Lists.

The Managers and Teachers appear to be alive to the convenience of having a Common Standard Series in respect to results examinations of Pupils, and annual examinations of Teachers and Monitors, as well as to the migrations of children from school to school, who, under the arrangement, are saved the cost of purchasing new books at every change. It seems, on the whole, a satisfactory thing to have a series generally accepted by the School Managers as safe and suitable.

The net cost of this Book System to the State is about £5,000 a year.

We have thus surveyed the main lines of the history and organization of National Education in Ireland. There are collateral lines within the scope of this wide subject that are of considerable interest, but too numerous to be even briefly dealt with, and they do not demand any special exposition. Such for instance is the history of the Model Schools, under the Board's own management, of which we may in passing observe, that having been built at heavy cost to the State, some £160,000, and been since maintained at considerable charge on the annual Estimates, they are now in many instances forsaken by the Catholic Pupils, the R. C. Hierarchy being opposed to schools under exclusive State management.

Lord Powis' Commission (1868—70) made what seems a reasonable recommendation, which, if adopted, would, no doubt, render these schools acceptable to Catholics as well as to all other denominations:—

" That all existing Provincial Model Schools which cannot be carried on by Local Committees as Elementary Schools on the present system, receiving only such sums as may be earned by their scholars on examination, or may be due to Teachers, may be granted on lease to anybody applying for them as Training Schools, on easy terms, such as will provide for their maintenance and repair."

As regards Agricultural Education in Ireland, we cannot do more, with our limited space, than state that the Commissioners have in active operation many schools in which practical Agriculture is taught, and others in which Dairying is taught, seven or eight hundred Dairymaids having within the last few years been trained in the industry.

There are also 84,676 pupils regularly instructed in Agriculture from the Text Books, as part of the obligatory course for boys in all rural National Schools.

Neither is it necessary to enter upon the examination of the means adopted from time to time by the Commissioners to further develop the industrial side of education, in the schools generally, for Boys and Girls, the indications, as above, in respect to the existing provisions in the Commissioners' Results Programmes being sufficient for our purpose.

SECTION 9.—*Compulsory School Attendance and Free Education.—Conclusion.*

But there is a word to be said, before concluding, in reference to the twin subjects mooted for Ireland,—Compulsory Attendance, and Free Education.

As to the former, we would observe that Ireland being almost wholly Agricultural, the children are unavoidably withdrawn from School for a considerable interval each year to help their parents in the fields, &c. Taking these intervals in connexion with periods of illness, wet weather, &c., we may fairly say that for about one-third of the year the children cannot attend School. Judging from the numbers on the rolls and the average daily attendance, we are disposed to conclude that there is at present an all-round attendance of about 140 full days in the year; and this cannot be regarded as unsatisfactory. Until, therefore, some well-pronounced demand is heard, we can see no possible result to ensue from legislative interference in the matter of School attendance, except irritation to parents, and additional unrest to the popular mind.

For the case of factory children, there is adequate provision under the Factory Acts; and the only other cases that invite attention are: (*a*) Children of beggars and vagrants, perhaps not as yet adequately provided for under the Industrial Schools Acts and Poor Law Acts; and (*b*) Youths who leave school before completing the full obligatory course prescribed by the Commissioners' Programme. For the latter class an extended application of the principle of the Factory Acts does seem desirable in the interests of the youths themselves, and of the country.

It is likely that a movement to largely increase the number and efficiency of Evening Schools—as Continuation Schools—would meet with general approval. But legislation in this direction must be accompanied by liberal provision towards the support of the Schools, which should not merely be organized to promote the literary education of their pupils, but also to give due opportunities for the development of the other side of education, namely the industrial.

Secondly, as to Free Education, we would observe that if the State is to bear all the cost, its direct guarantees must be increased, and so far the independence of managerial authority in Ireland be prejudiced. Besides, the question does not seem to arise from any necessity; for whereas in England half the cost of popular education is borne by the State, in Ireland the burden on the public funds is four-fifths. Practically, this means free education for the really poor, if we are to judge from the total pupils' fees for the year 1888—89, £108,284, which imposes on each pupil in average daily attendance the trifling charge of 1*d*. per week. We have also seen that the determination of the rate of fee, or the question whether any fee shall be charged to an individual child, rests entirely with the Managers, who, being nearly all of them Clergymen resident in the localities, can well decide what is best in each case.

In conclusion, we have to pay our tribute of acknowledgment to the course pursued by the National Education Commissioners and successive Governments in recent years, in harmony with the maxim of Burke—"Politic complaisance within the limits of Justice." We see an earnest endeavour to satisfy, without encroaching on the reasonable claims of any, the sentiments of the great majority of those for whose use National Education is established in Ireland, in the bringing to a close the long and vexatious controversy on the question of denominational training, in remedying the grievance of wholly inadequate pay under which the Teachers of Convent Schools—amongst the best taught schools in the Country — had lain, notwithstanding the successive scales of improved salaries granted to ordinary School Teachers, in removing the disability of members of religious orders to teach National Schools, and of Convents to have more than one school in connexion with the same Convent. Numerous other reforms might be mentioned that have been effected in a corresponding direction.

Such a policy we desire heartily — even from the Protestant standpoint—to endorse, as tending to remove any sense of unfriendliness or of inequality of treatment felt by the Roman Catholic community.

Whilst we find it hard now to point to any other substantial ground of dissatisfaction in regard to Irish National Education, we cannot withhold our opinion as to the reasonableness—and also the innocuousness—of the recommendation of the Powis Commission (1868—70), regarding which the Roman Catholic Bishops have within the last few years shown much anxiety, and they complain that it should not yet have been carried into effect. That recommendation is, that when there have been in operation in any School district, or within any City or Town for three years, two or more Schools, of which one is under Protestant and one under Roman Catholic management, having an average attendance of not less than twenty-five children, the National Board may, upon application from the Patron or Manager, adopt any such School without requiring any regulation as to religion, except that of the Conscience Clause.

PART V.

THE ENGLISH AND CONTINENTAL SYSTEMS OF ELEMENTARY EDUCATION COMPARED.

The most important and interesting points of comparison between the school systems of this and of Continental countries relate to religious teaching; school fees and State or municipal support; compulsory school attendance; physical exercises; technical instruction; and the efficiency of teachers; in all cases this refers to primary schools.

The rationalistic tone, and the general scepticism of the learned classes in Germany, has led many Englishmen to conclude that the German schools are irreligious and that the teaching of religion forms no element in the national system of education. This is far from being the case, and there is perhaps no country where less friction is to be found between the different religious denominations and the State in this particular connexion.

As a matter of fact religious teaching forms part of the national system,* and subject to conscience clauses provision is made by school managers, who usually represent the inhabitants of the parish or district in which the school is situated, for religious instruction in conformity with the views of the various denominations, Protestant, Catholic, &c. Religious toleration must be considered the normal feature in the German State system.

Switzerland even in a greater degree than Germany possesses a mixed population so far as religion and language are concerned; some cantons are almost exclusively Catholic, whilst in others Protestants largely predominate. In all, however, the children of each denomination are provided with religious instruction according to the wishes of their parents, sometimes during and at other times out of school hours, whilst a comparison of the reports from the different cantons shows that care is taken that there is no interference with the liberty of conscience, and no enforced attendance at religious exercises. Those consist of hymns, prayers, and reading the Bible, generally without comment.

There is perhaps no country in Europe where politics are so much affected by religious differences as in Belgium, and whilst until recently the system of State instruction favoured by the Liberals in power was purely secular (as indeed it is *nominally* at

---

* In Austria and Prussia it stands first on the Time Tables. See Sonnenschein, Educational Codes of Foreign Countries, pp. 189 et seq. London: Swan Sonnenschein, 1889.

present), and religious instruction was given only out of school hours, it may be said that under Conservative rule the greatest facilities are now afforded by the subsidies of Communes to denominational education. In rural or sparsely populated districts a certain number of parents may claim to have a school established in which their religion is taught, but in the large centres of industry the schools continue to be secular; and as already stated, each political party is intent upon fostering its own educational system, and great acrimony is thereby imparted to politics. The interference of the clergy in education is very active in Belgium.

In Italy also the priesthood claims to direct the education of the masses, but the changes which have taken place in the temporal rule have greatly restricted their influence. Speaking generally, religious instruction is only imparted once a week by laymen, and only to those children whose parents desire it. It does not form part of the national system, and, as in other Catholic countries, the clergy are bitterly opposed to education by the State as at present regulated.

The laws concerning primary education in Sweden and Norway, which date back to 1842 and 1848 respectively for the towns, are very much alike in essential principles. Religious instruction forms an integral part of the system in both countries. The objects of State education are "true Christian instruction and such knowledge and attainments as every member of the State ought to possess." The teaching of the primary school, which begins and ends each day with prayer and the singing of psalms, may be described as leading up to the "Confirmation," or the passing by the parish clergyman into the right to partake of the sacrament, and with it into responsible life. The clergyman plays a prominent part in the system, but religion is generally taught by the schoolmaster according to a recognised book of instructions. In addition to the religious instruction which they receive in school, all children above twelve are bound by law until two years after confirmation to appear in church at the public catechisms, which are conducted by the clergyman, and are held several times during the year. From the lowest classes in the elementary schools up to the highest several hours weekly are devoted to catechism, Bible history, &c., and the system is therefore unmistakably denominational. These remarks apply to those professing the State religion, but there is provision for the establishment of schools for dissenters under the supervision of the School Boards (one of which is to be found in every ecclesiastical parish), which see that the Standards are complied with.

In Denmark religious instruction is also part of the curriculum, but only for children whose parents are members of the State (Lutheran) Church.

In France the struggle for priestly ascendancy has exercised greater influence over State instruction than in any other European country, and entirely to the disadvantage of the Clergy. The department of education professes complete neutrality towards the religious denominations, but it is by exclusion and not by the concurrent endowment of education. Hence the State system, which is purely secular, is usually designated "Godless education," and it is no doubt one of the results of the reaction against priestly interference in other than religious affairs. No priest as such is permitted to take any part in the management of the public Elementary Schools, in some of which the name of the Deity is never mentioned. Instruction in morals is, however, an important feature in the educational course in all public Elementary Schools.

The supervision of the State over elementary instruction in England is secular only, and the Department does not profess to extend any support to religious or denominational teaching. Certain hours are set apart for secular teaching, during which time no instruction is given in any religious subject or book, and those are the only school hours to which the State pays attention. Moreover, where religion is taught, or where there are any kinds of religious exercises, children are not compelled to be present, and parents may ignore them without detriment to their children's secular education.

In practice, however, a widespread religious system of instruction obtains in Board as well as in denominational Schools. One may go into a Church of England School and then into a Board School, and find in both the same book in use treating of the Old and New Testament; the same hymns; the same Trinitarian form of prayer; the only difference being the teaching of the Catechism in the Church School. It is true that in an infinitesimally small number of schools religious teaching is excluded; in a few others the Bible is read without comment; but in by far the largest number, religion is taught either before or after lessons, or both.

Besides the general religious teaching in Board and denominational Schools, there is the strictly sectarian instruction in the latter. In the Church of England Schools the system is less uniform and rigid than in those of the Roman Catholics, just as in the former the religious system generally is less completely controlled by a central authority. In practice the Bishops and Clergy in both cases " set " the religious course. In a typical rural school of the Church of England, in Standards V., VI., and VII., the following is the course of religious instruction for a certain year : " The Second Book of Samuel; St. Mark's Gospel ; Morning Prayer to the end of the ' Te Deum ' ; the whole text of the Church Catechism, with explanation of the Lord's Prayer and the Desire ; four collects to be learned and understood ; four hymns." The Scriptures are read from 9 to 9.45 A.M. Pressure is frequently brought to bear upon children in order to " induce " them to attend religious exercises, where any such action is at all needed. It varies according to the character of the clergy or school managers in different districts. In the school of which the religious course is given above, " objections of parents to religious instruction are fully respected." This is, however, far from being the case everywhere, and a volume might be written on the subject. In a typical Roman Catholic School the following is the course of religious instruction : "*Infants:* Instruction on God; Our Lord; the B. Virgin; St. Joseph; Guardian Angels ; Death ; Judgment; Hell ; Heaven." Standards

I. to V.: Catechism; Prayers; Instruction on Sin, &c.; Sacred History.

The reason for entering with some minuteness into the religious aspect of education is because it is the stumbling-block in the way of most of the changes that are proposed in the national system. How will it affect denominational teaching? Who are the men that propose the change? Have they any ulterior motive? All other considerations would be more easily disposed of by the lay authorities, if the religious grounds of action or inaction were less prominent. In the present controversy on free or gratuitous education, for example, Catholics will tell you that they could not for a moment support any change in the system which would remove the management of their schools from the present superiors to the ratepayers. "What is to prevent an Orangeman from being foisted upon our committee," they say, "who would at once begin to interfere with our religious instruction?" And Churchmen in like manner fear the intrusion of dissenters and even of secularists.

Turning to the question of compulsion, it may be stated that in Germany the attendance is compulsory, and neglect may even be punished by fine or imprisonment in most States; but this is rarely needed, as the desire for education is universal. Like many other "paternal" customs in Germany, the method of enforcing attendance at school is sometimes very unceremonious, and a writer on the German system of education tells us that in some places "the school authorities are empowered to send a policeman to the home of the child and have him taken to school by the collar." This method, he says, is very salutary, as it creates a great sensation in the school, and is regarded as a serious disgrace.* From statistics collected by the same writer the necessity for imprisoning parents is diminishing, for whilst in the year 1881 in Königsberg 173 persons were fined and 15 committed to prison, the numbers in 1885 had fallen to 141 fined and 2 imprisoned. In Sweden and Norway the attendance of children is compulsory from seven or nine, as the School Board may decide, up to "confirmation," or until the final standard is passed. The means of compulsion are reminders, fines, and in case of gross neglect on the part of the parents, removal of a child from its home to a home approved by the Board, or in extreme cases to a reformatory. The Boards fix the minimum attendances, both as to days per week and school hours. In many large sparsely-peopled parishes the schools are held in one place after another, so as to make attendance possible; and where no school-house exists ratepayers have to provide accommodation in their houses. In fact the difficulties which impede education, in Norway especially, greatly resemble those which attend religious ministrations. Any one who has sailed along the coast of Norway knows how the clergyman has to travel from one place to another at intervals to administer the rites of matrimony, baptism, confirmation, &c., and how irregular are the services of religion over which he is able to preside. This naturally

---

* Perry. Reports on German Elementary Schools, p. 12, where cases are given. (Rivingtons, 1887.)

renders the necessity for religious instruction by laymen exceptionally requisite. In France, Switzerland, and Italy, attendance is also obligatory, but in the last-named country there is not sufficient school accommodation, and so far as we are aware the law is nowhere enforced. In Belgium attendance is not compulsory, and education is by no means universal: uninstructed children follow handicrafts in considerable numbers. In Great Britain a remarkable system prevails, and its most conspicuous defects are prominent in our large towns. All children between five and thirteen ought by law to attend school; if the parents are too poor to pay school fees they may apply to the guardians of the poor, whose duty it is, after inquiry, to supply the necessary means. In some places the parents have to walk long distances to the office of the overseers, and cases are known where the relieving officer treats them as paupers, and even uses language of a kind to deter sensitive parents from making the application. A respectable parent who cannot pay the school fees is liable to fine and imprisonment, and some are so imprisoned for a debt of a few pence, whilst unscrupulous traders who succeed in obtaining credit for thousands of pounds, and fail to meet their obligations, may seek relief in the Insolvency Court.

Notwithstanding compulsory legislation, and the severe penalties which are attached to it, the streets of our large towns swarm with children of school age selling matches, newspapers, &c.; and in spite of the Act recently passed for the protection of young children, many are sent out in their earliest infancy to beg, and sometimes, in order to excite sympathy, almost every rag of clothing is withheld from them, even in the severest weather. These are chiefly the offspring of dissolute parents or of the criminal classes, who would willingly part with their children and hand them over to the State for education and maintenance if it did not pay them better to retain their services in the infamous manner just described. It is this state of things that the ragged and industrial school system is intended to obviate, but with which it fails to cope effectively.

In France, Switzerland, and Italy, primary instruction is quite gratuitous; in Germany (as in England) school fees are allowed to be charged where the parents can afford to pay them, but exemptions are easily obtained when they are unable to do so: in all cases the fees are nominal, and in most of the large cities and towns elementary education is gratuitous to all. In Belgium the practice varies in different communes, but in every case declared poverty suffices to secure gratuitous instruction.

In Sweden and Norway, all State instruction, both in primary and secondary schools, is gratuitous, and parents whose circumstances are such as not to admit of their sending their children to school without injury, can obtain a grant from the poor-rates as a compensation for the loss of their services.

In Denmark, where school attendance is compulsory up to the fourteenth year, it is gratuitous in the country schools, and there is a number of free schools in Copenhagen also, but there the majority of poor parents take a pride in sending their children to the so-called "pay-schools," where the fees are one krone (about

1s. 2d.) per month, and there are also State-schools called citizen-schools where the fees are 3 to 5 kroner monthly. In Denmark, although parents neglecting the education of their children are liable to fines, they would as soon think of starving them as of keeping them away from school.

In Scotland primary instruction has recently become gratuitous in the lower standards, a portion of the grant from the State in aid of local taxation having been appropriated to that object. In England at the time of writing these lines an active agitation is proceeding to secure a similar privilege for children in our primary schools, and some concession may be expected to be made during one of the coming sessions of this Parliament. Until recently disinterested and liberal-minded educationists, such as the late Mr. Matthew Arnold, disapproved of gratuitous education being given, excepting in cases of extreme poverty. It was considered by many conscientious men that the State is no more called upon to give instruction free than to give bread or clothing gratis, and that to do so would diminish the sense of responsibility in parents. At present most of the members of the various denominations are agreed that gratuitous primary instruction (or "Free Schools" as they are called) is desirable, but the chief difficulties in the way of its accomplishment are, 1, the widespread feeling that where the State provides the funds there should be popular local control; and 2, that difficulties would arise in the method of appropriation. As it has been already stated in speaking of religious instruction, the first is the real difficulty. The State already makes grants in aid to denominational schools, without attempting to interfere with religious teaching, and if it be deemed necessary that local control should be extended along with increased State aid, that should be confined to the expenditure of public money for secular teaching, and there would not be much difficulty in securing the legitimate appropriation of State grants.

As to the question of apportionment, that is a matter of detail which would not stand in the way of the settlement of the question if the religious difficulty could be overcome. The object of these remarks is not to decide a controversy, but simply to state facts and to compare systems, and the fact that gratuitous education already exists in some countries where religious feelings and prejudices are much more pronounced than in England speaks for itself.

One of the chief defects in English primary instruction is the almost entire absence of physical training, to which, however, the Board Schools in Manchester, and some of those in other large towns, are an exception. In Germany, France, and Switzerland, gymnastics and drill are conspicuous features in the training of children. No doubt this arises largely from the necessity for keeping up a constant supply of soldiers. In Belgium also great attention is paid to physical exercises.

That physical training is neglected in Great Britain and the United States is no doubt due mainly to their not being military nations, but all the same it is a great disadvantage in a pacific sense, for the constant strain upon the minds of children, and the increasing area of instruction, renders a regular system of physical training an urgent necessity. In a very large proportion of the elementary schools there is absolutely no physical exercise besides the few minutes of play in the playground, snatched from or during the regular course of instruction. In many there is musical drill for the infants only; whilst in some of the Board Schools an hour per week is devoted to drill and exercise with small wooden or iron dumb-bells or clubs; but it must be apparent to the most superficial observer that sooner or later very evil results must follow from the present system of constant mental exertion without corresponding physical exercise for young and growing frames.

In France manual technical instruction is given in primary schools. Such instruction consists of drawing, cutting objects in cardboard, modelling, tool-making, wood-carving, &c., not only in day but in evening schools, and the various occupations are adapted to the different grades. Germany is provided with trade schools, and although workshops are not yet introduced into primary schools, drawing is taught, and there are apprenticeship schools in several German States. The same remarks apply to Switzerland and Belgium.

There has long been an outcry in this country against the educational authorities for neglecting to foster what has been called "Technical Education," but what was really intended to mean trade instruction, in which Continental nations are said to have left us in the background, and until the last session of Parliament no measure was passed for giving technical instruction in primary schools. Drawing has, however, long been taught in such schools, and although the system of science instruction, embracing theoretical and even practical training in many trades and professions, has not been associated with the curriculum of the primary schools, it has been provided to an extent far beyond anything that exists elsewhere for young persons and adults; and when, some years since, one of the writers of this article visited the United States, he was asked to read a paper, before the American Association for the Promotion of Science, on the "South Kensington System," as it was called, for the information of those who were desirous of fostering scientific education in America. Though an Act was passed for Scotland in the present year, even now technical instruction can only be given there in elementary schools to children who have passed the Fifth Standard.

It may be said in general terms that in Germany primary education is admirably conducted, bears excellent results, and is imparted by teachers who are thoroughly qualified for their duties. There are State normal schools, but they are only free to poor students; there are no pupil teachers; and generally speaking qualified teachers are badly remunerated. In France the same may be said of primary education as in Germany: there are many normal (State) schools in which instruction is gratuitous and of a high order; but as in Germany, teachers are in general badly paid. Even in Paris, where the payment has been nearly doubled, it is still much below our scale. Almost identical remarks apply to Switzerland, where the head schoolmasters take part in the public inspection of schools, sitting at the same tables with the Government or Cantonal Board. In Belgium there are many normal schools supported by the State, as also in Italy, where training of teachers is gratuitous; and the same remark applies to Sweden and Norway, where the expenses of all the normal schools are defrayed by the State. In this country the training schools have been founded and are managed by the various denominations, and they are liberally aided by the State. According to reports of the Education Department contributed by H. E. Oakley, Esq., and Dr. J. G. Fitch,* these institutions are fairly well conducted, and as far as they meet the requirements of the country little fault is to be found with them; but the returns for 1888 show that there are only forty-four such institutions in England and Wales, giving instruction to 3,277 students, whilst the number applying for admission far exceeds the annual vacancies. It is said that the supply of certificated teachers is equal to the demand owing to the employment of pupil teachers, a system which has either never existed or has ceased to exist in other countries.

In this hasty and necessarily superficial sketch we have not attempted to adduce all the evidence that is available to substantiate the opinions and support the conclusions at which we have arrived through a somewhat intimate acquaintance with primary education both at home and abroad; indeed we presume that some of the subjects which have been dismissed by us with a few passing words of comment will be treated in detail by writers who have made them a special study. We believe, however, that we shall have the concurrence of most persons who understand the question when we say that owing to two main causes, first, the removal of children from school at an immature age, and secondly, the extensive employment of pupil teachers and others inefficiently trained, elementary education has not reached the same high level in England as it has attained in several other European States.

* Eyre and Spottiswoode. "Training Colleges." 1889.

PART VI.

WESTERN STATE EDUCATION.

THE UNITED STATES' AND ENGLISH SYSTEMS COMPARED.

1. *Primary and Grammar Schools.*

It is not an easy matter to grasp the philosophy of a foreign educational system. Education is not an art, like the art of swimming for instance, where, though the methods of teaching and practice may vary considerably, yet the purpose which the art seeks to achieve, viz., how to propel the body along the surface of water without getting the head underneath, is, all the world over, the same. On the contrary, the purpose of a national system of education will differ very materially in different countries. Education is the organized and scientific initiation of the young into the duties of civilised life. Each different ideal of civilisation will, therefore, produce its own peculiar ideal of education.

Now there are undoubtedly strong differences between American and English ideals. Let us cite one conspicuous instance of such difference. The American people (by which here and elsewhere is meant the people of the United States) have always been their own law-makers, and so, from the earliest period of their national history, they have placed in the forefront, as their object in founding a public system of education, that of training up law-making, as well as law-abiding, citizens. But this object was certainly not the guiding principle of those who initiated and developed popular education in England. The voluntary and denominational movement of the early part of this century had confessedly no other than religious and philanthropic aims on behalf of the poorer classes; and as time went on it received recognition and support from the State almost entirely on these grounds. And, although our first really national movement on behalf of education, in the year 1870, received a great impulse from the middle and upper-class consciousness of the danger of leaving "our masters" in ignorance of their letters, yet the arrest of that movement at its present incomplete stage shows that we still realise only imperfectly that other ideal of education as a course of training for the law-makers of England. The English ideal in the past has not been that of an

American State which sets up as a fundamental axiom:—" Since the efficient government of the State requires the harmonious co-operation of the masses, it is a condition for the welfare of the State to provide schools in which the children of the people grow up together without class or sect distinction, so that a more homogeneous population may make the action of the Government harmonious and energetic." *

Again, neither is it an easy matter to master the details of a foreign educational system. This is especially true of the "American Common School system." And the reason is not far to seek—in one sense, there *is* *no* American Common School system. So difficult is it for an Englishman, with his Education Department administering the Education Acts, issuing its annual code of regulations, and thus virtually determining for all public elementary schools the duties of managers, the qualifications of teachers, and the course of instruction, to realise "local option" as the fundamental principle of a public school system, that it becomes necessary to emphasise this fact at starting. There is *no* American Education Department, *no* American Minister of Education. The Commissioner of Education at the head of the United States Bureau of Education at Washington is rather a Registrar-General for education than a Minister of State—a sort of statistical head centre who has no more control over educational bodies than the Registrar-General in England has over the births, deaths, and marriages of human bodies which he records and tabulates. In fact the functions of the United States Government in the matter of educational legislation are of the narrowest kind. Apart from the scientific military training of the Army and Navy, which is entirely in its hands, it limits itself to making endowments in the shape of land-grants to the several States for the purposes of common school education or for the promotion of scientific agriculture and the mechanical arts. It has also furnished endowments for the support of Universities in all new States formed since 1787. The duty and responsibility of making provision for the education of its population rests with the several States individually; and each State has, of its own proper motion, though some in the South only tardily, come to recognise this duty by establishing a common school system in its midst. And this system differs, or may differ, from the corresponding system of other States.

First, this individuality is shown in the different modes of election, the widely varied composition and functions of the several State Boards of Education. In some States the Boards are composed mostly of professional teachers, in others, chiefly of State officers. Then, in some States, the State Superintendent (*i.e.*, Inspector, though not with analogous functions to Her Majesty's Inspectors of Schools) is elected directly by the people, in others by the Governor, in others, again, by the Legislature, in others by the State Board of Education itself; and his duties, powers, and prerogatives are equally diverse.

* National Council of Education, Proceedings, 1887.

Again, some States enforce compulsory school attendance, others do not; and where compulsion *is* carried out, the "bye-laws" (as we should call them) regulating the ages between which they are enforced, the minimum number of attendances required, the penalties for their breach, and the conditions of exemption, vary with each State.

The principle of local self-government which underlies the social and political constitution of the United States asserts itself still further by each State assigning to the municipalities of cities and townships within its borders the power to elect their own School Committees or School Boards, only retaining the right of prescribing their organization, officers, and general powers. These City Boards have also been organized on every variety of plan. The New York Board is elected by the Mayor. In Philadelphia the Board is elected by the Judges, who are themselves elected by popular vote, and the Board is associated in its task of school management with certain "school directors," who are elected by the people, three for each ward in the city. In Cincinnati the Board is elected partly by the people in wards and partly on a "general ticket;" and so on. These City School Boards have power (subject to the State educational laws) to constitute school districts, elect school officers, collect taxes for school purposes, and arrange for the examination, appointment and rate of pay of teachers, to build schools, arrange courses of study, prescribe the regulations for the government of the schools, and to administer these schools. Hence there are further opportunities for diversity in educational machinery and policy owing to the individual local circumstances, the ever-varying political and social temper of each city and town. And it should further be borne in mind that America is far less homogeneous in itself than England. Over that wide area, varieties of race and tradition, of climate and environment, have impressed even upon individual cities, marked divergencies from a uniform ethical, social and political standard. Boston is not as New Orleans, nor Richmond as San Francisco.

But, amidst all this diversity of ideal and theory, of detail and practice, there is an underlying unity, an undercurrent of common sentiment in educational matters which is strong enough to set the course of the stream very much in the same direction all over the United States, in obedience to the "genius" of their national institutions. The Common School is universal; it is open to all classes; it is free; and it is either unsectarian or secular, *i.e.*, neutral, in religious matters. Let us glance at these points in order.

First, *the Common School is to be found everywhere*, in the remotest farming town where scarcely 20 children of school age can be counted within a radius of two or three miles, no less than in the large cities.* And every Common School is under the

---

* In America, a *town* (old English *township*) corresponds to the English village or group of villages forming a *rural* area; and a *city*, to the English municipal town, forming an *urban* area.

control and management of a local board, variously designated in different parts of the United States, but everywhere practically what, from the point of view of local *representative* control, we in England would call a School Board. The School Board is, therefore, universal. Its foundation rests on the idea that every locality is competent to manage its own educational affairs. But this only within limits. Each State has its own State Law, which is administered by the State Board of Education. The State lays down by law that Common Schools of a certain grade and range of study shall exist within a given area, that the schools shall be open for a minimum number of days, and (where it has adopted the principle of compulsion) fixes the requirements as to school attendance, and the penalties for truancy. The function of the State Board of Education is to obtain and publish the returns required by law from the School Boards, and to apportion the State Fund (where such exists) arising from grants of land, bequests or endowments. But the State Board has no *legal* control over the *management* of the schools, and can exercise no authority with reference to local taxation, the erection of school buildings, the appointment of teachers, or the organization, discipline and course of study in the schools. These matters are entirely in the hands of the local School Boards. The State Board does, however, exercise considerable influence in the form of "moral suasion" beyond the limits of its legal powers, by the acquiescence and good-will of the School Boards. It exercises this function more especially among the rural School Boards. Practically it leaves the city School Boards alone in the management of their schools; for experience has shown that the public spirit of a city community is an ample guarantee, in spite of occasional abuse of the position by struggling politicians, for the presence of a sufficient number of competent administrators upon the School Board, and for the efficiency, energy, and enterprise of its working.

In the rural parts of the States, however, it is frequently far otherwise. The only available members of the Board are farmers; they live two or three miles from each other, and from the school; they do not profess to be qualified for the work, and only serve on the School Board because "somebody must." A School Board so composed will not only frankly recognise its inefficiency, but will court the assistance and guidance which the State Board of Education is prepared most freely to render. For the discharge of these functions towards the rural Board the State Board employs Superintendents or Agents whose duty it is to collect and diffuse information as to the condition of the schools, to inspect and examine when invited, to point out weaknesses, and to make suggestions for improvement. But beyond this they are careful not to go.

Now contrast this with the English system; and, for this purpose, for "State Law" read "Education Acts of Parliament," for "State Board of Education" read "Education Department," and for "State Fund" read "Parliamentary Grant." Further, for "School Board," we must read "Managers of a Public Elementary School," for the English law recognizes equally as "Managers" either School Boards, or a body (of three persons at least), representing a voluntary or denominational agency. The analogy thus suggested between the English and American systems holds good very fairly, but the following points of differentiation will at once strike the observer. In both countries, the education of the people is regulated by a central law. But the strength of a law depends upon the degree to which it can be enforced, and with regard to education, the leverage which in both countries makes for the enforcement of the law is mainly the money grant which the administrators have at their disposal. That money is the "State Fund" in one case, and the "Parliamentary Grant" in the other. Now, in America, the State Fund even at its largest (as, probably, in Massachusetts) bears a very much smaller proportion to the sum raised by local taxation, than the Parliamentary Grant in England does to the sum raised locally either by rates and fees, or by subscriptions and fees. Consequently on this ground the power of the Education Department over Public Elementary Schools in England is much greater than the power of the State Boards of Education over the Common Schools in America. But, further, the Education Law in England is wider and more far-reaching. By "the Code," which is strictly an annual appendix to the Education Acts, the Education Department has a very direct control over the buildings, the teachers employed, and over the organization and internal management of a public elementary school; it appoints inspectors, who can claim admittance at any time into a school for a close examination and inspection of the school in all these particulars, and the amount of Parliamentary Grant, even to the extent of total withdrawal, is subject to a minute assessment of the merits of the school as to its condition, teaching-staff, and educational results.

It is admitted, by thoughtful Americans, that their policy (as regards the rural Boards) has its elements of weakness as well as of strength :—"It may allow to be left for a long time untouched many errors and defects in the management of the schools which might at once be removed if the State were to lay its hand directly upon them; and it may seem thus to fail, and may perhaps really fail, in bringing the schools with sufficient promptness to the best attainable results. But, on the other side, in its reliance upon the intelligence and carefulness of the people themselves in their several localities, and through the necessity of working only through such agencies, it may secure, in a more permanent form, the gains that are made." *

May not Englishmen admit that our policy also has its elements of weakness as well as of strength; that too much centralization and too little trust in local interest in education is a characteristic note of our system, just as too little of the former and too much of the latter is of theirs?

Secondly, *the Common School is open to all classes*, rich and poor, of every station or social rank. The "legal school age" (*i.e.* the

* Report of Massachusetts Board of Education, 1880-1.

range of ages between which a child or young person can legally claim to be educated at a Common School) is determined in each State by its State Law, and is accepted, with only a slight modification here and there, by the Cities or Towns which are entitled to have their own School system. The usual range of school age is from five or six to twenty or twenty-one. It is the function, then, of the Common School system to supply any demand for education which can reasonably be made on behalf of young persons between these ages. Obviously, therefore, there can be no such limitation in the American system to merely elementary education as pertains in England, where Parliament has limited State recognition to Elementary schools which are provided for the child-population between three and thirteen years of age, and practically turn the scholars out of school when they have passed the highest "standard" of an elementary course of instruction set forth by the "Code."

In America, then, every State requires by law that there shall be, first, a sufficient number of schools for the instruction of every child who may legally attend school in orthography, reading, writing, English grammar, geography, arithmetic, drawing, the history of the United States, the constitution of its own State, and of its own city or town, and in good morals. Higher subjects are required to be taught where expedient. These schools are, in working, universally divided into *two* departments, called Primary and Grammar schools; but this division has no foundation in the nature of things, but is made purely as a matter of convenience. The Primary School receives children from the youngest school-age up to about ten or eleven; and they then pass on to the Grammar School, there to complete what practically is the elementary course. The arrangement has the advantage of enabling small Primary Schools to be placed nearer the homes of the younger children, who are then transferred, when able to walk longer distances, to a large and well-grounded Grammar School, which is thus fed by a group of Primary Schools. But, secondly, the State law requires that there shall be maintained in every town of so many hundred (500 in Massachusetts) families, in addition, a *high* school, and, sometimes, makes further provision, as in Massachusetts, that every town of 4000 inhabitants must widen its high school curriculum by the introduction of such additional subjects as Greek, French, Astronomy, Moral Science and Political Economy.

There are, or were until very recently, no schools, in the Common School system, corresponding to our English Infants Schools, receiving children at three (or even under three) years of age up to about seven. Within the last few years, however, as a result of a number of experiments by private persons to adapt the Kindergarten or Froebellian system to American conditions—notably at St. Louis—Schools on the Kindergarten model (called Sub-Primary) have been established as part of the Public School system. Following the lead of St. Louis, Milwaukie and Philadelphia have Sub-Primary Schools firmly established. Boston has lately joined this goodly company, and has taken over the fourteen Kindergarten schools in that City, previously supported by private benevolence; and other cities are rapidly taking steps in the same direction.*

Before passing on to the work of the High Schools, a few criticisms on the work of the American Primary and Grammar Schools, based on the writer's own observation and examination, may serve as an estimate of the comparative efficiency of American and English public Elementary Schools, to be taken for what it is worth. The average age of children in the lowest grade (or class) on admission in American city schools is nearer seven than six, and, as a consequence of the child's first introduction to mental training at an age nearly two years greater than the corresponding age in England, where Infant Schools are universal, it follows that the average age of children doing work corresponding to any given English Code Standard is greater in America than in England. This disparity seems to hold good all through school life, though in diminishing degree, that is, American children never entirely make up for the time lost through the lack of Infant Schools, so as to be as young in any "Standard" as English children. As no payments to the teachers, either from the State Fund or the local taxes depend upon the "results" of examinations, the scholars are not driven at so great a pace. The pace might be somewhat increased, without physical strain. There seems to be a little too much "marking time." Promotion from stage to stage takes place at long intervals (sometimes as much as a year, as in England), and follows rigid rules. Consequently, as in England, promotion is not rapid enough for the more intelligent scholars. Those who complete the course, going right through to the highest class of the Grammar School, at fourteen or fifteen years of age, are comparatively few, more girls than boys, in the proportion sometimes as high as two to one; and these go through a "review" of the work of past years, and may be said to leave school with a thoroughly sound practical education. Large numbers, however, especially in those States which have no compulsory law (*i.e.*, in about half of the States), have left school by eleven, indifferently equipped, and these must soon lose most of what they have acquired. Those who leave between eleven and thirteen do not seem to have had the opportunity of being so well equipped with an Elementary Education as corresponding English children. Doubtless, this defect in their school training is largely made up for, afterwards, by greater adroitness and adaptability—the result partly of inherited faculty, and partly also of the wider education in the ways of the world, acquired during those early years up to seven, which are spent by English children in the narrower community of the Infant School.

2. *High Schools.*

In passing from the Grammar School to the High School, which is equally open to him under every State Common School System, the scholar is being lifted, by the enlightened provision of the com-

* Report of Commissioner of Education, 1887–8, p. 821.

munity, out of the region of elementary, into that of secondary, education. Herein America is in marked contrast with England. In England the provision for Secondary Education follows the track of the old endowments of the Tudors and Stuarts, and is almost wholly wanting outside of that track. But the distribution of these endowments is in no way based on the needs of modern England, so that a village like Ewelme in Oxfordshire has far more than it can profitably use ; a populous town like Sheffield, far less. In many small country towns, endowed Secondary Schools are to be found which neither Acts of Parliament, Royal Commissions, nor new Schemes of government have been able to galvanize into life. Vested interests have been too powerful for the masterly Recommendations of the Schools Inquiry Commissioners of 1868, which proposed to divide the country into educational districts, and to co-ordinate the endowments within each area by such redistribution as would meet the latter-day wants of the community. Though the composition and constitution of governing bodies have been largely, and, in many cases, beneficially re-modelled, it has not always been possible, even for Parliamentary Commissioners, to eliminate elements antagonistic to reform. Hence, even the funds derivable from endowments, scanty as they are for the needs of the England of to-day, are far from being appropriated to the best advantage ; and the late Mr. Matthew Arnold, preaching the doctrine of "organize your Secondary Education" incessantly for five-and-twenty years, felt himself to be only a *vox clamantis in deserto*, and the disregard of his voice to be a terrible "blow for the declining age of a sincere but ineffectual Liberal." *

But America knows nothing of these characteristic English difficulties. There, whatever Secondary Education exists (except that given by a few private schools and academies in the wealthier cities) is provided as part of the Public School System by the local School Board, and is supported out of the taxes annually raised from the whole community for the purposes of Education. This is, indeed, the most distinctive feature of each State Common School system. The facilities for higher education are not capriciously distributed, by the chances of ancient or modern bounty, but are to be found in the midst of all fairly populous cities and towns in the State.

But though the cause of higher education escapes our difficulties, it must not be supposed that it has not difficulties of its own. It is obviously essential to the proper management of any kind of higher education that the managers should be socially in sympathy with those for whom they are providing the education, that they should have an adequate conception of the value to the many of the higher mental training for the few, and be conscious of aims based on broad views of the fruitfulness of intellectual life in a nation. Now, unhappily, there comes across the usually healthy political life of an American city a sick season—a time when the unscrupulous, the mercenary, the self-seeking, to whom " everything human and divine has its

---

* See Matthew Arnold's article "Porro unum est necessarium," *Fortnightly Review*, November, 1878.

price," has full sway; it is then that the better elements either retire from public life in disgust at the treatment to which they are subjected, and in despair at their powerlessness to stem the tide of deterioration that has set in, or are elbowed out of the honourable posts they occupied by the mean devices of those who use these posts for their own dishonourable ends. Sad times these for higher education: for the selfishness of the demagogue immediately suggests to the burdened taxpayer, "Why should you be called upon in your poverty to pay for the Latin and Greek and other accomplishments which are of no use to your children, and which ought to be provided for the rich man's children at his own expense?" Most cities have had their days of re-action, when it has been a severe struggle to maintain a proper standard of secondary instruction in face of an outcry like this. But the struggle generally ends in the triumph of the better elements; and many of the State legislatures have checked the recurrence of such untoward times for higher education by changes in the mode of election and constitution of School Boards, which have made them less directly dependent on popular whim and less capable of manipulation by political machinists. "In this direction, however, much remains to be desired." *

The English Endowed or Public School and the American High School being thus the outcome of such different circumstances as have been described, present numerous and marked points of contrast. An English Endowed School would admit scholars of *all* ages, from eight or nine years old and upwards; its standard of attainment qualifying for admission would vary with the age of the candidate; and each pupil, on being admitted, would be placed in that class in the school where the attainments were as nearly as possible similar to his own. The batch of admissions at a particular entrance examination, though the greater proportion would be entered in the lowest class of the school, would be distributed over a wide range of classes. But in America the almost universal rule is to make the condition of admission to a High School either that the candidate shall have passed at least the previous year in some upper elementary school (*i.e.*, Grammar School, so called), and have *graduated*, *i.e.*, satisfactorily completed the course of instruction there, or, shall show in an examination attainments equivalent to such graduation. Consequently, all the pupils entering a High School at a given time are as nearly as possible of the *same* age and attainments. Having previously reached the first grade (or class) of an American Grammar School, they will average fourteen or fifteen years of age; and will have all reached a certain standard in the subjects named above (p. 87) as forming the course of instruction in Grammar Schools. Consequently, though of such an advanced age, they will, as a rule, have studied no *foreign* language whatever, ancient or modern.†

* City School Systems, by Dr. John D. Philbrick, Circular of the Bureau of Education, 1885.
† Except, possibly, German, if they should happen either to be of German parentage, or of American parentage living in cities with a large German population, when, as is the case with Welsh children in a public elementary school in Wales, they will have received a *bilingual* training (English and Welsh) in the elementary school itself.

The High School course (in a city) usually extends over four years, but sometimes, as in the newer cities of the West, only three years. But the average length of stay in the school is only a little over two years, and in the case of boys, even less than that;[*] while the number of those who complete the course only ranges from one-third to as low as one-sixth of the number admitted to the school. It follows that a High School accommodating 300 scholars will admit nearly 150 from the various Grammar Schools at one annual or two semi-annual admissions. The scholars enter the same class and travel more or less *pari passu* through the school. This class will be divided into sections, and a large amount of choice will be allowed to each pupil, according to the parental views as to his (or her) future career in life. In some cities, the popular demand (to which the High School must bow) has compelled the introduction of three or even more " elective " *courses* of study (not subjects merely) in the same school—a classical or commercial or a general English course.† The pupils in the several sections belonging to the same year are taken together in those general subjects which are common to one or more of these courses, such as History or Algebra, and where any branch of a subject is pursued to a greater extent by one set of pupils more than another, further subdivisions may be formed. As a consequence of this great liberty of " election " on the part of scholars as to the course of study they will pursue, the High Schools of America are almost all taught upon the " departmental " system, *i.e.*, each member of the teaching-staff is a specialist, having his own special department of school-work—one, or, it may be, two subjects which he teaches throughout the school—one teacher taking all the Latin, another Algebra and French, another Geometry and History, another English, and so on. This system is not the usual one in English Endowed and Public Schools (though it is largely practised in the High Schools for Girls which have lately been established), where each master has his own class for a given half-year, which he takes in a wide range of subjects, only passing his boys on to " departmental " masters for modern languages, mathematics or science. But such a plan would be impossible where electiveness of studies is carried to such an extent as in America.

As may well be imagined from this description, the difficulties of elaborating an effective school programme, which shall ensure the full employment of every teacher and scholar during the school hours are considerable. But the Departmental system in America has its drawbacks as well as its difficulties.‡ In the Grammar Schools from which the pupils have been drafted into the High

---

[*] In many of the High Schools, especially in the centre and west of the United States, boys and girls are taught in the same school, and the proportion of girls to boys in the highest class of the High School is 3, 4, or even 5 to 1. This, of course, means that the women of America are better educated than the men.

† Sometimes there are *two* English courses, one for children of English-speaking, and the other for children of German-speaking, parents, and called respectively the English-English, and the German-English courses.

‡ For the latest references to the " Departmental plan," see Report of Commissioner of Education, 1887-8, pp. 196, 388.

School, they have been accustomed to the class-teacher system, where scholar and teacher are thrown together for the greater part of the day's programme for a half-year or even a year at a time, and the relations between them become intimate, and even parental, in character. But all this is changed when they come to the High School. There each teacher gives instruction to perhaps 200 different scholars every day, and consequently teacher and scholar do not get, even at the end of the year, much beyond an attitude of amiable neutrality. It is admitted that the pupils feel this reduction of personal interest in themselves keenly, and that this is one reason of their abandoning the High School course so frequently soon after admission.

Coming now to the special studies of the American High Schools many circumstances will occur to the mind as militating against the attainment to the same high standard of work which is reached by a thoroughly efficient Endowed or Public School in England. It is obvious that, where the study of a foreign language is only commenced at the advanced age of fourteen or thereabouts, no such proficiency in Latin and Greek is attainable as compared with that which an English boy can show who was introduced to one of these languages at eight or nine years of age.

Again, a very general age for admission to an American University, even to the older institutions of Harvard and Yale, is seventeen; consequently a boy who showed marked capacity or taste for classical studies would be passed out of the High School and on to the University at a much earlier age than in England, and the High Schools would not be called upon to carry the classical course beyond his requirements at seventeen years of age. In a word, the head scholars of an American High School are just three, or at most four, years removed from their Latin declensions; in an English High School they would be more nearly eight to ten years from that initiation into the Latin tongue. The fundamental difference between these schools in the two countries cannot be more concisely put. Latin or Greek Verse Composition is unknown; the Professor of Classical Literature at John Hopkins University (Baltimore) told the writer that he thought he was the only man in America who could write Greek Iambics, and he was an Oxford man. Latin Prose Composition is not taught to any great extent. Most of the classical work that would be shown up by the scholars of the first class of an American High School, aged seventeen or thereabouts, would only pass muster in an English Public School for boys of fifteen. Great attention is, however, paid to Mathematics. Pupils do not, as a rule, study more than *two* foreign languages, so that those who are following the complete classical course, and taking up both Latin and Greek, are not taught any modern language. It is not usual, even among those who have elected for the English or Commercial courses, to find more than one modern language studied, which would be either French or German. German is the most popular of these two "Electives," and naturally, because of the large German-speaking element to be found in most of the great cities. Several branches of Science :—Physics, Physiology, Botany are included in the possible curriculum. Much more attention than in corresponding Schools in England is paid to English Language and Literature, Constitutional History (of the United States), and General Geography. The complaint is still frequent in the Reports of Superintendents that in these and the science subjects the tendency is to require of the pupils mere memorizing of the paragraphs of their text-books, " dull as a bill of lading and scrappy as an invoice." The slavery to text-books has never been so conspicuous in English High Schools, though it cannot be said that the schools of this country are altogether free from it. Teaching here, as there, is frequently an artificial, not a natural, process. And it must be so in any part of the world where more people profess the art than those who have a natural aptitude for it, or have taken the pains to study its principles. The moral of all which is—train your teachers.

But there are two institutions which must be excepted from most of the foregoing criticisms on American High Schools—the Latin High School, and the English High School, at Boston. That city is, as everybody is aware, the nursing-mother of American National Education. *Noblesse oblige*, and whatever Boston does in the matter of Education is always worthy of its traditions and its enlightened educational faith. It has recently (1881) erected for the Boys' Latin and English High Schools, under one roof or series of roofs, what may be indeed called a school-palace, vieing in the completeness of its equipment and architectural fitness with anything of which Vienna—that city of school-palaces—can boast. The late Bishop Fraser visited (in 1865) the English High School when it was in its old premises, and said of it even then, in his Report to the Schools Inquiry Commission, that " it ought to be put in a glass-case and carried over to England," as a specimen of what a school for the training of the English Middle Class for professional and business avocations should be. Would not his heart sink within him in despair at England ever rising to the same lofty conception of what is true wisdom in regard to the education of the middle-classes, if he saw this school as it is now, in all the magnificent surroundings of its new home, with the most perfect class-room arrangements, with science lecture theatres, laboratories and gymnasium, and with every newest device for securing the orderliness, health, and efficient instruction of its pupils! The English High School for boys was originally founded in 1827, but the Latin High School is by far the oldest American Public School, dating from 1635, five years after the original settlement of that city and a year before the founding of Harvard University. This latter school, alone of American High Schools supported by public funds, bears a close resemblance to our Public Schools or First Grade Endowed Schools in England. The object of the school is distinctly to prepare boys for the University, and parents are required to signify their intention of giving their sons a University education. It is not a Finishing School, preparing boys for business life, as the American High Schools of the ordinary type profess to be, and as the other—the

Boston English High School—is, but it is a Preparatory School for the University. Instead of admitting boys only on condition of their having completed the Grammar School course, they are encouraged to enter much earlier, and the admission Examination only requires a standard to be reached equivalent to the third class of the Grammar School, instead of the first. Thus boys of twelve, or even eleven, find their way into the Latin High School, and as they stay till seventeen, and sometimes till eighteen years of age, and devote their time mainly to the classics—with some mathematics and science in addition—it follows that the majority of them go to College with six or seven years of thorough classical training as a foundation for further study.

Recently also, the Board School for Boston has erected Girls' Latin, and Girls' English High Schools in another part of the city, and with courses of instruction precisely the same as those in the corresponding schools for boys. These schools are the result of an agitation carried on over many years to obtain for girls the privilege of being trained to an intelligent womanhood on the same grounds, and by the same means, as boys had long been trained to an intelligent manhood. The maxim of *co-education*, which is that boys and girls should be educated together, up to any age, in the same school and in the same class-rooms is not accepted in Boston. This principle has been very generally adopted in High Schools in the cities of the newer Western States of America, and in towns of small population in the Eastern States, for obvious reasons of economy; but it does not meet with favour in the larger of the old communities in the East, and has led to considerable abstentions from the use of the Public High School on the part of the wealthier classes in the West, who prefer to send their daughters at all events, and even their sons, to private Academies. Though co-education finds many able and honest advocates among prominent educationists on *à priori* grounds, parents of families find that it bristles with practical difficulties. The question is a wide one, and cannot be satisfactorily dealt with in this essay. But with regard to *High Schools*—and we are now speaking exclusively of such Schools—where the scholars are of ages from fourteen to eighteen and are drawn from homes of widely-different surroundings and social ideas, it may be assumed—to quote Dr. Philbrick's words—" that separate education of the sexes and not co-education in the High School grade of the city schools is the normal finality to which all civilisation tends." With this verdict, most English people will, doubtless, agree.

In closing these remarks upon American Secondary Education as part of the Common School System, we conclude, as we began, by emphasizing the one great and glaring point of contrast between America and England:—Whatever the shortcomings of the American High School, its glory is that it exists everywhere; maintained at the public cost of the tax-payer, within reasonable reach of every family of the middle classes, and accessible to the brighter intelligences among the poorest; while, whatever the excellences of the English Endowed School, where it is found in good working order, the crying grievance is that it exists only in a few favoured but

isolated spots, and the bulk of the middle classes of England as
well as the exceptionally gifted of the working classes,

> "look up, and are not fed,
> But, swoln with wind and the rank mist they draw,
> Rot inwardly."

In lifting up his lamentation over this glaring defect in our
English educational system, Matthew Arnold, though dead, yet
speaks words of wisdom and of justice when he says: *—" The
existing resources for secondary instruction, if judiciously co-
ordered and utilised, would prove to be immense; but undoubtedly
gaps would have to be filled, an annual State grant and municipal
grants would be necessary. That is to say, the nation would perform, as a corporate and co-operative work, a work which is now
never conceived and laid out as a whole, but is done sporadically,
precariously, and insufficiently. We have had experience how elementary instruction gains by being thus conceived and laid out,
instead of being left to individual adventure or individual benevolence. The middle class, who contribute so immense a share of the
cost incurred for the public institution of elementary schools, while
their own school supply is so miserable, would be repaid twenty
times over for their share in the additional cost of publicly instituting secondary instruction by the direct benefit which they and theirs
would get from its system of schools. The upper class, which has
bought out the middle class at so many of the great foundation
schools designed for its benefit, and which has monopolised what
good secondary instruction we have, owes to the middle class the
reparation of contributing to a public system of secondary schools."

3. *Free, Compulsory, and Secular Education.*

Thirdly, throughout the American Common School System—alike
in Primary, Grammar, and High Schools—and in all the States
without exception, instruction is gratuitous, or, in ordinary parlance,
free.

The adoption of the principle of Free Schools has only become
general in the United States within the last quarter of a century.
In Massachusetts, and in those of the New England States where
the original settlements were made, and the State system set up, in
the 17th century, by Presbyterian exiles from England, the " Free "
School was adopted from the very first. The explanation of this is,
that the *Presbyterian* exodus from these shores (which is not to be
confounded, as is often the case, with the *Puritan* exodus to Ply-
mouth in the " Mayflower ") was largely composed of men of means
and of fair social position among the middle classes—country
squires, clergymen, lawyers and merchants, such as the Winthrops,
Vanes, Eatons and Bellinghams; and these men had been educated
in English Endowed Grammar Schools, in all (or almost all) of

---

* See his article in the *Fortnightly Review* quoted above, p. 89.

which instruction was entirely (or almost entirely) gratuitous. These men, therefore, carried the principle of *free* education with them from England; and it is their *special* glory that they enlarged the conception of this "free" principle so as to cover the educational needs of every, even the poorest, citizen of the new communities across the Atlantic, all the while that "the poor," *i.e.* the labouring classes in the mother country, remained without any education till the present century, and even now do not receive it at the public cost, without school fees. But the difficulty of raising sufficient funds for educational purposes, as the population of the community increased faster than its wealth, led even the New England States to fall back upon the expedient of school fees, except Massachusetts, which has under all financial stress remained true to the spirit and letter of its earliest Education Law. And so, school fees were exacted in the form familiarly known as "rate-bills," from all parents (except in cases of poverty, which had to declare and prove itself) in all but this State until about the middle of the present century. Then an agitation commenced against them, largely on the ground that "attendance was repelled by directly taxing it"; and this, gaining force and volume as it progressed, slowly and steadily prevailed, first in one State and then in another, until, by the year 1871, the rate-bill had entirely disappeared, and instruction in the Common Schools of every State became entirely gratuitous. The effect of the removal of direct taxation from school attendance has been just what was anticipated: greater enrolment and more regular attendance have been characteristic of the school returns uninterruptedly since the abolition of fees.

A further movement is gaining ground for the gratuitous supply of text-books and stationery. The arguments for this extension of the principle of gratuitous instruction are partly economic and partly moral: (1) Expense would be saved, because the books would be purchased on more advantageous terms by the School Board, and, when they had served their purpose with one batch of scholars, would be available for use by the next batch coming up to that grade; and (2) The invidious distinction between the well-to-do who can afford to buy books and the poor who, under present regulations, can only obtain their books gratis on a personal plea of poverty, would be obliterated. The policy of supplying free books has been adopted for seventy years in Philadelphia and for fifty years in New York, and its success has led to its adoption in many other cities. The State Law of Massachusetts, which made the provision of text-books by a city or town optional by an enactment in 1873, has since 1884, made it compulsory upon all cities and towns to furnish all pupils in the public schools with free books and stationery.*

This is the place to say something about *compulsion*, or the en-

---

* "The free text-book Act has undoubtedly been a large factor in filling our high schools and the upper classes of the grammar schools." Report Boston School Committee, 1886-7. In Massachusetts in 1888, the average attendance was 90 per cent. of the average membership (Rep. Mass. Board of Education, 1888); in England, the average attendance for the same year was 77 per cent. of the number on the books.

forcement of attendance at school by legal enactment. The American States have shown very great reluctance thus to interfere with the legal rights of parents over their children, and to assert the legal rights of children as against their parents. But they are rapidly recognising the stern logic of facts which, presented in the form of annual statistics of child-vagrancy and adult-illiteracy, are convincing them that parental indulgence, negligence and greed, are greater sources of danger to the community than any encroachment could be on parental liberty to deprive his offspring of education. "The State, though it has provided a free gift to its children, yet finds it necessary to compel its acceptance"—this is the painful conclusion to which the American mind is coming, but only very slowly and unwillingly. Barely one-half of the States (only 16 or 17 out of 38) have as yet adopted any compulsory laws, and these, where they are in force, are generally very mild in character, and are still more mildly administered. The most stringent compulsory law does not require attendance for more than half the number of weeks in the school year, and then only from children above eight years of age; the offence of truancy rarely touches more than exceptional and flagrant cases; the penalties for the breach of the law on the part of parents and guardians are (except in Massachusetts) slight and ineffectual, and only in Massachusetts, and perhaps in one or two cities, are truant officers appointed to search out cases of illegal employment, or are penalties attached to such illegal employment of children of school age. In many States where the law (as in New York State Law, 1875) looks strong, it is practically a dead letter.*

The contrast with England in this respect is most striking. Though England has *not* provided education as a *free* gift to her children, she has yet determined to enforce its acceptance. And, having determined this, she has set to work in spite of the retention of the school fees to carry out compulsion with a rigour which is in marked contrast to the mildness of American compulsion. In England, the Law, first introduced in 1870, and strengthened by further enactments in 1876 and 1880, is now universal; it applies to all children over *five* years of age; it requires regular attendance morning and afternoon for five days in the week all through the school year; it imposes penalties upon parents for the irregular attendance of their children as well as for their truancy and vagrancy, and upon employers for illegal employment of children who should be at school; and it has armed School Boards, and School Attendance Committees in non-School Board areas, with very large powers, which they are obliged to exercise, for following up and detecting offenders, whether children, or parents, or employers of labour.

The question that is now arousing considerable public interest in England, and pressing upon practical statesmen for solution, is whether the community can fairly and reasonably enforce such a

---

* See Parliamentary Blue Book, Royal Commission on Education, Foreign Returns, 1888, p. 295.

stringent compulsory Law without making the education to which it applies a free gift for the compelled, at the public cost.

Fourthly, and lastly, instruction in the Common Schools is confined to *secular* subjects entirely in three-fourths of the States;* and in the remaining States, religious instruction of an unsectarian character is either required to be given (in New Hampshire alone), permitted to be given, or not forbidden to be given, by the teachers, with the right of children to absent themselves; and this permission is very variously made use of, the amount of religious instruction in most cases being limited to reciting the Lord's Prayer and reading the Bible without comment.

The Common School is only one of the agencies recognised as operating for the development of the perfect manhood of an American citizen, and, as the School does not usurp, so neither does it ignore, the functions of the Church and the Family as copartners with it in this development. This is the explanation of the attitude of America towards religious instruction. Moreover, there are practical considerations which have influenced this division of labour. The existence of a Roman Catholic population in a city—if these children are to have the same educational rights as those of all other American citizens to the schools to which all alike contribute by taxation—has of itself the effect of confining the teaching exclusively to purely secular subjects. The Roman Catholics will not accept unsectarian religious teaching at any price; they will not allow the children to be present at the reading from a version of the Bible (the Authorized Version) which, though accepted by Protestant Churches, is repudiated by their own Church. Protests are raised, from time to time, against what is considered so disastrous for morality and religion as a school system which, though it enjoins the teaching and inculcation of moral principles, largely precludes reference to the highest moral sanction. American State and City Reports are very reticent on this subject from fear, possibly, of stirring up a heated discussion which would hinder the progress of the school system; but on the whole it seems as if the secular platform is maintaining its ground in spite of an occasional charge of "godlessness" which can be so readily met, as it has been met by the following words of Secretary John W. Dickenson of the Massachusetts State Board of Education:†
"The public schools are condemned by some because they are godless institutions. The charge should be carefully examined for its meaning. If it means that theology is not one of the branches of study required or permitted to be taught, the charge is true, and the public Common School could not live a day if it were not true. If it means that the schools are anti-religious in any sense, the charge has already been shown to be unqualifiedly false. It must be false, unless the cultivation of good intellectual and moral habits is opposed to a faithful consideration of the highest truths that refer to

---

* Twenty-seven out of the thirty-six States who furnished Returns to the Royal Commission on the Elementary Education Acts, see Blue Book, Foreign Returns, 1888. The remaining nine States are Florida, Maine, Michigan, New Hampshire, New Jersey, Oregon, Pennsylvania, Vermont and Virginia. Ohio made no Return.
† See Report, Mass. Board of Education, 1888, p. 78.

our future, as well as to our present, well-being. What harm can come to a true religion from the ability to read, or to perform arithmetical problems; from a knowledge of the constitution and uses of things in the natural world; from an understanding of the principles and forms of our civil Government; from the power to reason correctly; from a training in the practice of good manners; or from the cultivation of the virtues, which are the ornament of society and the basis of a republican constitution? It seems hardly possible that in this age of the world, and in this civilised State, religion should stand in fear of general intelligence, or of personal freedom."

4. *The Training of Teachers, and " Teachers' Institutes."*

No survey of American Common School Education would be complete which did not include some account of the provision made in the several States *for the supply of teachers and for their efficient training.* The right to select the teacher is possessed, and tenaciously clung to, by each local School Board, and the only control, which each State can and does exercise over the qualifications of the teachers employed within its area, lies in fixing the conditions under which it is prepared to grant licences to teach (after examination by the State Superintendent), and in refusing all "appropriations" from the State Education Fund to any City or Town Board which employs unlicensed or uncertificated teachers. Most of the States issue such licences or certificates, and exercise the power of the purse—with greater or less effect upon the Boards according to the length of that purse—to exclude uncertificated teachers from the Public Schools. The qualifications required are very various, and for teachers in the rural districts, often deplorably low; but, as a rule, no one is allowed to undertake any subjects except those for which his certificate shows him to be qualified. The School Boards of the great cities, in like manner make the possession of a certificate from the City Superintendent a condition of employment as a teacher.

The source of supply of Teachers is found in the 'Graduates' of the Grammar or High Schools, or from those who have spent one year or more in Normal Schools or at the Universities. The age at which young persons commence teaching may be as young as 16 or 17, but is rarely less than 18 in cities and populous towns. The English "pupil-teacher" system is not found anywhere in the States. By far the larger proportion of teachers engaged in the common schools are women. The teachers in the primary schools, all but the principals (and sometimes even the principals) of Grammar Schools for both sexes, and some of those in High Schools for boys are women. They stay in the profession longer than the men, intending, unless they marry, to make a livelihood by it. The men, on the other hand, largely use teaching as a stepping-stone to other literary professions, or to the many avenues of commerce which are continually opening up in such a country of new enterprises and new conquests over primitive nature as America. The scale of pay for men (except in Massachusetts) is not at all calculated to counteract this influence, being decidedly low, considering the high rents and great cost of living; and is often (in the Western States) very slightly higher than that of women. Then, most of the Boards, especially those outside the cities, make the appointments of their teachers terminate at the end of each school year; and the shortness of the engagement, and the insecurity of re-engagement, greatly favour and encourage this tendency to treat "school-keeping" as a temporary occupation.*

By way of comparison and contrast, it may first be noted that, in England also, the appointment of the teacher rests solely with the School Boards or Bodies of Managers, while Parliament (through the Education Department) lays down as a condition of sharing in the Goverment grant, that the Head Teacher, at least, shall hold a Government Certificate, and that the rest of the staff shall possess certain qualifications; and here, also, small schools in rural districts are allowed to be in charge of head teachers with qualifications of a comparatively low standard (known as the "provisional certificate"). The Teachers in English Elementary Schools are mostly recruited from the Elementary schools themselves—a state of things rendered possible, and indeed purposely created, by the "pupil-teacher system," whereby young persons of both sexes may, and do, enter the profession at the early age of 14. The numerical preponderance of women over men engaged in teaching is not so great as in America, in spite of the existence of Infant Schools staffed wholly by women, because here, as a rule, boys are taught, after the infants' stage is passed, entirely by men. Again, in marked contrast to the American phenomenon, the vast majority of the men who enter the profession (certainly if they get beyond the pupil-teacher stage and become assistants, or go to a Training College), take it up as a means of livelihood and adopt it permanently. This great advantage to education which the English schools possess over the American is largely secured to them by comparative fixity of tenure, and by the higher rate of salaries for men (taking into account the smaller cost of living) which generally obtains in England, no less than by the tendency characteristic of this country to choose a career and stick to it.

But the American States have not remained satisfied with simply requiring, where they could, that the teachers employed should possess some kind of certificate attesting to a certain amount of knowledge of the subjects to be taught, but they have, most of them, realised the paramount necessity of some training for them in the art and science of education. Accordingly, second to none of the means by which each State—as a State—influences the Common School instruction within its borders, its great concern has been to secure this professional instruction. The last half-century, com-

---

* "The tenure of office of teachers is becoming more permanent, and it is a sign of progress." Rep. Mass. Board of Education, 1888.

mencing with the year 1839, when the first State Normal Schools were established by Massachusetts at Lexington (transferred to Framingham) and at Westfield, has witnessed the founding of nearly one hundred of these Normal Schools (or Training Colleges, as they would be called in England); and, if we add to these the Normal Schools and Teachers' Training Classes set up by counties and cities, a grand total of 134 Public Normal Schools is reached, maintained by public funds, and, in most cases, free of charge to those students who declare their intention of following their profession in the Common Schools.* Of these Normal Schools, Wisconsin alone supplies five, Massachusetts six, New York State nine, and Pennsylvania no fewer than eleven. The demand for professionally trained teachers is still largely in excess of the supply, and the States are every year founding additional Normal Schools. In the Southern States, where the need is most felt and the State resources are subject to most strain, the Peabody Trust has stimulated and assisted local effort (as in Virginia, South Carolina, and Tennessee) with liberal appropriations.

In the Cities which have taken professional training in hand, the machinery for this training assumes various forms, adapted to local circumstances. The High School for Girls at Philadelphia, which has been presided over for the last twenty-five years, by the veteran Principal, George W. Fetter, is the Normal School for that city. Out of a total of nearly 2000 Pupils (Rep. Bureau of Educn., 1887–8), 228 Pupils were enrolled for the Teachers' Training Course, and 575 Students were in the Practising Schools attached, which embrace boys, girls, and Kindergarten departments. This Normal School has a three years' course, commencing at about fourteen years of age, and a fourth year of studentship in the Practising Schools, before teaching certificates are awarded. New York City has a corresponding institution on an equally large scale, and it is estimated that nearly one-half of the students who have graduated at this School (here called a College) are teaching in the Common Schools of the city. In other cities, we find a Training Class formed as an extra year's course in the High School, or a Normal Department attached to the State or local University which may happen to be situated in its vicinity. The State Normal Schools, which are mostly for women only, though some are for both sexes, usually arrange for day or non-boarding students only, each student making private arrangements for residence in the neighbourhood of the School; but some of them receive Boarders, while there are three or four State Schools (in Massachusets and New Jersey), which are restricted to boarding students. Each State makes its terms of admission, which are dependent upon examinations equivalent to the higher Grammar, or middle High School, grades. The usual age of admission is sixteen for women, and seventeen for men. The "graduating" course varies considerably in length, from one

* Report, Bureau of Education, Washington, U. S. A., 1887-8. Ohio is the only one of the older States which has not established a State Normal School, but there is a Normal Department at the State University at Athens, and Normal Schools at Cincinnati, Cleveland, and two other cities.

year in some States, to three or four in others. No religious instruction is given in Normal Schools.*

In treating of the professional training of teachers in America, mention, and very conspicuous mention, is merited by a piece of machinery entirely of American origin, and quite peculiar to that country. This is "The Teachers' Institute." This kind of organization, the first experiment in which was made by the voluntary efforts of Dr. Henry Barnard, at Hartford, Conn., in 1839, has since been universally recognised as a most valuable supplement to, or substitute for, professional training in the Normal School proper, so that all the States with few exceptions, have now incorporated into their School laws regulations for the holding of Teachers' Institutes, and have set apart appropriations for their support, even making attendance compulsory in some cases upon all teachers engaged in public schools.

A Teachers' Institute may be defined concisely as an "itinerant normal school" for the professional education of teachers actually engaged in teaching. The Institute is organised under direction of the State Superintendent, who associates with himself one or two principals of Normal Schools, and some of the ablest City or Town Superintendents in the district in which the Institute is to be held, and thus a Normal School is extemporized at a given centre, which holds a session for some days or weeks there, and then migrates to another centre, passing from place to place during the autumn months. By this means an Institute normal training is brought within easy reach of every teacher in the State once every year. The instruction is generally given gratuitously at the expense of the State, and, wherever the Institute is held, all sections of the residents combine to reduce the cost which would fall upon the teachers for board and lodging by hospitably housing or entertaining them during the session of the Institute. The duration of each session varies inversely with the other provision which the States, Counties and Cities have made for normal training. Where, as in Massachusetts, a large proportion of the teachers actually employed in the schools have already received normal training in a Normal School proper, the Institute session lasts for only one clear day.† But where, as in the more Western and Southern States, the large majority of the teachers are not normally trained, the Institute Session is made to extend to two, or even three weeks. Other supplementary aids to the professional training and general culture of teachers are to be found in Township Institutes, Teachers' Conventions and Associations, which exist in nearly every town having a graded system of public schools; also in Teachers' Reading Circles for the study of works on Pedagogy and Moral Science; and in Holiday or Summer Normal Schools, where recreation, social intercourse, and professional study and discussion combine to pro-

---

* For some insight into the inner working of American Normal Schools, the reader is referred to "Notes on American Schools and Training Colleges," by Dr. Fitch, Her Majesty's Inspector of Training Colleges for Schoolmistresses, Blue Book, 1889.
† Nineteen such one-day Institutes were held in the State of Massachusetts in 1887-8. See Rep. Mass. Board of Education, 1887-8.

mote healthiness, good fellowship, homogeneity and a high standard of educational ideals among American Teachers.*

5. *Conclusion.*

In bringing this survey of the American Common School system to a close, the writer is again impressed with the inefficacy of facts and figures, reports and statistics, however deftly handled, to strike the characteristic note of the American system, so as to convey to an English mind all that it conveys to an American. The system is the creation of the all-pervading democratic idea, which, Minerva-like, leapt into full being in the seventeenth century: in England, the feudalism of the middle ages still survives, and is only slowly being transmuted by the infusion of the democratic idea of the nineteenth. When our English Royal Commission on the Education Acts sent its paper of inquiries the other day to the several American State Boards of Education asking, among others, the question, "From what class of society are the teachers drawn?" that State,† which gave back the laconic reply, "We are democrats," put the fundamental *differentia* between the English and American mind into the clear view which a flash of lightning momentarily produces on a landscape in darkness. "Among the important virtues," says Mr. Secretary Dickenson,‡ "which the public school is adapted to cultivate, is patriotism or love of country. The love of benefactors is a natural affection. It springs up in the mind on the perception of favours received. The public school is the free gift of the State. It is the best gift of a government to its people. As the scholar comes to understand its value to him as an individual and a citizen; as he becomes aware that his intelligence and the free government which protects him are, in an important sense, the results of its developing influences, his love of country grows stronger, and his desire to promote its welfare increases. In the same way it may be shown that the public school, by its organization and exercises, is adapted to cultivate all the social virtues, and at the same time to train the children to that self-control and independence in thinking which are the necessary characteristics of the people of a self-governed State."

No doubt there is much to be avoided by England in the methods and working of the American Common Schools. But is there not also much that may be prudently imitated? After all, we English

---

* The idea of Reading Circles and Summer Schools has recently been presented to the English Public through the attention which has been drawn to them by Dr. Paton of Nottingham, Dr. Percival of Rugby, Professor Stuart and others (see Dr. Fitch's description of the annual summer assembly by Chautauqua Lake in the *Nineteenth Century* for October, 1888). In connection with the University Extension Movement, a somewhat similar "Summer School" meets at Oxford for its third session in August next.

† The State of Mississippi, see Blue Book, Royal Commission on Education Acts, Foreign Returns, 1888, p. 273.

‡ Report of Secretary of the Massachusetts State Board of Education, 1888, p. 77.

may well take a lesson from the American people of enthusiasm for, and a genuine belief in, education *as a civilizing and ennobling force.* No one in America *fears* (secular) education, or looks with dread upon any of its possible consequences to society. There it is reverenced, deeply reverenced, as *a saviour* of society. And the teachers, as Education's priesthood, share in that reverence, and receive accordingly that respect and deference which goes so far to compensate priesthoods all the world over for meagre material prospects and emoluments. We cannot be said to have yet learnt that lesson in England.

E. F. M. MacCarthy.

PART VII.
NOTES ON EDUCATION IN CANADA AND AUSTRALIA.

I. CANADA.

IN his "Problems of Greater Britain," Sir Charles Dilke draws attention to the fact—"a phenomenon," he calls it, "never seen before in the World's history, and never likely to be seen again"—that "two countries (the United States and the Dominion of Canada) with a common frontier 4,000 miles in length, three-fourths of which is an artificial frontier, two countries under different flags, inhabited by people to a great extent of identical race, speaking the same tongue, and each governed by free Federal institutions, are each now provided with independent parallel railway lines of communication" from ocean to ocean. An equally remarkable phenomenon is exhibited in the fact that each of these countries is provided with independent systems of public education, which have travelled, along with these peoples, on parallel lines, ever farther and farther westward, placing Vancouver educationally in touch with Quebec, and San Francisco with Boston. And another striking fact—these systems are not only independent, but characteristically different. All along the route of westward movement of the population in the United States one traces the pervading spirit of that educational system, so largely (as we have shown in the preceding Article) political in its motive, which was set up by the Presbyterian settlers in Massachusetts in the seventeenth century; while along the parallel route in the Dominion, one is constantly reminded, in spite of distance and difference of development, of the methods of England of the nineteenth century, which, when the century was still quite young, grew out of the educational impulse identified with the names of Lancaster and Bell, and finding its most prominent exponent in the "National Society," whose headquarters are under the shadow of Westminster Abbey.* At one point, curiously enough, these systems almost touch. On the Michigan (U.S.A.) side of the Narrows, through

---

* The first impulse on behalf of public education in Lower Canada (Quebec) was made in 1787 ; but, owing to sectarian differences, no general plan of education was set on foot until 1841. In Upper Canada (Ontario) the first legislative enactment in favour of general education was passed in 1807. (See Rev. J. Fraser's Report, Blue Book, Schools Inquiry Commission, 1867.)

which the waters of Lake St. Clair travel on their way to Lake Erie, stands Detroit, while on the opposite shore, barely one mile across, stands Windsor (Upper Canada), and steam-ferries ply hourly between the two towns; and yet, in educational as in other characteristics, Windsor smacks of Old England, but Detroit of New England. The resemblances to England are sometimes slight, and not visible to the superficial observer, for Upper Canada and New Brunswick, being more closely in geographical contact with the United States, have developed and perfected their systems (in the last 30 years) on New England rather than English models. But still they are there—sometimes it is the architecture of a school building, sometimes the methods of a Training College; here it is the "standards" of the curriculum, there the text-books; but even as regards Ontario itself, the most educationally Americanized (next perhaps to New Brunswick) of the Provinces of the Dominion, the writer of this Article was told at Toronto, its capital, that Canadian Schools were not visited by Englishmen "because the amount of *differentia* was not sufficient to justify a journey all that way."

Each Province of the Dominion enjoys local self-government, having a provincial legislature and a Lieutenant-Governor appointed by the Federal (Dominion) Government. Counties, townships and municipalities have likewise the management of their own affairs, subject, of course, to the supreme control of the Provincial and Dominion legislatures. Education is almost entirely a matter under provincial and local control. The Federal Government has very little power in its hands, except to keep the peace in the presence of religious differences by securing the observance of the *concordat* between the Protestants and Roman Catholics, in the Provinces (chiefly Lower Canada, Upper Canada and Manitoba) where the community is thus divided in opinion. In Lower Canada (Quebec and Montreal), and in Manitoba (Winnipeg), the law runs that "whenever in any municipality the regulations and arrangements of any school are not agreeable to any number whatever of the inhabitants professing a religious faith different from that of the majority of the inhabitants," the inhabitants so dissentient may appoint their own trustees who shall have power to establish and manage "dissentient" schools. They form a corporation, constitute their own school districts, fix and collect the assessments to be levied on the dissentient inhabitants; and are "entitled to receive, out of the general school fund appropriated to the municipality, a share bearing the same proportion to the whole sum allotted as the number of children attending these schools bears to the whole school population in the municipality: and a similar share in the building grant." *

Practically, though this *concordat* makes for peace, it does not always secure it. The reason will appear from consideration of the circumstances of the city of Montreal. There the School population is divided between Protestants and Roman Catholics in about

---

* See Rev. J. Fraser's Report (Blue Book), pp. 308, 309.

the ratio of 28 to 72; but the wealth (to which the taxation bears a direct proportion) of the two communions is about in the ratio of 50 to 50. Consequently, while the Protestants would contribute one half of the municipal school fund, they would only get the benefit of a little more than one quarter.* They further complain that, while they thus largely contribute to Roman Catholic schools, these schools give the children only a bare minimum of secular instruction, while the Protestant schools are pinched for want of the funds which are required for the wider and more intellectual curriculum at which they aim. In Upper Canada (Ontario) the liberty to dissentients of establishing separate schools is more circumscribed. There "Protestants can only establish a separate school when the *teacher* of the common school is a Roman Catholic," and *vice versa*.

New Brunswick—here, as elsewhere, showing distinct signs of American influence—has no separate schools for religious denominations, and its schools are by law required to be unsectarian. The Ontario public (protestant) schools are also largely unsectarian; but the clergy of any denomination, or their authorised representatives, have the right to give religious instruction to the pupils of their own church in each schoolhouse at least once a week, after afternoon school.

Each *Provincial* Government determines the main outlines of the School system for its Province. Acting through a Department of Education, it settles what Schools or Institutions shall be maintained, what shall be the duties of School Boards or Trustees of municipalities, appoints Public School Inspectors, and determines the qualifications of the Teachers to be employed, and awards Teachers' Certificates by examination. The grant at its disposal for distribution among the School Boards is called the Legislative Grant.

The *local* control over Education on the lines thus laid down is administered by School Boards or Corporations or Trustees (as in the United States) elected by the ratepayers of the city, town, village or rural school "section," as the case may be. The money locally raised for educational purposes is called the Municipal Grant.

All through the Dominion, then, the public schools are supported (as in the United States) by a Legislative and a Municipal grant (State School Fund and local rate), but, unlike the United States, the scholars are not free in every Province. In Ontario, all children between the ages of five and twenty-one can attend school free, and therefore the High Schools as well as the Elementary Schools are free. The Model Schools and Training Colleges are also open free to *bonâ fide* teachers in the Province.

* This inequality in the distribution of the "city school tax" has been partially remedied at Montreal by the formation of separate rating-lists or panels; setting out the value of all real estate belonging to (1) Catholics, (2) Protestants, (3) Public Bodies or Neutrals. The rates collected on the Catholic panel are handed to the Catholic School Board (School Commissioners), and similarly to the Protestant School Board, but the amount collected from property entered on the third panel, which is considerable, is still divided between the Catholic and Protestant Boards in proportion to *population*.

The University and University College of Toronto, by means of Endowments, "Scholarship Gifts," are enabled to give an almost gratuitous education to students. In the Provinces of smaller population, education in the primary schools, and also in the superior and grammar schools (where they exist) is *free* to all scholars residing in the school area. But education is not free in Lower Canada (Quebec and Montreal),* although remission of the fee is readily granted on the plea of poverty, so that, in Montreal, for instance, about one-sixth of the scholars in attendance in the public schools pay no fee. It is also provided with regard to the fees charged in high schools in that city, that, if fees are demanded at all, they shall be so moderate in amount that no one shall be excluded by poverty. Taking population into account, it appears that school fees are payable on behalf of every two out of seven of the school children in the Dominion.

Coming next to compulsion, the law itself affecting school attendance is widely different in the several Provinces, and the actual practice still more divergent. In Ontario and the four smaller Provinces, British Columbia, Manitoba, Nova Scotia, and Prince Edward Island, where education (as has been stated) is free, it is also compulsory; but in New Brunswick (which is most under United States influence), where education is free, it is not compulsory; and in Quebec, where it is not free, neither is it compulsory. But even in the Provinces which have compulsory clauses in their Education Laws, it is extremely doubtful whether the law in this respect is ever put into force, even to the extent of a fine, and certainly not, in any case, to the extent of imprisonment. In Ontario, however, the authorities may possibly show a degree of firmness not prevalent elsewhere. The compulsory law in that Province provides that the school trustees *shall* impose upon neglectful parents a rate-bill not exceeding a dollar per month for each of their children not attending school; and the school trustees *may* appoint an officer to ascertain the names of persons violating the Act in this matter. The highest penalty is a fine by the magistrate not exceeding five dollars for the first offence, and double that penalty for every succeeding offence. In Prince Edward Island, the method exhibits an interesting divergence from the ordinary forms of compulsory attendance law :—the Government grant being paid on average attendance, the amount of this grant which the school board loses through the non-attendance of children is levied upon the parents of those children.

Throughout the Dominion all teachers are adults, and the pupil-teacher system is unknown. Teachers enter the profession, males at 18 years of age (usually), and females at 16; and are trained in the Normal Schools, which are supported by the Provincial Governments; or at County Model Schools, which are supported at the

---

* There is a monthly fee, payable compulsorily by the parent, for every child from 7 to 14 years of age residing in the municipality and capable of attending school. This fee is payable for eight months of the year, and is levied with the other Assessments directly upon the parents. See Foreign Returns (Blue Book), 1888.

joint cost of the Municipality and the Province. They receive their professional education almost entirely free of cost to themselves.

Very little has as yet been done in Technical Education in the Dominion; but mention should be made of the excellent work in this direction done at the School of Practical Science, the Schools of Art, and the Agricultural College in Ontario, and at the Polytechnic School, Montreal.

II. AUSTRALIA.

The transition from the British Colonies in North America to the British Colonies in the Southern Hemisphere is, educationally, a passage from State systems of public education largely tinged with Denominationalism, to State systems which are, now, universally undenominational or secular. The Australian Colonies are essentially democratic, and so, like the United States, they all base their common school systems on the principles of religious freedom, and the non-establishment of any particular form of religious belief.* But the Governments in Australia are more distinctly bureaucratic, and less decentralized, than those in the Dominion; and the administration of Education Law, especially, has been retained in the hands of a central Government Department. Consequently, we find that those local influences which make against the local initiation of penal enforcements of neglected parental duties have far less power, and school attendance, which is universally compulsory, is far more rigidly enforced than in the Dominion or in the United States, even to the extent—unknown in English-speaking countries except England itself—of a summons before a police magistrate, and possible imprisonment. On the other hand, the Colonies of Australia share with the Provinces of the Dominion in the presence of a difference of opinion on the subject of non-payment of school fees. Public education is free only in Victoria and Queensland (and New Zealand), but fees are charged in New South Wales, South Australia, Tasmania, and Western Australia.†

The Central Department (called the Council of Education, or Education Department), to which reference has been made, is in each Colony or Province presided over by a Minister of Education, and has had assigned to it by an Act of the Provincial Legislature

---

* Religious instruction may, under certain conditions, be given out of the ordinary school hours by ministers of religion, and others, to children whose parents are willing that they should receive it. In South Australia, teachers may *read* portions of Scripture in the authorized, or Douay version, to such scholars as may be sent by their parents before 9:30 A.M., but they must strictly confine themselves to Bible reading.

† Dr. R. W. Dale, in his "Impressions of Australia" (see *Contemporary Review* Feb., 1889), makes the following pertinent comment on this divergence in practice between the several colonial systems:—" Where the schools are free, the people whom I met seemed satisfied that they should remain free; where fees are charged, I could not hear of any serious agitation for their abolition. In the absence of large masses of extremely poor parents, the question is not a 'burning' one. There are no such serious administrative difficulties as those with which we at home have to deal in collecting the fees and in discriminating between parents who are able to pay and parents who are unable."

the determination of the number of schools required, the purchasing of the sites, the building of school premises, the number of school hours per day and school days per year, the amount of the fee (where charged), the course of instruction, the nature of the school-staff, the appointment, remuneration, promotion, and dismissal of teachers. It appoints an Inspector-General and Inspector of Schools, whose functions correspond in the main to those of Her Majesty's Inspectors under the Education Department in England, but who have greater power, as the future prospects of the teachers depend more intimately on their reports. It also establishes, maintains and manages Training Colleges, and awards the several grades of Teachers' Certificates, on the results of general and special examinations which it holds for that purpose, and on proved skill in actual teaching. The powers exercised by the Education Department of an Australian Province (or Colony) will thus be seen to be much more extensive in scope and jurisdiction than those of the English Education Department, or of the Government Department of a Province of the Dominion. The functions, therefore, of the *local* educational authorities will be proportionately smaller. And this is plainly indicated by their title: they are simply "Boards of Advice." These are elected by the local ratepayers in Victoria alone; in all the other Provinces they are appointed by the Governor. Their constitution and general duties are, (1), to exercise general supervision over educational matters in their school district, and report to the Minister of Education on any matters affecting the general welfare of the schools; (2), to maintain the school buildings in repair out of funds placed to their credit by the Minister; (3), to put themselves into close communication with the teachers, and to intervene in any cases of friction between them and parents; (4), to determine the uses which may be made of school buildings out of school hours; (5), (in the Provinces where fees are charged), to consider and adjudicate upon all applications for free education and for reduction of fees, subject to the general regulations of the Education Acts; and (6), to see to the effective carrying out of the compulsory clauses of the Acts, by summoning parents before the Board, and ordering such legal proceedings as may be necessary; but all legal proceedings are conducted by officers specially authorised by the Minister, after receiving the recommendation of the Board of Advice.*

The prescribed school age varies in the different Provinces. In South Australia it is from 7 to 13, in Victoria from 6 to 15, in Tasmania from 7 to 14, in New South Wales from 6 to 14, in Queensland from 6 to 12. In South Australia, and perhaps elsewhere, the children may attend at five years of age, and Infant Schools may be established as departments of public schools for children between five and seven. The public schools are everywhere in Australia strictly elementary schools, but South Australia

---

* See Acts and Regulations of the Education Department for South Australia. The duties of the Boards of Advice (or Public School Boards) in the other Provinces are defined in almost identical terms.

supports an Advanced School for girls to meet the deficiency in the supply of high school education, which is met in the case of boys by the three high schools at Adelaide; and the New South Wales regulations provide that if in any public school a class can be formed of not less than twenty pupils who have reached a certain standard of attainment, the school may be declared a "superior public school," and in addition to more advanced work in the ordinary subjects, boys are to be taught mathematics, Latin, science, and drawing, and the girls, French, drawing, and sanitary science.* Even German and Greek may be taught in these superior schools at the discretion of the Minister of Education. In addition to the superior public schools, New South Wales supports three or four regularly organized State High Schools. Liberal provision is, however, made in the other Colonies for the passage of deserving scholars from the public schools to the high schools which have been founded by denominational bodies or by private persons, and even to the Universities, by means of Exhibitions, Bursaries, and Scholarships.

There is one leading feature of the Australian public school systems which differentiates them from either the United States or the Canadian systems, and which at once reflects the influence of the home Country upon its Colonies in the Southern seas, and that is, the presence of the pupil-teacher. In South Australia, candidates for pupil-teachership may be admitted at $13\frac{1}{2}$ years of age, and after a period of probation go through a further term of service of four years, unless they have matriculated at Adelaide University and are not less than fifteen years, when their period of service may be reduced to three years. As in England, they are eligible for admission to a Training College on having satisfactorily completed their term of apprenticeship. Similar regulations are in force in Victoria, Queensland, and New South Wales.

E. F. M. MACCARTHY.

* These have been established in most of the large towns of New South Wales. Formerly a special fee was charged for these subjects, but, as it was found that the imposition of the fee acted injuriously upon the teachers, and prevented many children from receiving the full benefits of this provision, the fee was abolished. See the "Schools of Greater Britain," by John Russell.

PART VIII.

NOTE ON COMMERCIAL EDUCATION.

GREAT BRITAIN is the chief trading country in the world. Her merchants and shipowners are amongst the most enterprising and honourable representatives of commerce; her mercantile houses are to be found wherever barter exists; and yet there is hardly a country in Europe where so little attention is paid to Commercial Education. There has been undoubtedly considerable improvement of late in the preparation of our youth for the mercantile career, but until recently every school of any pretensions was a "Classical, Commercial, and Mathematical Academy," where the Classics, to the exclusion of those modern languages which are so useful in everyday life, consisted of reading and learning off by heart a little of Virgil or Tacitus. What part of the course of instruction could be called " Commercial " it is difficult to say, unless it was writing and arithmetic up to vulgar fractions, decimals being a novel innovation of "foreigners"; and as for "Mathematics" they usually enabled the student to cross the bridge upon which the " Claimant " came to grief and nothing more. Even now a lad who receives what is called a liberal education, and who is supposed to be training for commerce, generally leaves school without any knowledge of book-keeping; in modern languages, he has probably acquired a smattering of French and German, which will not be of the least value to him in practical intercourse with foreigners or in correspondence; and in consequence of the useless information which he has laboured to acquire, he begins his commercial career under less favourable conditions than the son of an artizan who has received an elementary education at a Board School. That parents of the trading classes are beginning to appreciate these facts any reader may convince himself by inquiring as to the changes in relative attendances at Board and at Proprietary Schools, for he will find that the attendances at the latter have fallen off in many of our large towns, notwithstanding the increase of population, whilst the children of the lower middle classes are crowding into our Board Schools, not only because the school fees are lower, but because the *practical* instruction which is given there is of greater value as a commercial training. Let us inquire for a moment how these inconsistencies are to be explained, and why the commercial education of our youth is so greatly neglected. Does it not arise chiefly from the very predominance which we enjoyed amongst the trading nations of the world? A preponderance which was until lately so unquestioned that our countrymen abroad hardly took the trouble to learn the languages of those with whom they traded. It was *their* business to learn *our* language, and in our insular hauteur we compelled them to do so if they wished to enjoy the privilege of dealing with us. We are almost the only trading nation that adheres to its old-fashioned system of weights, measures, and coinage, and for no other reason than the repugnance to change and novelty. In one or two extensive branches of trade, as the corn trade for example, centals are taking the place of the " hundred weights " of 112 lbs., and florins *were* superseding half-crowns. Now and then you meet in one of our offices a young gentleman who has spent a year or two abroad, and who would not exchange his knowledge of French or German for all the dead languages, but as a rule we still expect foreigners to adapt themselves to our customs, to our metrical system, and to our language.

And if he is insular in his commercial methods John Bull is equally eccentric in his commercial literature and phraseology, and it will soon be as difficult to teach a lad the jargon of the markets as the language of neighbouring nations. It is a kind of *volapuk* which is understood alike in London and in Liverpool, in Glasgow, Cork and Belfast. Oats are " firm " and sugar is " steady " ; oils are " quiet " and lard is " stiff " ; in iron, pigs are " nominal " ; in dyes, logwood is " strong," and so forth, until nearly every adjective, appropriate or otherwise, is imported into the category. But when the trader gives free play to his imagination, or soars into the higher regions of rhetoric, then he excels himself! " A waiting policy is being pursued " by the holders of lambswool, a " profound secrecy characterises the operations in the cheese market " ; whilst " the illusion is dispelled " in the tobacco trade, and " operators are rising to the occasion " !

Changes are, however, taking place in the relations between the trading nations of the world and between the classes of producers and consumers which will necessitate corresponding changes in all our commercial methods. The old-fashioned ways are no longer suited to telegraph and telephone; middle-men are being gradually displaced, and the producer abroad is entering into direct relations with the consumer at home, or *vice versâ;* the travellers of one nationality are invading the trading ground and securing the connection of neighbouring peoples; and the German who knows English enjoys a great advantage over the Englishman who does not know German. Only recently the Consuls in one of the newly enfranchised States of South-Eastern Europe sent home reports that English manufactures are being supplanted by those of Austria, although the latter are of inferior quality, through the pursuasiveness of " polyglot " Austrian commercial travellers. In this country the demand for French, German, Spanish, and Italian correspondents is increasing rapidly, and, owing to the ignorance of our own youth, it is found necessary to engage young clerks from abroad who are prepared to serve for low salaries, or even in many cases gratuitously, as " volunteers," in order that they may make themselves acquainted with our systems of trade, and may thus gain access to our markets.

STATE EDUCATION.

Here and there an enterpising English firm may be found carrying the war into the enemy's country and sending some accomplished member of the house abroad to deal direct with continental consumers, and no one who is paying the least attention to the subject can fail to see that if we are to maintain our prestige as a trading nation, the youth of this country must receive a *practical* commercial education, and Latin and Greek must give place in our ordinary schools to French, German, and other modern languages. As the Lord Mayor recently remarked at a meeting which was held in the Mansion House to promote Commercial Education, the question has become one of "bread and butter," and it is well that the leading citizens of the metropolis are alive to its importance. The London Chamber of Commerce has made a commencement in the right direction, the great collegiate schools of the Metropolis have been enlisted in the cause, a couple of hundred leading firms have agreed, in the engagement of clerks, to give a preference to youths who possess certificates of competency in commercial knowledge, and there is little doubt that if the movement spreads, if the course of instruction is sound, and if the young gentlemen who succeed in obtaining certificates, don't give themselves airs of superiority when they enter into practical life, they will not only secure more lucrative employment at home, but will be found occupying situations of trust in foreign countries.

It is not sufficient to teach young people to read and write French and German, but they should be taught to speak them fluently; they should be made thoroughly acquainted with the weights, measures, and coinages of the most important trading countries, with exchanges and bookkeeping; they should learn shorthand, and be able to make rapid calculations by the decimal system. In driving a bargain a smart German or Frenchman will often make a calculation of profit or loss before a slow Englishman fully comprehends what is proposed. As for geography and a knowledge of the products of various countries, those are now better taught in many of our Board Schools than in Colleges and High Schools for the upper classes.

Where a youth is preparing to enter any particular branch of commerce or industry he cannot be too early familiarised with such details as are likely to be of use to him in after life. It is not at all unusual to meet with clever French or German traders who possess a good technical knowledge of the nature and manufacturing uses of the substances in which they deal, and even a fair general acquaintance with the manufacturing processes of their customers; such men are not likely to throw away new products in ignorance of their value to the manufacturer. Economic botany (which is already taught in some of our best Board Schools), zoology, chemistry, &c., will ere long form a necessary part of a purely commercial education.

And there are one or two other aspects of this question which are entitled to a passing notice. We hear a good deal about the danger of divorcing religion from education, and great pains are taken, especially in our denominational schools, to impart accurate knowledge in the three C's, creeds, catechisms, and ceremonial. No doubt the moral virtues are also inculcated, but does it ever occur to the teacher to impress upon the young that a lie is a lie under whatever circumstances it may be uttered; that is it no less culpable, however common it may be, to misrepresent the value or quality of an article of produce offered for sale, or to mis-state any fact or circumstance relating to a bargain for the purpose of securing some advantage in trade, than it is to mislead a teacher or parent by a falsehood uttered to screen a fault or to escape punishment? There never was a more abominable maxim in trade than "Caveat emptor," and it will be far better to teach a child in its earliest years that the motto of a true merchant should be honesty, truthfulness and plain dealing with one's neighbour. A great advantage, too, to the cause of education generally, will be the partial if the not complete substitution of the living for the dead languages, the application of arithmetic to the transactions of actual trade, and the study of the productions of different climes in their natural as well as in their manufactured state, inasmuch as they will lend an attractiveness to school hours which they do not at present possess. Indeed, every consideration and all the circumstances and changes in modern civilised life call for an improved course of instruction as a preparation for a mercantile career, and none will be rendering a greater service to their country than those merchants and others connected with our trade and manufacturing industries who employ their means and influence to secure so desirable an object.

PART IX.
THE EDUCATION AND STATUS OF WOMEN.

The task has been deputed to me to treat of the status of women in civilised countries, as illustrated by their condition in France, England, and America, and to show in what degree the material improvement thereof is related to the progress of education. If by education High Schooling is meant, there would not be much to say in regard to France, the Camille Sée law for girls' secondary instruction only dating from 1880. This law will doubtless, when looked back to by future generations, mark a new, and there is room for hoping, glorious epoch in French national life. But up to its date French women owed little to school tuition, and a good deal to their personal ambition, mothers' wit, sprightliness, grace, persevering courage, and practical good sense. It is a mistake to suppose the French woman frivolous. She is practical in taking the world as she finds it. When a small class of idle men held the all-power, they did not want helpmates, but amusing mistresses. The demand was supplied, and with so much talent that fashionable idlers all the world over looked to Paris for hints and ideas when they wanted to give zest and elegance to frivolity. Women kept at the head and front of French civilisation, and, indeed, of European, until a system sprung up of higher education for boys, in which girls had no part.

But before going further into the subject of education in its bearings on the status of women in France, it may be well to glance at the place women have held in that country from the earliest historical times.

We find that among the Gallic Celts women were high-hearted, intrepid, and the inspirers and helpmates of the men. They helped, not because they were forced like Indian squaws in the wigwam, but because such was their good pleasure. Having, as Joan of Arc said of their high standing, at the coronation of King Charles, helped to bear the brunt, it was only right that they should share the reward. When the chiefs went to battle, their ladies and hand-maidens followed them to, in miry ground, push forward the chariot wheels. Savagery had no part in this helpful courage. Gallic female slaves in Rome were most sought after by patrician dames to serve as tire-maidens, they being deft, tasteful, and inventive. As religious martyrs when Christianity dawned, they led the way. Long before Saint Blandine's martyrdom, druidesses were venerated as sacred beings. Imperial Rome did not counteract in Gaul the race tendency of the Celt to place women on the highest social plane, or rather to let them rise to their own level. The Roman patrician lady filled a great place in the general Roman life, was mistress of her own fortune (save the dotal part), and enjoyed liberty pushed to the degree of licence. We may suppose that either the Franks were the German tribes which Tacitus best knew, or that the Roman historian knew little of the domestic usages of the Germans. That Salic law, which the Franks hastened to declare as soon as they overran the Gallo-Roman country, does not bear out the character which Tacitus gave their forefathers. It was, on the other hand, very Gallic of Clotilde at once to turn it.

Gaul and Rome thus worked to give French women power outside laws and constitutions. This power has been used in general to embellish national life, and to toughen the moral fibre of the people. It went into every national movement, bloomed out in the Mariolatry of the middle ages, which bore the fruit of chivalry, and it was the cause of the first crusade. All historians, so far as I know, overlook this cause. It lay in a Russian princess, the daughter of a Byzantine Emperor, being called to wear the crown matrimonial of France. Her mother took to Moscow her sacred images and relics, and had, we may assume, that yearning for the Holy places which became a neurosis of the women of the Lower Empire. Long before Joan of Arc, maids, supposed to be inspired, were employed to serve as standard-bearers of French armies, and to advise and admonish kings and great nobles. Their intuition was believed in. They were called *voyantes*, or seeresses, were deemed heaven-sent, and sacred as long as they remained pure. Impure, they were limbs of Satan. There was no prejudice in ancient France against the foreign woman. Blanche of Castille was submitted to, and waged successfully a seven years' war against the vassals of the crown. She was the first female Regent, and had common traits with Isabella of Castille, who is to be the tutelary divinity of the next Universal Exhibition in the United States, because the American ladies so desire.

Three women, Yolande, Queen of Sicily, Duchess of Anjou, and Countess of Provence (*née* Princess of Lorraine), Agnes Sorel, and Joan of Arc, fill the reign of Charles VII. Yolande had the strongest political head of her time, and despised no means, however humble, to compass her ends, one of which was to make her son-in-law Charles the overlord of the King of England. Anne of Beaujon, her great granddaughter, inherited her brains, and ruled with a gentle temper and a firm hand through the minority of Charles VIII. Feminine influence was not brilliantly asserted in the reign of Louis XII., but Anne of Brittany, an obstinate little woman, took her head nevertheless. Francis I. was a ladies' man, all deference for his mother, whose vices he overlooked, fixing his eyes only on her statesman-like capacities, and loved with tender and admiring, though a selfish and exacting affection, that Pearl of Pearls, his sister Margaret. A maxim of Francis's was that a court without ladies was like a spring without flowers. Clouet's portraits show how the riches of the east, of Genoa, Venice, and the Low Countries were lavished on the dress of those who held a high social status in the reign of Francis. Their head-light was great for the time. There was a Ladies' Peace, which delivered Christendom from the evils of war, and the king from captivity. The Higher Learning was first brought into fashion by the fair negotiators of this peace—a fashion which spread to England, and directed the early growth of Queen Elizabeth's mind, and indirectly her reign. Grand ladies were as proud of their manuscript editions of Greek and Latin authors as of their jewels. Even those who devoted themselves to the king's pleasure had choice libraries. The wreckage of Diane de Poitiers, which has come down the stream of time to our day, is keenly hunted after by bibliophiles. Diane's mental culture explains why she was first in the exercise of power through two reigns. A woman of beauty and of mind is not to be toyed with like a doll and then cast aside.

Catherine de Medici, the Lady Macbeth of French history, was not worse than her age, and had a theory of government which she steadily kept in view, and which in after ages enabled France to withstand the German Empire. National unity, as opposed to the feudalism of the Guises and Montmorencies, and the federalism of the South and of the Protestant nobles, was her objective. This foreign woman was uppermost in two reigns and in the part of a third. Her only serious rival in her long widowhood was another foreign Princess, Mary Stuart. They were both women of great mental parts. Mary had brilliancy, beauty, and superior birth, the Medici in the recollection of old people in Catherine's time having been dealers in quack medicines, and having made most money, like all the druggists of the Middle Ages, as dealers in *la poudre de succession*.

Gambetta was fond of following the bright trace women left in all ages in French history. He maintained that they in all cases owed their power to their personal efforts. The great merit of Frenchmen was in Gambetta's estimation having recognised these efforts. Madame de Sevigné was the letter-writer, we know her because her girlhood was serious, and she faced trouble in a brave spirit, burying herself for years at a time in the wilds of Brittany to be the steward of her youthful son's estate. Her pastimes were country work, reading, meditation, and correspondence. Madame de Maintenon was raised to wifehood with the King, for being of a cultivated mind, sagacious, and mistress of herself under all circumstances.

The first attempt to give regular school instruction to girls of high family was made by Saint Marie de Chantal, grandmother of Madame de Sevigné, in the foundation of the Visitandines Convents. But there being no body of trained teachers, not much was to be learned in the schoolrooms of these houses. Catechism, reading, writing, enough of mythology to understand the great painters, dancing, curtseying, and fancy needlework, were thought enough for the culture of young minds which, however, might have run to weed, but were not warped. Madame de Maintenon and her friend Archbishop Fenelon· deplored the uneducated state of women of quality in their time. The former (as Gambetta liked to remind his friends when he made up his mind to help forward a scheme for higher education for girls) made educational experiments at temporary schools which she set up and directed herself in those hours which she was able to steal from the King. These trials encouraged her to found St. Cyr for 250 daughters of poor and noble families. Her plan of education was solid, and did not exclude brilliant accomplishments. What should we now think were Lord Tennyson to write a religious drama meant to elevate taste and feeling, strengthen faith and refine diction, and cultivate the sweet voices of the young, for Girton, and Her Majesty and the Royal Family to go and see the students play it. This is what Racine did for St. Cyr, where the King and Court witnessed the first representations of "Esther," with its lovely canticles, and of "Athalie." Limits of age were from ten to seventeen, and the outgoing pupil received a slender dowry, which her education helped her to turn to account. Reading, writing, arithmetic, mythology, history, geography, dancing, music, singing, and drawing, were taught. Senior pupils were expected to wash and dress the little ones, and mend and make for them, the mistresses and servants to keep house accounts, and take turns in the kitchen, laundry, and in floor-scrubbing. Lafayette's mother graduated at St. Cyr. Eliza, the only sister of Bonaparte whose head was not turned by rising to a throne, was brought up there also. Napoleon found at St. Cyr his model for daughters of Knights of the Legion of Honour.

Under the Ancient Monarchy ladies of illustrious birth only were on view as governing influences. Rousseau seems, towards the Revolution, to have quickened the middle-class womanhood of the country and raised them to a higher state of feeling, and to nobler ambition. We find proof of this in Madame Roland's life, and the diary kept by Lucille Desmoulins before her marriage. Later, under the spur of misery, the labouring-class women burst out and precipitated the Revolution. Moved by pity, vanity, and a longing for quiet after the storm, the women of Thermidor hastened reaction. Both classes were ignorant. But absolute ignorance was less unfavourable to the feminine status than the semi-instruction given since 1815 in the high-class convents. The former did not twist the female mind and place it out of touch with those of the other sex.

On the morrow of the Reign of Terror Bonaparte wrote to his brother: "Women alone deserve to govern here. The men have no will of their own, and do nothing but what the women tell them. They see through the women's eyes, follow their advice, and live to please them." Bonaparte followed the crowd for a while in seeing through Josephine's eyes. He then made war on all women who ventured to have strong opinions. Maternal love was sure to rise in rebellion against his hecatombs, and so it rose. He said, after Waterloo, "I fell because all the women were against me."

The Constituant, Convention and Legislative, decreed equal civil and educational rights to men and women, boys and girls. Two churchmen, Talleyrand and the Abbé Desrandes, who were used to the corrupt and uneducated women of rank of the fallen Monarchy, thought them delightful. But they also thought it better that they should not have the power that education secures. Charged by the Constituant to draw up a scheme for public instruction, they reported that in theory men and women had equal rights, but that in practice women served their interests in waiving them. The home was the best school for girls, and the mother the best teacher. This doctrine was not accepted, and it was proposed to teach girls and boys alike, and the former handicrafts suitable to their sex. A decree embodied this proposal. The Legislative ordered another report on public schools; Condorcet was the reporter. He recommended for both boys and girls secondary State schools. Lakanel and Carnot studied a scheme of national education which should be a preparation for the workshop, the farm, the dairy, &c. Wherever there was a schoolmaster there should be a schoolmistress. Each school was to have a boys' and a girls' division. The technical instruction was to be different. War absorbing all available funds, this scheme fell through. On founding the Empire, Bonaparte decreed primary schools for boys, set apart no money for them, and did not deign to notice working-class girls.

It has been constantly brought against French women of our day that they love despotism and darkness. This charge is unfair. For more than two hundred years there has been a great and continuous organised movement, showing itself under different forms, to give head-light to boys. The religious orders began it, and kept it up until the Revolution. Ecclesiastics imparted most of the higher instruction, and in no narrow or warping spirit. This we may deduce from what Voltaire and d'Argenson thought of their preceptors. Girls were neglected. Sometimes, if they married men of education who treated them well, they picked up more than a gloss of scholarship. Madame de Boufflies was an instance. Occasionally paternal affection, as in the case of Madame Campan, led fathers to be their daughters' tutors. Sometimes girls longed to rise to high intellectual consciousness, and educated themselves, as in the case of Madame Roland. Madame de Stael's mental training in girlhood was unique, and she was detested by the ladies of the Court for the brilliancy of her mind. But there was a general forward movement for many generations of boyhood towards the light, while, on the whole, girlhood was kept stationary. The mental state of the fair sex explains why it was that for every step which French men advanced, after the Revolution, the upper class and bourgeois women dragged them back another. Napoleon gave France a national system of higher instruction for boys. He did nothing beyond the creation of three Legion of Honour schools for girls.

Napoleon fell. A Court, soured by the hardships of a long exile, and hating every work of the Revolution, and of its 18th century precursors, took his place. All lay teachers were obliged by a law passed under Louis XVIII. to undergo test examinations of capacity, and to obtain at them diplomas. The examination standards were high. At the first blush this would seem a public benefit. But it was merely intended to throw education into the hands of the religious orders, who at once began to spring up. Members of sisterhoods had only to show certificates of obedience to a Superior in setting up to teach, to be dispensed from showing diplomas. They soon swarmed. Laics were kept out of the field by the close combinations into which the convents entered with each other. Few, also, were the rewards offered to the lay schoolmistress, and the cost of preparing a girl for a teacher's diploma fell heavy on her family. Conventual schools under the old monarchy did not give feminine education a polemical bias. Submission to the Catholic Church and monarchy were taken for granted, and young minds were not influenced for or against political institutions. It was far otherwise after 1815. In the reign of Louis Philippe there was no primary State instruction for girls. M. Guizot, who venerated his mother, and had a blue-stocking wife, attempted, in bringing in his bill for primary instruction, to endow every commune with a boys' and girls' school. But he was only able to legislate for the boys. The Queen, a Neapolitan Princess, was devout according to the manner of her country. She was secretly brought round to oppose the bill, which was greatly docked in the clauses that dealt with boys' schools, whilst those dealing with girls were suppressed altogether. The King, in his Cabinet Council, said to his ministers, " Gentlemen, whatever you do, don't make me quarrel with my wife." The device hit upon to cover the retreat of M. Guizot was want of money. Just the same amount was voted for boys' schools that had been granted as an appanage to the Duke of Orleans. All such schools in 1833 were dens, and nests of contagious diseases. As to High Schools for girls nobody dreamt of them at that date. Protestant families sent their daughters to Lausanne, which became a sort of collegiate town for women. Catholics relegated theirs to convents, of which, touching some points, much good should be said, and will be said further on.

On a highly educated German Princess, Helena of Mecklenburg-Schwerin, being placed by her marriage with the Duke of Orleans on the highest step of the French throne, women of means began to feel ashamed of their ignorance. Her mind was steeped in what was best in the literatures of Germany, France, and England. She was pensive, and sought to rise above the flatness of Court life through intercourse with Victor Hugo, Guizot, Michelet, Cousin, and would, if she had dared, have brought Edgar Quinet into her circle. From this she was debarred by the agitation to which his lectures at the College of France gave rise among the Clergy, and the consequent suspension of them. Quinet was a man of a religious soul, and it might be said of the Duchess of Orleans as Madame de Stael said of Schiller, "*elle avait la nostalgic du ciel.*"

A Madame Bachellery, a *protegée* of M. and Madame de Lamartine, was the first to awake to the need of a high class of schools taught by laics for girls. She set up a day-school, in which she was aided by all the illustrious men of liberal minds who took an interest in educational questions. Her staff of professors caused her house to be nicknamed by her friends "*Le Petit College de France.*" Omnibusses were chartered by her to fetch pupils to and from the classes. She originally planned the high schools now existing under the Camille Sée law, and wanted Lamartine and Carnot to turn the Château and Parc de Monceau into a normal school for high-class governesses. The reactionist press attacked her, and she ultimately fell. But imitators arose. Pensionnats,

where out-door pupils were taken in, sprang up, as did also classes.
However, the courses were not of a kind to nourish, strengthen, and
beautify young intellects. History was a mere dictionary of dates
and names, and dealt, unless in the upper classes, entirely with
France. In the geography classes, a general sketch of the world
was given. But when details were to be gone into, they were reduced to a list of French watersheds, rivers, chief and county towns.
Occasionally a Professor who was moved by a love of young souls
put life into these dry bones, and awoke and nourished mental
faculties in his pupils. The late M. Richard Cortambert was one
of these teachers, who seemed to have a mission from on high. A
M. Alvarez Levy founded also classes on which there was an extra-
ordinary run, he having perfected the dry bones system, using it
successfully to coach young girls wanting to obtain teachers'
diplomas, or to give others the means, without much learning, to
pass off for having a great deal. A generation of mere parrots were
turned out in these classes. Families who were not Voltairian,
Jew, or Protestant, continued, when at all rich, to send their girls
to convent boarding-schools. The convents stood in vast gardens.
That of La Délivrande, near Caen, had a playground of twenty
acres. The park-like garden of Les Oiseaux, in the Rue de Sèvres,
in Paris, was nearly as large. Les Dames Augustines, at Roule,
Le Sacré Cœur, in the Faubourg St. Germain, were as well provided.
Schoolrooms and dormitories were scrupulously clean, lofty, well
lighted. Infirmaries were faultless. The staffs of teachers and
monitresses being numerous, and free from cares as to what they
should eat and drink, and how they should pay rent and taxes,
came to their class-room and other duties unjaded. Manners and
deportment were carefully attended to: the best bred nuns were
the monitresses for recreation hours. Respect for all that it was
agreed was to be respected was taught by precept and example.
A kind of emotional piety, closely associated with the rather finical
prettiness of the chapel, was inculcated. The world was described
as a horrible place where bad passions raged. Self-reliance was
not a plant to grow in these warm conservatories.

In 1848 a few eminent women and MM. Hyppolite, Carnot (father
of the President), Barthelemy, Saint-Hilaire, and Jules Simon took
up the questions of primary education for girls and of the reform of
primary schools for boys. Their idea was to combine the school
with industrial apprenticeship, and to render attendance obligatory
and gratuitous. A boys' and girls' school was to be set up in every
commune with 800 inhabitants. The law was nearly passed when
Prince Louis Napoleon was elected President. He, wanting the help
of the clergy to make himself emperor, shelved it; and so the women
of the masses were consigned to ignorance until M. Duruy arose
nineteen years later. One great work, however, was accomplished
in that interval, and by the group which was with M. Carnot in
1848, namely, the creation in Paris of technical schools for girls,
where a high-class of primary instruction is given, and technical
education for many handicrafts, arts, and trades. The creating
spirit of these schools was a Madame Lemonnier, the daughter of a

South of France pastor and wife of a Saint Simonien lawyer. She was a high-strung being, filled with an enthusiasm which never became the wildfire of zeal. In one respect she was a Saint Simonien. It was borne strongly upon her mind that the movement to enfranchise women must come from themselves, and that they must be prepared for it by an education which would make them self-reliant, useful, and capable of enjoying the things of the mind. There are now three of these schools in Paris. The Empress Frederick, as German Crown Princess, found in them a model for her Victoria and Sophia Schools at Berlin. For nearly a quarter of a century they have been turning out about 500 pupils yearly, armed at all points for life's struggle. Few of these young women have been unsuccessful in any of the careers for which they were specially prepared, and in which they command the market. Business houses are on the watch to pick up girls educated in these schools, to keep books, direct commercial establishments, make dresses and mantles, underclothes, cut-out, embroider, engrave on wood, paint from nature for industrial purposes, paint glass, porcelain, and design for textile manufactures. Thoroughness is the aim of the mistresses, who are directed by a committee of ladies, some brilliant, all practical, and several filling great positions. They are aided with a consulting committee of eminent scientists, traders, and artists, who look closely to the work done in the school, and give help in opening new channels for activity.

These schools were begun with a fund collected little by little and day by day by Madame Lemonnier, who spent twelve years gathering it. Her heart burned within her, and she communicated her sacred fire to those whom she recruited. She seemed a being in whom there was no dross. Born a sweet poetess, all her poetry in her mature years went into beneficent action. She sought neither personal profit nor glory, and died just as she began to realise that the great idea and work of her life was no mere dream of an enthusiast. Her schools have been liberally patronised by the Jews, to whom they owe a yearly income, taking the form of subscriptions, of about £3,000, for they are not yet self-supporting, though in a fair way to become so. Their most active patronesses are Mesdames Jules Simon, Floquet, wife of the Speaker of the House of Deputies, Manuel, wife of the poet who sings in heart-awakening verse the trials of the poor, the joys of honest family life, the happiness of guiding one's actions according to duty, and the loveliness of justice, human brotherhood, and kindliness towards all God's creatures.

Boys' schools of every degree, kept by religious brotherhoods, were, in regard to pedagogic education, far above nuns' schools, low and high. This was due to young men having to start out in life in callings and professions to which ignorance would have been a bar. They had to pass test examinations for the civil service, enter cadets, engineering, polytechnic schools, also through examinations. Besides, the teaching brotherhoods were subject to the competition of the Lyceums, which stirred them up. While the sons of rich liberal and reactionary families were being educated according to a high standard, the daughters were being trained, how, I have already shown. In good society thirty years ago, in consequence of this divergence in the education of the two sexes, a great chasm began to yawn between them. In drawing-rooms, ladies were as much isolated from gentlemen as if they were in a Turkish seraglio. A man of sense could hardly, with any pleasure to himself, converse with a "well-educated" lady. Her mind bristled with small and touchy prejudices. At *soirées* the ladies seated themselves, as they unfortunately do yet, at one end of the room, where they whispered flat gossip or silently scanned each others dresses; the gentlemen standing at the other, solemn as at a funeral. There was no gay *badinage*, no collision of the flint-and-steel sort between masculine and feminine minds, no presentation of serious ideas in light and graceful forms. When there was not the noisy mirth of vacuity there was pretentious dulness. This stagnation was unexpectedly disturbed, owing to the following causes.

About the middle of the sixties the Empress Eugénie wanted, the Emperor's health being bad, to prepare her way towards a Regency, and began to take an active part in public affairs. He and she then happened to go to an agricultural show at Orleans. The bishop and his clergy furbished up their local erudition and scholarship to display it before the Empress and her ladies, as in another reign they had before the Duchess of Orleans. But what M. Dupanloup had to say was, he found, Greek to Eugénie and her fair following. His disappointment and ire at not finding them responsive were given vent to in a series of articles for *Le Correspondent*, in which he wrote at them. Though not exactly for Equal Rights, he was a Joan of Arcist, and could not endure ladies not learned enough to seize the classical and historical allusions with which he studded his conversation. M. Duruy came about this time into office as Minister of Public Instruction. He had lost the idol of his life, an only daughter, with whom he was one in heart, thought, and all the knowledge she had acquired from him. M. Duruy felt like Jeremiah lamenting over Jerusalem as he realised, in the grand world to which he was admitted, to what a degree the sexes lived apart, and how mischievous, from ignorance and a mind-distorting education, the power the fine ladies still exercised had become.

Below, things were almost as bad. Statistics showed that three-fourths of the women felons and misdemeanants did not know how to read and write. There was not among them, from 1850 to 1860, a single woman who had received a good education. Whilst the number of illiterate men had decreased at the rate of 103 per 1,000, the ratio of diminution, notwithstanding all the schools of Saint Marie, was only 49 per 1,000. Out of 1,200 women tried for infant murder, but six knew how to read, write, and cast up accounts. In the west and central departments the proportion of illiterate women, many of whom could not read the clock-dial, had remained what it was in 1848, when M. Carnot made his educational census, namely, from 794 to 895 per 1,000. The advance, as shown at the universal exhibition of 1867, of Switzerland, Germany, Holland, and even Austria through the school, came home to the Imperial

Government. M. Duruy took advantage of all this, and of the anger of the Empress at finding herself written at by the Bishop of Orleans, to advance the cause he had at heart and on his brain. He decided that Mlle. Daubie was to be given the University B.A. degree for which she qualified six years before, carried a law obliging every commune of 500 inhabitants to open a primary school for girls, and taught according to the wish of each commune by laics or Sisters. Women and girls were admitted by his order to the Sorbonne lectures, to which the Empress sent her nieces, and classes for higher instruction were opened for girls in the chief county and other towns where there were Schools of Faculties and Lyceums, the professors of which were to teach at them. It became *bon genre* to go to the Sorbonne, where M. Caro lent grace and other charms to moral philosophy, and M. Paul Albert awoke a thirst for history and classic literature. But in the provincial towns the new classes met with violent hostility. Parish priests and vicars stood at the lecture-room doors to make lists of the young girls who went in or out, and put them and their families under a ban. An order came from Rome for the Bishop of Orleans, who was "the father of the mischief," to eat his words, and he explained them away. The Empress took her nieces from the Sorbonne, and M. Duruy was dismissed. In 1870 his provincial classes had, in all but 14 Republican towns, died out. But they were so missed by the women who attended them as chaperons, and the young girls, that on the Camille Sée law being passed in 1880, the great county and manufacturing towns asked to co-operate with Government in creating Lyceums for their girls.

There was a hard fight in the Senate over this law, in favour of which were MM. Henry Martin, Carnot, Jules Simon, St. Hilaire, Pressensé, Schœlcher, and De Freycinet. Gambetta was its fervent advocate publicly and privately. He disliked the company of women who were insensible to the ideas that rolled from him with splendid richness when he talked at the table or fireside of a friend. The women-writers of France, De Sevigné, De Maintenon, Roland, De Stael, Sand (when she described country life and landscapes), and Louise Ackermann, gave him the most pleasure. He never enjoyed living in the south of France, because women did not go with their husbands to the cafés, and were not in companionship with men.

Whatever may be the final result on France of the uprise of the race which M. Drumont hates, the advance made by women within twenty years could not have been as rapid as it has been since 1880 without Jewish help. That help was strenuous and practical. If, as M. Drumont believes, the Jews want to ruin France, they have worked hard, in the matter of education, to secure to French Gentiles the advantages to which they themselves owe the power that they exercise. Jews and Protestants form a small minority of the whole French population. The great situations both fill are out of all proportion to the numbers of these communities. This is because they lost no educational advantage, and were ready to take the Republican tide. The Protestants are not as rich as the Jews, but are more to the front as occupants of high places. Both have co-operated heartily in all questions that touch the advancement of public instruction. A Jew of rare personal distinction, M. Camille Sée, is the author of the law under which France has twenty-seven girls' high schools, and will soon have thirty-six—a law that Belgium has copied. It was elaborated by M. Jules Simon, a Jew on his father's side of the house, by MM. Cohn, the Poet Manuel (Jews both), Zevort, Bréal, and Gréard, Vice Rector of the University of France, and biographer of Madame de Maintenon, whom he has set right in the eyes of all who have read his penetrating criticism on her time, life, surrounding circumstances, work, and writings.

It was a pity there were not women as well as men on the Grand Council of Public Instruction when the courses which are followed in the girls' Lyceums were being elaborated. The programmes are overcrowded. Too much time must be spent in lessons and preparation. Madame de Maintenon's plan of varying class work with hard physical work and elegant arts was a healthy one. Short hours for class leave time for such variety, and afford rest, without which there can be no unconscious cerebration, and, therefore, no strong flashes of head-light. Nobody more than M. Camille Sée regrets the overcharged programmes. But when women enter the Grand Council they will probably reform as he would wish. The quality of the teaching leaves nothing to be desired. Morals are treated as a positive science, growing out of the social needs of human beings. Religion is taught to pupils of different denominations in separate rooms by their priests, pastors, or rabbis.

Secondary instruction has not yet had time to improve the material status of French women, but we may hope that it will rapidly improve their condition and speed forward evolution. Girls who study in Lyceums generally belong to families of good means. A fair proportion of poor ones enter on scholarships. It is decided that, all things equal, women professors are to be preferred to men in these establishments, and that in every case the principals are to be women. What is very remarkable is that young girls educated in the new secondary schools outstrip young men at the university examinations for diplomas—not in Greek and Latin, but in science. The girl's mind in the new Lyceums more easily takes in mathematics and physics than classics, history, and moral science. Young women who have striven successfully for medical diplomas have been without exception classed as super-excellent by their examiners. But the number of French who attend the medical schools of Paris is less than that of English, Americans, and very much less than the number of Russians. French and foreign female undergraduates are admitted to compete at examinations for house studentships in hospitals. An Anglo-French young lady, Blanche Edwards, was the first to get in. The next was Miss Klumke, a Californian, who is counted one of the first among living anatomists, and has gone deeper than any one else into the remote nervous causes of paralysis. The Town Council of Paris has resolved that doctresses are only to be employed (when there are enough of them) in the infant and girls' communal schools. A similar rule has been made concerning the offices in which women are employed in the posts and telegraph department. Infant schools are exclusively under female teachers. The communal schoolmistresses are mostly women of superior parts, and far above the schoolmasters of their class. In Paris they are received in the best society, and are well off, though not as well paid as their masculine colleagues. These are the relative scales of salaries:—

SCHOOLMASTERS.

Class.	Salary.	Number now employed.
1st Class	4,500f.	42
2nd ,,	4,300f.	44
3rd ,,	3,700f.	71
4th ,,	3,300f.	17

UNDER MASTERS.

1st Class	3,000f.	300
2nd ,,	2,700f.	306
3rd ,,	2,400f.	277
4th ,,	2,100f.	285
5th ,,	1,800f.	155

SCHOOLMISTRESSES.

1st Class	3,800f.	42
2nd ,,	3,450f.	52
3rd ,,	3,100f.	77
4th ,,	2,750f.	23

UNDER MISTRESSES.

1st Class	2,500f.	225
2nd ,,	2,250f.	278
3rd ,,	2,000f.	334
4th ,,	1,750f.	301
5th ,,	1,500f.	175

Masters and mistresses of all classes and degrees of seniority, who are not lodged in schoolhouses, are allowed, according to the dearness or the cheapness of the neighbourhood where they teach, from 400f. to 500f. for rent. The mistresses, as has been pointed out, are not so well off as the masters, and yet they have, in addition to the usual pedagogic task, to teach sewing, cutting out, washing, clear starching, ironing, and plain cooking. Ten francs a day per girls' school is allowed for edibles on which the cook is to demonstrate. What she cooks goes to the poorest or "assisted" class of children to whom food is given by the City. She and the senior girls have also to instruct the junior or "non-assisted" ones who bring the materials for their noontide meal, how to dress them.

Sometimes a lesson is given in association, by making out of what each brings common dishes. Ten children, say, have raw eggs. Would they like them in an omelette instead of boiled, or would they by combining to buy some rice, milk, and sugar, have a pudding? If the eggs are to be boiled the names of the several owners are written on them, with, according to the taste of each, the words, "well done," "done to a turn," or "underdone," the French for which last is *bareux*. The reason schoolmistresses are paid less than schoolmasters is that the latter have votes and can be useful to candidates at elections. Political parties are always trying to have and to hold the communal schoolmasters, and the Republic has delivered them in rural districts from all servitude to the Church. In Republican places the schoolmistress, if a woman of character and pleasant manner, is on a good social footing. In Clerical communes she is often attacked behind her back, and constantly denounced in anonymous and signed letters to the Board of Public Instruction and to the Communal Council. Paris is the heaven of the primary schoolmistress, because of the personal independence she enjoys out of school hours, and the social relations she may form with distinguished people who value usefulness and love the fruits of the mind. There is an average of fifty vacancies for schoolmistresses, upper and under, in the Paris communal schools. The candidates this year came to 6,479, and next year there must be a great many more.

Mlle. Maria Deraismes, an all-round, strong, brilliant, highly-educated, and a wealthy woman, is working to push the law for granting civil rights to women through the Senate. She is first among the orators of France, deserves to rank as a classic polemist, and is hearty, generous, and in all things right minded. This lady was carefully educated by her father, and is a well of erudition. She holds the Town Council in her hand, and has for her lieutenants in the Chamber MM. Yves-Guyot, and Clemenceau. A thing to recommend her is her freedom from pedantry and small vanity. According to statistics with which she has furnished me, 23,000 women are employed on French railways (1) to signal, (2) as junior clerks and to issue tickets, and (3) as senior clerks. The Post Office employs 10,000 as clerks, assistant and district postmistresses, not to speak of telegraphists and telephonists. But it has lately ruled that daughters of postal functionaries are to be preferred. M. Magnan, Governor of the Bank of France, opened many departments there to women. He says they scent forged notes with unerring sureness. There are 200 women clerks there, entitled, like the men, to pensions. The Crédit Foncier employs 260, and gives them pension rights. Not a few private banks are directed in chief by women. As book-keepers and auditors they top the market, and are very well paid. Women buyers only act as such for themselves and husbands. Madame Jaluzot made the fortune of the Printemps by her taste as a buyer of fancy wares, and Madame Boucicaut of the Bon Marché.

French women who move forward owe a good deal to the example of their American sisters. It stirred them up to see English and American and then Russian girls attend the Schools of Medicine, walk the hospitals, live as decent girls should, without chaperons, and distinguish themselves at degree examinations. There is long headway to make before they come up to the daughters of Brother Jonathan, who have equal rights at the Bar, in the reporters' gallery (of which the *entrée* is still denied to them in "the first Assembly in the world"—the British House of Commons), the school, college, pulpit, editorial room, and hope soon to have political rights in all the forty-two States of the Union.

Last February, Senator Blair, Chairman of the Select Committee to report on a resolution proposing an amendment of the United States Constitution, reported in favour of a change favourable to woman's suffrage. The committee thought denial of that suffrage on a par with negro slavery in its injustice. Unless the United States Government should be made and kept Republican by such suffrage, the ballot could not accomplish great reforms, nor disintegration in the body politic be checked. Corruption of male suffrage was a well-nigh fatal disease. The ballot was withheld from women, whose moral sense, when they are regarded as a mass, is far higher than that of the other sex, because men did not wish to part with one-half of the governing power. Ignoble and tragic catastrophes had engulfed all past Republics, which, without exception, denied equal rights. The United States Republic would founder, too, if it kept on being a male Republic. What Senator Blair said was needed, was a Republic in which both men and women should be free indeed.

The State of Wyoming has Woman's Suffrage, and Kansas gives municipal rights to its women, and finds there is advantage in doing so. The cities which have lady Mayors, and town councils that do not include a single male member, are the ones in which the whisky saloons are on their good behaviour and the town concerns best managed. One of the greatest organisations in the world is Frances Willard's and Mary A. Livermore's Women's Christian Temperance Union. It covers the whole ground from East to West, and nothing escapes its vigilance. The three planks of its platform are the temperance question, the labour question, and the woman's question. Married ladies joining it are requested to register themselves under their own, and not their husband's names. This organisation is becoming a school for women journalists. It has its foundling homes, city nurseries, kindergartens, inebriates' reformatories, and some of the central unions from which district ones branch have their lady attorneys, and no Sally Brasses either. A Mrs. Ada Bitterden is the attorney for the organisation at Chicago. The light of legal science for the whole organisation is Leila Josephine Robinson, author of "The Legal Rights of Women, and the Law of Husband and Wife," a new text-book which already is accepted by lawyers as an authority. There are mixed guilds and women's guilds of art and learning, and there is a social guild at Philadelphia where young wage-earners of both sexes meet in evenings to follow classes, debate, sing in glees, chorals, and soli, and on Saturday evenings to dance; Friday evenings are Eleusinian. Gentlemen absent themselves because the ladies want drill exercise. The Bryn Mawr University maidens have overflowing biological laboratories. Miss Goff, a graduate, is the demonstrator and an authority on ferments. Miss Randolph, fellow in biology, has lately delivered a lecture which ought to make Sir John Lubbock claim her as a sister scientist. The subject is, "Do Animals think?" She and Miss Goff are engaged on special work, the one studying the regeneration of lost parts, and the other the action of drugs on the heart. At Chicago, the young ladyhood have a medical college of their own. Scientific ladies in the United States have lost none of the charm for which in past ages women were mostly valued. If there is a sight on earth which should cause joy to a believer in the ever-mounting, ever-widening spiral of human progress, it is that of bands of white-robed American girls on degree day. Head, firm character, impressionability, are expressed in the fair young faces, the mien, the slender figures. Sentimentality has been crowded out, but there is no incapacity for sentiment or ideality. The most intellectual women in America have been the most humane. Mrs. Beecher Stowe wrote her wonderful book because she had a wonderful and finely-cultivated mind, and a heart that bled at the sufferings of the negro slave. Boston is famous for its good works. And what a fidget the Boston woman is about her "mind." High intellectual and moral consciousness form the heaven to which she is ever soaring. New England spinsters often settle down into happy, useful, and dignified old maidenhood. They don't marry, because they don't want to, and not from want of asking. Ladies all over the United States are coming to the front as preachers. Out West, there are a number in the pulpits of the Unitarian churches, and they are thought the most active and progressive ministers there.

The Reverend Miss Carrie J. Bartlett, of Kalamazoo, Michigan, who has been three years in the ministry, is making Brooklyn forget the Rev. H. Ward Beecher. She started in life as a reporter, then rose to be assistant editor, in which post she got sick of newspaper sensationalism, political intrigues and other uglinesses, and determined to devote herself to the pulpit. The churches in Clinton Street and Gale's Avenue, Brooklyn, have been lent her by their vestries. To judge from her looks, she might be twenty-six, is of average height, has a strong, speaking face, large, eloquent eyes, and mobile and delicately formed lips. Her voice carries far, is firm and under control. The diction is delightful, her articulation being distinct, tones well modulated, and those of a finely-organised contralto chest and larynx. The gestures are graceful, and she has a sculptural hand, elegantly finished at the finger tips. At home in the pulpit, and speaking out of the depths of her own emotion, she easily sways her hearers. When she preaches, she dresses in a neat black silk dress, with box pleats falling the whole way from the back of her neck. Since God made roses, and human industry developed their beauty, she does not see why she should not wear a cluster of them in her corsage when she preaches. Perhaps they might be better on the desk or communion table. The Reverend Miss Carrie Bartlett's central idea is that happiness is in ourselves, depending on our view of life in its relations and its bearings. She holds the present phase of the world's history to be one rich in Divine Grace and influx, and indeed a sacred phase.

The excellence of the public schools, and the spread of higher instruction, are making the American woman fit for everything that does not require muscular strength. Fitness is shown in Arts: witness Miss Hosmer, Margaret Foley the cameo carver, Miss Elizabeth Gardner, Miss Strong, the animal painter, Miss Fanny Currey, who is growing famous as a landscape painter, and with ease, in modesty and retirement, making quite a fortune. I never met, it now occurs to me, a talented American woman artist who was not quite reserved, free from extravagance, tastefully dressed, versed in social amenities. The lady lawyer also dresses well. Victoria Woodhull and her sister, both great Wall Street operators, made conquests after they had made fortunes, of two English millionaires, one of whom has an English and the other a Portuguese title. Even Mrs. Hetty Green, the richest woman in her own right, and in regard to three-fourths of her wealth by her own exertions, does not impress one as a disagreeable person. She looks motherly. The point of a nearly straight nose is just a little suggestive of hardness, but the eyes are blue and kindly, and she has a straightforward manner in which there is no peremptoriness. Mrs. Hetty came years ago into a fortune of $9,000,000 after she had started out in her present course. She is now worth $40,000,000, and is not yet on the downhill slope of middle age.

Journalism now gives a field to thousands of American women. Editors, shorthand and type-writing clerks, are mostly young ladies. Miss Hutchinson, for years the editor of the *New York Sunday Tribune*, the best weekly paper, perhaps, in existence, is one of the most accomplished critics of the age. Gail Hamilton, Mrs. Blaine's cousin, stands at the top of the American press as "a letter-essayist." Syndicates give her any price she chooses to ask for articles to be copyrighted.

To realise how far English girlhood and womanhood have advanced since the Social Science Congresses first timidly aired the woman's question, one should live a good deal out of England. To do so has been my fate. Whenever of late years I returned there, my breath was almost taken away by the speed with which this question had advanced to many solutions. In France, "the cause" is held back by the habit of intrigue contracted by French middle-class women since the First Empire in overcoming the difficulties of their position. No men are more respectful than the French towards well-conducted women or girls. But none are more quick to take a bad advantage of levity, or a taste for gallant intrigue. Women are shut out from many advantages for this and no other reason. They are recognized as art critics, and Madame Rouvier had a permanent seat in the gallery of the Chamber as a press woman. But railway boards refuse them free passes. In England there is a different state of mind. There is also greater candour and good faith in the British than in the French mind, which is often apt to be cynical, and to bow rather to routine than to what is fair. Maria Deraismes and Louise Michel are the only women in France ready to go on political platforms to address meetings. Mrs. Gladstone, Lady Sandhurst, Lady Dilke, Lady Carlisle, Mrs. Ashton Dilke, Mrs. Ormeston Chant, Mrs. Labouchere, Miss Cobden, Lady Aberdeen, who is all grace, goodness, and a rock of sense, and many others of light and leading, have come forward as public speakers. Nobody since Wesley has so leavened the poor inhabitants of English towns as Mrs. Booth of the Salvation army. The philanthropy of Elizabeth Fry was wondered at in her time, and justly. I doubt whether she worked such wonders as Mrs. Percy Bunting, whose modesty prevents fame from finding her out. Mrs. Amos, Miss Clementina Black, Mrs. Price Hughes and her band of "sisters" are an angelic influence in the horrible parts of London, raising the weak and fallen, inspiriting to better effort, showing what may be done by organisation and by doing one's best. Nor should Mrs. Besant be passed over. She is right-minded and true hearted. Her work will not be in vain. English women have learned to stand together. I had many opportunities of seeing the "advanced" ones among them at the Women's Congresses held last year in Paris. Some of them were successful as agreeable women at the *soirées* given in honour of these congresses by members of the French Government and the Prefect of the Seine. Miss Balgarnie, a straightforward, unaffected, soft-mannered and handsome girl, a Una who might lead any lion, tamed or otherwise, represented an association to obtain the political franchise for British women. I never spent more enjoyable days than at the Universal Exhibition of last year with her and some of the distinguished *consœurs* who came over for congresses with her. Doctors Kate and Julia Mitchell, the incomparably beautiful Madame Anna de Ritzius of Stockholm, were in the company, with Mrs. Magnusson, who is likely to become the Elise Lemonnier of her native Iceland.

These are a few thoughts regarding the education and status of women, as they occur to one of themselves, in three of the most highly civilised countries in the world. Intellectually, Woman may be said, even more than Man, to be in her infancy; but when it is considered how the growth of her mental faculties has been stunted, and how in past times in Europe, as even now in Eastern lands, she was regarded as an inferior being, and by some denied the possession of a soul, it is marvellous that in the course of a few years she should have advanced by leaps and bounds, until she has proved herself the equal of Man in some, as she may one day prove herself his superior in many departments of human knowledge.

Mrs. EMILY CRAWFORD.

PART X.
TECHNICAL INSTRUCTION, AND PAYMENT ON RESULTS

MANY circumstances have combined to bring the subject of Elementary Education prominently under public notice. The general demand for Technical Instruction, which is now in a fair way towards being satisfied, directed attention to the foundations on which all education rests, and showed that the provision of technical instruction for artisans depended for its success on the efficiency of the preliminary teaching in our primary schools.

The Royal Commissioners on Technical Instruction, appointed in 1881, soon discovered the close connection that existed in all European countries between elementary and technical education, and that no satisfactory and general scheme of technical education could be introduced into this country which did not presuppose various alterations and improvements in our system of elementary teaching. In the introduction to their Report they say: "It is necessary in order to understand the position of the purely Technical Schools, of which we shall have to treat subsequently, that an outline should be given of the system that has been adopted for the general education of young people of both sexes, from the commencement of the school age onwards;" and, in the concluding chapter, are found many important recommendations with respect to primary instruction, all of which have received careful consideration, but can scarcely be said to have passed beyond the stage of enquiry. A general feeling that our whole system of elementary teaching required to be remodelled in order to better adapt the instruction to the practical needs of artisan life was one of the causes which led to the appointment, in 1885, of the Royal Commission of enquiry into the working of the education acts; and although from the constitution of that Commission no general agreement could have been expected, the recommendations of either section, if adopted, would effect considerable improvement in the character of the teaching given in our Public Elementary Schools.

Notwithstanding the imperfections of the Act of 1870, the beneficial effects of this first attempt to nationalize our education and to bring the rudiments of knowledge within reach of all classes of the community are generally recognized. But twenty years ago the principles of education were not so well understood as they now are; and apart from the difficulties and delays which arose from the necessity of getting School Boards into working order, of erecting new schools and of training efficient teachers, the aims of elementary instruction were not clearly understood, and the results of the teaching were consequently found to be less satisfactory than had been anticipated.

Children left school able to read and write and do simple sums, but their intelligence had been very little quickened by the instruction they had received, and of the knowledge they had gained little or nothing remained a year or so after their schooling was over. Even the mechanical ability to read and write was partially lost through neglect, and the power of using writing as a means of expressing thought can be scarcely said to have been acquired. The influence of mediævalism, which had moulded all our Secondary Schools to one pattern, had stamped its mark upon our elementary system of education, and had made the exercise of memory the main purpose of instruction. Other circumstances had tended to accentuate this position. The system of distributing the Government grant by payment on the results of the examination of individual pupils has had much to do with placing before teachers an altogether erroneous idea of the real aim of education. Of this fact, I think there can be now no reasonable doubt; and whilst the Code unduly encouraged the teaching of literary subjects, the effect of the annual inspection was to intensify the efforts of the teachers to make the children remember such facts and phrases as would pay best in the examination. In learning to read and write, as in learning any other art, in which skill has to be acquired, a certain amount of drill is absolutely necessary, but such mechanical methods of instruction are of little use in awakening and stimulating the intelligence of the child.

Some of our best educational authorities have pointed out that the fault of our teaching is that it is too "bookish;" and this conclusion has been reached by those who have approached the subject along very different and almost opposite lines of enquiry. The late Mr. Matthew Arnold knew our schools from within. He was familiar with the methods of instruction. He had seen our teachers at work, and had tested, time after time, the results of the teaching, and his conclusion was that the teaching was "mechanical," and did not succeed in adequately developing the child's whole mind. In contrasting school teaching abroad and in this country, he tells us: "The methods of teaching in foreign schools are more gradual, more natural, more rational than in ours, and in speaking of foreign schools, I include Swiss, and French schools, as well as German. I often used to ask myself, why, with such large classes, the order was in general so thoroughly good, and why, with such long hours, the children had in general so little look of exhaustion or fatigue, and the answer I could not help making to myself was that the cause lay in the children being taught less mechanically, and more naturally than with us, and being more interested . . . . The fault of the teaching in our popular schools at home is, as I have often said, that it is so little formative. It gives the children the power to read the newspapers, to write a letter, to cast accounts, and gives them a certain number of pieces of knowledge, but it does little to touch their nature for good and to mould them."

Professor Huxley, who examined the question from an altogether different standpoint, has arrived at a similar conclusion. Our Education, he says, is too bookish, it appeals too much to the memory, too little to the senses and to the reasoning faculties. The concurrence of two such authorities, whose training and habits of thought would naturally lead them to approach the problem with very different educational sympathies, supported as it is by the opinions of many other educational authorities, may be considered as conclusive. But this testimony receives further confirmation from practical men of business, who generally endorse the views of Lord Armstrong, that "a man's success in life depends incomparably more upon his capacity for useful action, than upon his acquirements and knowledge, and the education of the young should therefore be directed to the developing of faculties and valuable qualities rather than to the acquisition of knowledge."

The fact is that during the twenty years that have elapsed since the passing of Mr. Forster's Act, our ideas of the aims and purpose of elementary education, and of the means by which they may be attained have undergone a considerable change. It is not so much knowledge as the power of acquiring knowledge and the means of developing the faculties of observation, which we expect education to confer upon us. This shifting of our position is due to a truer recognition of the real object of school training, and has been assisted by a comparison of foreign methods of instruction with our own. During the last ten years, a belief in the defects of our present system has been gradually growing, and Code after Code has been introduced with the view of indirectly improving the course of study pursued in our elementary schools. I say, indirectly, because all new regulations necessarily operated through the measure of the amount of grant they produced. In too many cases the aim of managers and teachers has been to secure, not the most efficient and useful instruction for the children, but the largest amount of Government grant. The importance of Science-teaching as a means of training the observing faculties, and of affording useful knowledge has long since been recognized; but nothing has hitherto been more unsatisfactory than the failure of payments on results to encourage Science-teaching in our schools. Owing to the fact, that the grant on Geography, as a class subject, was equal to that on Science, and that geography was more easily taught, there has been an actual falling off in the number of children who have been presented in Science.

The number of schools, or departments of schools, which have taken Science as a class subject has decreased from 51 in 1883-4 to 36 in 1887-8, and if we look to the statistics showing the number of children examined in any branch of Science as a specific subject we find the results equally unsatisfactory. From the following table, prepared by Dr. Gladstone,* it will be seen that whilst the number of

* Journal of Society of Arts, Nov. 29th, 1889.

children taking Science has fallen in the five years ending 1888 from
82,965 to 79,985, the number of children in the Standards V., VI.,
and VII., in which the subject might have been taught has increased
during the same period from 286,355 to 472,770, and very note-
worthy are the decreases in such subjects of practical application
as Animal Physiology, which underlies the laws of health, and
Magnetism and Electricity, a knowledge of which in various industries is every day becoming more and more important.

Specific Subjects—Children.	1882-3.	1883-4.	1884-5.	1885-6.	1886-7.	1887-8.
Algebra	26,547	24,787	25,347	25,393	25,103	26,448
Euclid and Mensuration .	1,942	2,010	1,269	1,247	995	1,006
Mechanics	2,042	3,174	3,527	4,844	6,315	6,961
Animal Physiology .	22,754	22,857	20,869	18,523	17,338	16,940
Botany	3,280	2,604	2,415	1,992	1,589	1,598
Principles of Agriculture .	1,357	1,859	1,481	1,351	1,137	1,151
Chemistry . . .	1,183	1,047	1,095	1,158	1,488	1,808
Sound, Light and Heat .	630	1,253	1,231	1,331	1,158	918
Magnetism and Electricity	3,643	3,244	2,864	2,951	2,250	1,977
Domestic Economy . .	19,582	21,458	19,437	19,556	20,716	20,787
Total . .	82,965	84,499	79,774	78,477	78,122	79,985
Number of Scholars in Standards V., VI., VII.	286,355	325,205	352,860	393,289	432,097	472,770

According to our present system, it is the grant-producing quality
of the subject rather than its practical usefulness or its educational
value that determines the extent to which it is taught in our public
elementary schools. There is no doubt that the Code of 1889, which
was introduced into Parliament and withdrawn, would have tended
to remove many of the defects of the system of which we continue to
complain. The new Code about to be introduced will certainly be
an improvement on any previous code, and will further tend to
encourage the teaching of Science, Drawing, and Manual Exercises.
But how will this be effected? By making the pecuniary grant sufficient to induce schools to teach these subjects. The regulation
requiring Cookery to be taught in girls' schools, as a condition of
paying a grant for Drawing, may be withdrawn, and girls showing an
aptitude for Art may be allowed to learn Drawing without occupying
their time with Cookery. The teaching of Science may be
encouraged by placing it in a more favoured position as regards
grant than other subjects. Freedom may be given to school authorities to introduce the teaching of subjects for which there exists a
local demand, without incurring pecuniary loss, and Manual Training may be recognized as a part of primary education. But when
all these alterations are made, the curriculum of our schools will be
determined by that selection of subjects which will produce the
maximum of grants, without any necessary reference to the capa-
bilities of the pupils or the requirements of the locality. The
commercial element will continue to enter into the consideration of
every change in the subjects of instruction. Can it be right that
the character of the course of study shall be determined by these

monetary calculations? Members of School Boards and managers of elementary schools are well aware of the extent to which this commercial consideration affects the teaching. Not only is the course of instruction the product of careful calculations which have for their object the securing of the greatest possible amount of grant, but the teachers themselves keep this object in view in all their lessons. Each class must yield its maximum number of passes. There can be no doubt that so much reason as existed in the cry against "over-pressure" was due to this cause. The effect of all examinations in merely acquired knowledge is to obscure somewhat the true aims of teaching; but when the income of the school partly depends on the results of such examinations, their effect in this direction is necessarily more marked. When we are told by the most competent authorities that the teaching is mechanical, that it appeals to the memory rather than to the understanding, that it is "so little formative," and when we know, that in many schools, reading is taught so as to secure fluency on the part of the pupil without regard to the meaning of the words read, that answers to questions in history are too often a jumble of phrases, that in other subjects verbal accuracy is secured at the expense of intelligent thought, one cannot help feeling that undue stress is laid on the results of the examination, which controls, instead of merely guiding, the teaching. Various modifications of the Code have been suggested, and some have been adopted with the view of remedying these evils. The examination of classes has been partly substituted for that of individual pupils. A general merit grant has been added to the other numerous sources of revenue. The instructions to inspectors have been issued with the greatest care, and with the evident desire that the examination should test ability and intelligence rather than acquired knowledge, but all this availeth nothing whilst the mercantile spirit pervades the atmosphere of the school-room, and the Code under which the teachers work, reads like a price-list of pieces of knowledge. He who knew the real worth of that instruction which is truly formative of character tells us that "it is more to be desired than gold, Yea, than much fine gold;" but the Code duly assesses its value in current coin. Only recently, the "Association for the promotion of Technical and Secondary Education" has issued to its members some suggestions for the new Code of 1890. The objects aimed at by these suggestions are excellent; but how are they to be attained? By making higher pecuniary bids for the teaching of those subjects, which in the opinion of the Association need to be encouraged. "The teaching of Science as a class subject to be encouraged in the Upper standards by an *additional grant.*" Alternative courses in specific subjects, "to *receive a grant* on the same principle as the subjects enumerated in Article 15" of the Code. Instruction in the use of simple tools to be introduced in the Higher standards, and "*grants to be paid* thereon." Elementary modelling to be taught and "*a grant to be made* in connection therewith," and so on. Can it be wondered at, that teachers, many of whom have been educated under this system, who have served an apprenticeship as pupil teachers in these schools, who have been trained in Colleges among other students exclusively of the same class as themselves, and who have heard the question of the amount of grant constantly discussed by those in authority over them, shall grow up with a mercenary idea of the true aims of education, and shall pursue their high calling under the influence of an inseparable mental association between good teaching and large money grants?

It would surely seem that the time has come when, instead of adding grant unto grant, we should recognise that possibly the mechanical teaching of which we complain may be the result of the mechanical methods by which its value is assessed. To many it may seem that to throw over the system of payment on results would be to destroy the foundations on which our national education rests. Those who whether as teachers, managers, or inspectors, have worked under this system throughout their entire life, naturally ask what substitute can be suggested for the premiums, now offered, of half-crowns and four-shilling pieces for isolated scraps of knowledge in different branches of learning. The answer is, no substitute is needed. Do the Charity Commissioners dole forth their endowments to the governors of secondary schools according to the number of pupils who pass the Oxford and Cambridge Locals or any other public examination; or do they make the amount of their contribution depend on such results? I have elsewhere stated: "The restrictions under which the elementary schoolmaster works require to be relaxed. There is no essential difference between his duties and responsibilities and those of the head master of a middle class school largely dependent on endowments for support."* The system which is found to work well in schools of higher grade would work equally well in elementary schools. "What is needed in both cases is that the teacher shall be well trained, and that the inspection shall be thorough." We have only to attempt to realise the effect of introducing payment on results into our secondary schools to recognise the full force of the arguments for abolishing it in our elementary schools. I venture to prophesy that if all reference to grants for special subjects or individual passes were removed from our Code, the directions of the Code would be no less faithfully observed than they now are, and the character of the teaching would be gradually improved. Moreover, if such a new departure could be made, very few years would elapse before the staunchest advocates of the system would express surprise that it was so long tolerated, and that the results were not still more unsatisfactory than they have proved to be. There exists a general impression, which the mercantile spirit of the Code tends to foster, that teachers are only kept up to the mark by the knowledge that the amount of Government grant depends on the result of the Inspector's report. So strong was this belief for many years, that the Government grant formed part of the teacher's salary, and in many places the teachers continue to have a share in it. But experience has shown that this particular kind of incentive to painstaking teaching is productive of more harm than good, and the system of paying the teacher a fixed salary is now

---

* "Industrial Education" (Kegan Paul & Co.), p. 118.

generally preferred; and where this system has been introduced, as in the case of the School Board for London, the teaching is found to be improved. But if the teacher's salary is made independent of results the main argument in favour of the retention of the payment on results loses its force.

It is the opinion of many of H. M.'s Inspectors, that if they were deprived of the power of making the State contribution towards the school income depend, to some extent, on the efficiency of the teaching as tested by results, their influence in screwing up the school to higher excellence would be seriously impaired. But I very much doubt whether in actual practice, this would be found to be the case. The importance rightly attached to the report and to the recommendations of the Inspectors is quite independent of the grant-distributing quality with which they are weighted. Indeed, in many cases the system works most unfairly, the larger grant being withdrawn from a school, which on account of its less efficiency is often the more in need of funds. Teachers are not permanent institutions: they are liable to dismissal if found incompetent; and sufficient incentive to good teaching, apart from its own stimulating effect, is found in the praise or blame they receive on the result of the Inspectors' reports.

But it will be said that whilst "payment on results" might be easily abolished in the case of the majority of schools under School Board management, the stimulus it affords is needed in the case of Voluntary Schools which are under no similar public control. I think, however, it may be assumed that what the public really care for, is not so much the control of Voluntary Schools as the assurance and guarantee that they are thoroughly efficient and properly managed. Voluntary Schools, receiving state aid are even now subjected by H.M.'s Inspectors to some measure of public superintendence. If the inspection is imperfect or inadequate, if it is not sufficiently frequent, or sufficiently thorough, to afford the guarantee which the public has a right to require, of the efficiency of the schools inspected, the remedy lies, not in continuing the system of payment on results, which is after all a mere mechanical method of testing the efficiency, but in improving and strengthening the inspection; and in this suggestion, I venture to think, will be found the looked for substitute for payment on results.

If grants on results were abolished, schools would be maintained as they now are from two or three sources, according as school fees are retained or abandoned. The sources of income would be: (1) Local Aid, whether in the form of rates or subscriptions, supplemented or not by school fees; and (2) Government Grant. What is wanted, is that the Government grant should be a fixed sum per unit of average attendance, and that the payment of this sum should be independent of results. To secure, and to afford the necessary assurance of, efficiency, changes would have to be made in our system of inspection. In addition to H.M.'s Inspectors, who would visit each school, as now, and report to the Education Department, district Inspectors should be appointed by the School Board or other local authority. It would be the duty of the district

Inspectors to visit the schools under their charge more frequently than they are visited by the Government Inspector, to report to the authority appointing them, and to assist the managers and teachers in giving effect to the recommendations and suggestions of H.M.'s Inspectors. The withdrawal of the Government grant, which would lead to the closing of the school, would be the ultimate penalty of inefficiency; and it would be better that inefficient schools should be closed than that they should continue to be carried on with means inadequate to their proper maintenance. It may be, that the managers of voluntary schools would resent this further outside interference with their work; but I cannot help thinking that the supporters of denominational schools, if they wish to continue to retain in their own hands the practical management of their schools, must be prepared to give the public some further guarantee of efficiency, than is at present afforded by the annual report of the Government Inspector.

In France, the system of inspection is much more developed than in this country. "French schools," says a recent writer on the subject, "are certainly not under-inspected. They are subject to six or seven inspections; to wit, inspectors-general, rectors and inspectors of the academy, primary inspectors, members of the Departmental Council (who are *not* teachers), the mayor and Cantonal delegates (for sanitation) and the medical inspector."* In the French system, there are three grades of inspectors; the Primary inspectors, the Academy inspector, and the Inspector-General. The Primary inspector has to report on each separate class, with observations on the condition of the school, the course of instruction and suggestions for improvements, and he also reports on each teacher. The Academy Inspector, whose duties comprise the inspection of all educational institutions in his district, inspects the schools to see that the Education Acts are properly carried out. He has also " to arrange for the examination of teachers and training colleges. It is his business to oppose the opening of a private school where, in his opinion, it is undesirable. He also has to undertake the censure, reprimand, and provisional suspension of unsatisfactory teachers. The actual dismissal of a teacher is the duty of the Prefet or chief magistrate of the Department. The Academy Inspector reports to the Departmental Council of Education, which is responsible for establishing and maintaining schools in the Department. The Inspectors-General are few in number and act as advisers to the Minister of Education." †

With the abolition of payment on results, the Education Department would continue to prescribe, through its Code, the course of study to be pursued in all elementary schools receiving state aid; and it would be the duty of the Government inspector to see that the provisions of the Code are faithfully observed. Within the lines laid down by the Code, there should be considerable latitude for the

---

* "Elementary Education at the Paris Exhibition,' by J. G. Rooper (*Charity Organisation Review*, February, 1890).
† *Ibid.*

adaptation of the teaching to local needs; but it is far better that the general character of the instruction should be settled by a competent central authority than that it should be left to the caprice and independent judgment of different groups of managers or teachers. The fund-subscribing public will always look to the fund-distributing government for a guarantee that the children receive a thorough and serviceable education.

As regards the Code itself, there is now some approach to agreement as to the character of the changes needed to make our elementary instruction more practical and more useful. It is generally admitted that all boys, from whom our future artizans will be selected, should learn linear drawing, and that the teaching of freehand and model drawing should be encouraged both among boys and girls, and especially among those who show any artistic skill. To these, also, modelling in clay should be taught; but it is very undesirable that such instruction, except as a Kindergarten exercise, should be given to children, who have no taste for it, with the mere object of earning a grant. Teachers and managers may be trusted to develop the artistic aptitude which any of the children in their schools may exhibit, if, without injury to the school income, they are free to substitute drawing and modelling for some other branch of study, or some other form of manual training.

On the advantage of instruction in the use of tools, as a form of manual training, public opinion is no longer divided. The hesitating recommendation of the Commissioners on Technical Instruction in their first Report, followed up by the more decided recommendation in their final Report, and supported by the strenuous efforts of more than one member of the Commission, has resulted in the introduction, with excellent results, of workshop instruction, sometimes under the name of Slöjd, into a large number of schools. These results have received no encouragement by way of grants, but they have been none the less satisfactory. The experiment tried by the School Board for London, with funds supplied by the City Companies, has been sufficiently successful to justify its extension. Other School Boards, notably that of Liverpool, are now engaged in giving workshop teaching in some of the schools under their charge, and many of the voluntary schools are adopting it. There is no doubt that children are deeply interested in any form of teaching which occupies their hand; and the advantage of manual training as an educational discipline consists in this, that it arouses attentiveness, exercises the eye in observing accurately, and at the same time stimulates thought. Drawing, by itself, is a most useful part of manual training, but it needs to be supplemented by some constructive work. The experience of the well-known school of the Rue Tournefort, Paris, that the time devoted to manual exercises in no way interferes with, but rather stimulates, the children's progress in other studies has been generally confirmed by the results obtained in other schools. Every one now knows, or should know, that handicraft instruction in a school is quite distinct from trade-teaching in a shop. The methods and the end in view are different. In the school, as well as in the shop, skill is necessarily acquired, but in the one it is intelligent, in the other mechanical. In the school, the aim is to develop thought by means of hand and eye training; in the shop, the aim is to secure manual dexterity only.

To the French people is undoubtedly due the initiation of this important movement in popular education. During the last ten years, manual instruction has been gradually introduced into nearly all the primary schools of France, and is continued and developed in the higher elementary and apprenticeship schools. Student-teachers, in French normal colleges, are now required, as a part of their training, to take a course of workshop instruction, and the most sceptical observer must have been convinced of the value of this teaching, by the splendid show of school work at the Paris Exhibition. "It is quite safe to say that no such exhibit of educational buildings, apparatus, furniture, methods of teaching and work accomplished by scholars has ever been seen before," writes Dr. Butler of New York. The advocates of manual training have had to encounter two classes of objectors:—those who fail to see the difference between teaching carpentry as a trade and as an intellectual exercise, and those who argue that as the majority of children, trained in our elementary schools, will be occupied during their whole life with manual pursuits, their too brief school life should be devoted to studies that tend to inculcate a love of reading, and will afford them useful knowledge. The inspection of school children at work under a competent and trained teacher, not a mere mechanic, but one who understands the objects and methods of manual training, will at once indicate the difference between school teaching and trade teaching in the workshop; and the experience already acquired shows that practical instruction in woodwork and drawing is not only helpful to a child in his subsequent work, but enables him to give closer attention to his ordinary studies and to derive more real benefit from them. Lord Armstrong very justly says: "Except in teaching the art of drawing, no attempt is at present made to educate the hand. The addition of drawing would be a step in the right direction and would afford a useful accomplishment, but would not supply all that is needed for giving dexterity to the hand. Appropriate exercises ought to be devised for cultivating its mobility, precision and delicacy in touch; and, if in so doing, the ability to use simple tools were acquired, it would be advantageous in any line of life that might be ultimately adopted." *

Notwithstanding the practice of the school of the Rue Tournefort, it is now generally recognized that children should not commence to use tools at a very young age, and that the instruction is most profitably pursued in the 5th, 6th, and 7th Standards. To prevent any break of continuity in the manual training of the child from the time when he leaves the Infant School, some continuation of Kindergarten exercises is needed; and this, it is now suggested to supply, under

* "Nineteenth Century," June, 1888.

the name of Advanced Kindergarten. A scheme for such instruction has been carefully thought out by Mr. Ricks, the London School Board Inspector, and comprises exercises in paper-work, colour-work, cardboard-work, clay-work, and wood-work. These exercises continue the Kindergarten teaching, from the time when children leave the Infant school, till they are fit to commence workshop instruction. Throughout these exercises drawing is combined with construction and design. The children have to make patterns involving arrangements of form and colour. They construct geometrical and other models out of simple materials, and thus combine outline ornamentation with the application of colour to design. In this way, besides acquiring some skill in constructive work, they learn the simple geometrical properties of surface and solid figures, and the rudiments of ornamental art. Modelling in clay is a valuable addition to such exercises, and one of never-failing interest to children. Mr. Ricks is quite right in saying that "unless the element of construction is added, drawing must fail to yield the full measure of good which may be expected from it." The hand and eye training which this system of Advanced Kindergarten helps to develop, affords an opportunity of determining to some extent the taste and special aptitudes of the children under instruction, and of ascertaining which of them might with advantage receive further training in drawing and designing.

Another development of Kindergarten should be in the direction of Natural Science, which, by means of object-lessons, should be taught throughout the Standards. The failure of the grant system to promote sound science-teaching has been already referred to. There is little doubt that if the amount of grant no longer depended on results, as tested by examination, and if all schools to be accounted efficient, and so to receive State aid, were required to give some instruction in Science, this blot on our present system would be removed.

It is quite possible, that owing to the consensus of opinion on this subject, the new Code may give further encouragement to the teaching of Science in our schools. But even so, the principle that will regulate the selection of subjects, the methods of teaching, and the time devoted to it, will be a wrong one. Monetary considerations, rather than local needs, will enter into the calculations of most school managers.

If drawing, handicraft, and science, are to be taught throughout the Standards, it necessarily follows that time must be found by sacrificing some subject of the present curriculum; and it is, I think, generally agreed that the more advanced parts of English grammar can best be spared. The children of our working classes will find themselves very little, if any, worse off in later life, if during their short school course they devote considerably less time to the study of the complicated rules for the analysis of sentences. In the hands of a good teacher some amount of mental discipline may be evolved from lessons on the several forms of the extension of the subject and predicate of a sentence, and on the definitions of the different parts of speech. But how much of this acquired knowledge will a child retain a year after he has left school? It has been fixed in the mind by nothing that appeals to the senses. Acquired with great difficulty, it is never likely to be applied. It is altogether out of touch with the future thoughts, experiences, and occupations of the child. The links of association necessary to revive it are not likely to exist. Can it be said that such exercises create,—what is most desirable,—a love of reading, or even an intelligent appreciation of the beauty of the passages that are subjected to this process of analysis? Surely school life is too short to be occupied with cumbering the memory with useless freight that will be thrown overboard as soon as the child is fairly launched in life. The science of education has happily shown that there are other subjects of instruction which yield even more mental discipline and are at the same time practically useful. Let grammar, then, and, to some extent, spelling also, give place to them!

If our elementary education is to be reorganised on some such lines as I have indicated, a certain definite direction must be given to it, which managers and teachers, unfettered by any considerations of the grant-earning capacity of the scholars, will be required to follow. This direction should be indicated by the Code, and it would be the duty of the inspector to see that the regulations of the Code are duly enforced. The Code should determine the general curriculum of the school. It should prescribe the studies and the degree of efficiency in each subject, which each standard might be expected to reach. It should regulate the division of time between practical and other studies, and the time-table of each teacher should be approved, as now, by the chief inspector. But, within certain limits, considerable freedom as to subjects, methods and arrangements should be left to the managers and teachers. The Code should assist the managers and teachers by indicating the range of progressive lessons in different groups of subjects, from which a selection might be made, adapted to the circumstances and local requirements of each particular district. If the fetters of "payment by results" were removed, there would be more elasticity in the teaching, and each school, within the general lines laid down, would develop according to its needs. Moreover, a better educated and more cultivated class of persons would be attracted to the teacher's profession; and before long, we should find, that intelligent teaching had taken the place of the mechanical drill, which is incidental to the present system of distributing State aid.

There is another change, more closely connected with the one here advocated than is generally supposed, to which many of us now hopefully look forward. As a measure of justice to the poorer classes, and as relieving the teachers from irksome, onerous and anxious duties, which largely interfere with strictly educational work, the abolition of school fees is a reform urgently needed, and one which in many interests should not be long delayed. I believe, however, that this reform might be more easily accomplished, if undertaken in conjunction with such changes in our Code, as would enable us to dispense with "payment on results."

The three planks that constitute the platform of the new

educational departure are (1) Abolition of payment on results; (2) Practical teaching; (3) Free Schools; and I have placed them in the order of importance. I believe that a great part of the difficulty raised by the question of the existence and public control of voluntary schools might be met by extending and strengthening our system of inspection. Indeed, I think that the two questions of "payment on results" and "school fees" might be more easily considered together than apart. The question of "free schools" is no longer an open one. The principle, at least, is conceded. What we want is to discover a means of reconciling with free education the continued existence of really efficient voluntary schools, and of providing, whilst leaving them to a great extent under denominational control, a public guarantee of their efficiency. The problem, although a difficult one, should not defy solution. It demands, however, separate and careful consideration. What I now urge is, that precedence be given to the question of "payment on results"; and, I believe, that the means to be adopted to ensure the efficiency of our schools, without recourse to this much-abused system, will open the door to a solution of the problem of Free Schools.

Philip Magnus.

PART XI.
NEW CODE FOR 1890.

THE new code for 1890, which has recently been laid before Parliament and which is to come into force on the 1st September next, marks a very distinct advance in the system of elementary education in this country. The recommendations of the late Royal Commission on Education have been much more extensively embodied than in the ill-fated draft code of last year—a circumstance which largely accounts for its more favourable reception.

It is questionable, however, whether even this measure treats with sufficient boldness the various points needing improvement in our educational system—witness, for instance, the hesitating manner in which ampler opportunities of self-culture are claimed for pupil teachers. Compared, however, with previously existing arrangements, and viewed merely as a considerable instalment of the improvements needed, the new Code of 1890 is an important step in advance.

In the following sketch of its contents the provisions have been grouped under different heads, and in notes at foot have been given, as far as possible, references to the recommendations of the Royal Commission upon which the new regulations have been based.

Though the general framework of the Code is similar to that of its immediate predecessors, the document differs so much from them, both in substance and in wording, as to be practically an entirely new one. Accordingly the schedule of changes which is usually appended to each new edition of the Education Department's regulations is omitted on the present occasion. Many of the changes, however, are merely formal, and have in view rather the rendering of the document self-consistent and in harmony with the actual practice of the Department than the introduction of new provisions.

General Conditions.—Except in one respect these do not differ very materially from those in previous editions of the Code.

The school must be a public elementary school; children must not be refused on other than reasonable grounds; the provisions of the Elementary Education Act, 1870, in respect of Time Tables must be complied with; the school must not be unnecessary; it must not be conducted for private profit—this provision being, not altogether unnecessarily, emphasized on the present occasion by an added prohibition of the school being "farmed out by the managers to the teacher;" it must, if a day school, have met not less than 400 times—with exceptions in case of epidemics or elections, &c., &c.—

with certain conditions as to premises, staff, furniture, apparatus, instruction and registers, upon which later provisions dwell more in detail. A schedule of building regulations is added to which in future all new schools or enlargements of existing schools must conform, but which are not otherwise to apply to schools now in operation. The material change is that which provides for the entire withholding of the grant in case of continued inefficiency; before however this course can be resorted to, the Inspector must report " specifically the grounds " of his adverse judgment, and " the Department must, with the report, give formal warning to the managers that the grant may be withheld . . . at the next annual inspection, if the Inspector again reports the school . . . to be inefficient;" while even in the event of a second unfavourable report the managers are to be allowed an appeal to the Chief Inspector against the Inspector's decision, and in that case it is only in the event of the unfavourable report being confirmed by that of the Chief Inspector that the grant is to be withdrawn.

A copy of the accounts of the school and a notice that the report may be seen at the school is to be posted for at least 14 days on the school-door or on some other public place in the school district immediately upon receipt of the annual report.* In these accounts express permission is now given to include the salary paid to a teacher of drawing, manual instruction or laundry work whether such teacher is " at a central class " or is " a peripatetic teacher "; this is an extension of the like permission previously given in respect of teachers of drill, cookery, or any other special subject.

Subjects of Instruction.—The subjects for which grants may be made, are, as in previous Codes, divided primarily into " Obligatory" and " Optional " subjects, and the latter subdivided into (1) such as are " taken by classes throughout the school," and (2) such as are " taken by individual children in the upper classes of the school "—a third group, consisting of subjects taken only by girls, being added in the present Code. The " obligatory " subjects consist of the three " elementary subjects "—Reading, Writing and Arithmetic—of Needlework for girls in Day Schools, and of Drawing for boys in other than Infant Schools†—the grant, however, for this last subject is to be made by the Science and Art, and not by the Education, Department. The " optional subjects " taken by classes consist of Singing, Recitation, Drawing for boys in Infant Schools, and of the subjects called as heretofore " Class Subjects," viz. :—English, Geography, Elementary Science, History, and (for girls) Needlework—the special preference hitherto given to English being abolished.‡ The " optional subjects " taken by individual children are, as before, called " Specific Subjects " and consist not only of those included in former Codes—Algebra, Euclid, Mensuration, Mechanics, Chemistry, Physics, Animal Physiology, Botany, Principles of Agriculture, Latin, French, and (for girls) Domestic Economy—but also of four others introduced now for the

---

* Recommendations 13 and 21.
† Recommendations 99 and 117.
‡ Recommendation 90.

first time—Welsh (for schools in Wales),* German, Bookkeeping, and Shorthand. The "optional subjects" taken only by girls include the new one of "Laundry Work" as well as the former one of "Cookery." It is further provided, as before, that any other subject besides those previously enumerated may, "if sanctioned by the Department," be taken as a Specific Subject for a grant; and the right of Managers to provide instruction "in other secular subjects, and in religious subjects" for which no grant is made, again receives distinct recognition. It is not, of course, contemplated that all these subjects shall be taken by the same children or even in the same school. Of the optional subjects, no scholar may take, in addition to Singing and Recitation, more than two of the Class, and two of the Specific Subjects—the latter being moreover limited exclusively to children presented for examination in a Standard above the Fourth. Girls who take Cookery do so to the exclusion of one of the Specific Subjects, and Laundry Work to the exclusion either of Cookery or of the other Specific Subject.

Besides the subjects for which grants are provided, permission is given for Manual Instruction, Physical Exercises, and (for boys) Military Drill to be taught in the two hours required in a Day School to make "up the minimum time constituting an attendance;" and also for instruction in these subjects—as well as in Drawing, Science, Cookery, and Laundry Work—to be given elsewhere than "in the school premises" and by other than "the ordinary teachers of the school." No syllabus for "Manual Instruction" is laid down nor any grant for its instruction provided—the subject being scarcely more capable of individual examination than Cookery or Laundry Work, and therefore not one that can be taken as a Specific Subject. The suggestion that is made in Art. 85 (*b*) that Manual Instruction may be directly connected with Drawing may perhaps point to its being, like that subject, encouraged by a grant from the Science and Art Department.

Syllabuses.—Of the Elementary Subjects and of those of the Specific Subjects which were included in previous Codes, syllabuses not differing materially from those of former years are given in the Schedules. But of the new Specific Subjects syllabuses have not yet been prepared, and those of the Class Subjects have been largely remodelled—that for History being entirely new.† With regard to the Class Subjects, however, a most valuable feature has been introduced in the form of "Alternative Courses," ‡ of which no less than four are given for the one subject "English," three for Geography, one for Geography and History combined, and as many as eight for elementary Science,§ each of which provides for a series of systematized object lessons being given in Standards I. and II. preparatory to the more definite teaching in the later standards.‖ Of the alternative courses in English and Geography, one is in each case

---

* Recommendation 108.
† Recommendations 95 to 98.
‡ Recommendation 88.
§ Recommendation 120.
‖ Recommendation 121.

specially prepared for use in small rural schools. Not content with even this provision for elasticity, the Code concedes to Managers permission, in respect both of Class and of Specific Subjects, to frame courses of their own, merely requiring that they shall obtain the approval of the Inspector of the district.*

Examination of Scholars.—With regard to Infant Schools no alteration is made in this respect; but in the examination of schools for older scholars most important changes are introduced. Individual examination in the elementary subjects is no longer to be universal; but, instead, "the scholars will be examined, as a rule, by sample, not less than one-third being individually examined," though "if the Managers so desire," scholars in Standards III. to VII. "may be examined individually throughout." The examination is not to be limited, as heretofore, to scholars "whose names have, at the end of the school year, been on the registers for the last 22 weeks that the school has been open," but may include any child whose name is on the register. If proper care is taken, that the credit of the school shall not be unduly affected by the success or failure of children who have been only recently admitted, the extension of examination to the whole school will be a valuable improvement; for it will take away one of the artificial obstacles which have hitherto retarded the progress of scholars. Another, and perhaps a more serious one, will be removed by the new provision, that " the Standards in which scholars are presented for examination need not be the same for each subject."†

The methods of examination in Class, and Specific, subjects remain unchanged; but it is provided, that the children need not be examined "in the same standards in Class subjects as in Elementary subjects, nor need they be presented in the same Standards in both Class subjects," and that the Class subjects "taken may be different for different classes."

Grants.—The grants to Infant Schools remain practically as before ‡—the only changes being that if the boys are taught drawing instead of needlework a grant of the same amount may be made for the former as for the latter subject; that the merit grant is now denominated "a variable grant;" and that the determination of its amount is reserved to the Department instead of being left to the Inspector. With regard, however, to schools for older scholars the system is very considerably changed. The "fixed grant," the "merit grant," and the "percentage grant" on elementary subjects disappear, and are replaced by "a principal grant" of 12s. 6d. or 14s., and "a grant for discipline and organization" of 1s. or 1s. 6d. The lower of the two amounts is in each case to be a "fixed grant," to be reduced only in case any of the general conditions of annual grants are not fulfilled. The determination whether the lower or the higher grant is to be given is reserved to the Department after consideration of the Inspector's report and recommendation—subject,

---

* Recommendation 87.
† Recommendations 78 and 115.
‡ Recommendation 169.

however, to the condition that the higher principal grant will not be given "unless the Inspector reports that the scholars throughout the school are satisfactorily taught Recitation." The "needlework grant," the "singing grant," the "class grants," and the "specific subjects grant," are practically unaltered—except that the determination whether the higher or lower class grant shall be given is reserved to the Department, and that specific subjects grants are not to be made to "any school in which, at the last preceding inspection, the managers did not obtain a Principal Grant of 14s." As the latter is, among other things, conditional upon Recitation being satisfactorily taught, it follows that the specific subjects grant can be obtained only by schools in which Recitation is taken. This result, if intended, appears to attach a somewhat exaggerated importance to the learning of a number of lines of poetry. The "grant for cookery" remains as before, except that in future the school of cookery which certifies the teacher must be one "recognized by the Department," the lessons must be of not less than 1½ hours' duration, not more than 8 hours in any one week may be devoted to this subject, and demonstration-lessons may not be given while the pupils are engaged in practice-lessons. For the new subject of "laundry-work" a grant of 2s. is made on account of any girl presented in Standards IV. to VII. "who has attended not less than 20 hours during the school year at a laundry class of not more than 14 scholars."

The special grants for evening schools, pupil-teachers, assistant-teachers, and small schools respectively, will be referred to later in the paragraphs dealing more particularly with those subjects.

Staff.—The requirements under this head are somewhat increased.[*] The head teacher may still be reckoned as sufficient for an average attendance of 60 scholars, but a certificated assistant-teacher is to count for only 70 if trained, or 60 if untrained instead of 80 as heretofore, an assistant for 50 instead of 60, and an "additional female teacher" or a pupil-teacher for 30 instead of 40—a "candidate" on probation continuing as before to count for 20. In the case of Infant classes, also, the requirements are slightly raised—an adult teacher being required if the class exceeds 30 (instead of 40) and a certificated teacher being demanded when the attendance reaches 50 (instead of 60). In case, however, of a casual vacancy for any but the principal teacher occurring during the school year, temporary monitors may, for the remainder of that year, be employed instead—one being accepted as sufficient for 30, and two for 60, scholars. "Lay persons alone are recognised as teachers in a day school." For small schools, to which on that account additional grants are to be made, a somewhat stronger proportionate staff than that above mentioned will be required.

Pupil Teachers.—The general regulations with regard to these young teachers remain much as before, but additional precautions are taken to secure greater care in their selection and training.

---

[*] Recommendation 22.

NEW CODE FOR 1890.

Before they are apprenticed they must not only as heretofore pass an entrance examination and produce certificates of good character and good health, but "must" also "be presented to the Inspector for approval." It is further provided that the managers must "see that the pupil-teacher is properly instructed during the engagement," and that if "this duty is neglected" the Department "may decline to recognise any pupil-teachers as members of the staff of a school under the same managers." The managers are further required to report annually on the manner in which the head teachers have performed their duties to the pupil-teachers. The right of superintending pupil-teachers may be withdrawn from any certificated teacher whom the Department may consider to have neglected his duty in this respect. It is no longer required that the instruction received by a pupil-teacher shall be "out of school hours,"—a change which will facilitate the grouping of pupil-teachers for central class instruction, by permitting such instruction to be given, on other days than Saturday, in the day-time, and not as at present, exclusively in the evening. The annual examinations are to be continued, and two consecutive failures to pass either of the required examinations, unless from illness or other sufficient cause, is to entail the consequence that the "pupil-teacher will no longer be recognised by the Department;" but before the managers are informed that the pupil-teacher has failed in either of the first three years' examinations "the papers will be further revised in the Department." For the present fourth year's examination that for Queen's Scholarships is substituted; which may be taken either during the fourth year of apprenticeship or, in the cases where the apprenticeship terminates on the 31st December or the 30th June, or at any time between those dates, on the first occasion "following the conclusion" of the engagement. If the latter date is chosen it will be "the duty of the managers" to see that the pupil-teachers "are properly instructed up to the date of examination," and the pupil-teachers will continue to be recognised as such by the Department until the result of the examination is known. The withdrawal, as contemplated by the draft Code of last year, of the grants hitherto made towards the cost of training pupil-teachers has been reconsidered, and instead, the apportionment of the grant has been revised. In place of a uniform payment of £3 and £2 respectively for a pupil-teacher who passes the annual examination well or fairly, no matter at the end of what year, there is in future to be a scale of payments increasing with the progress of the apprenticeship. £2 is to be paid for each first or second, and £3 for each third year pupil-teacher who passes well, £1 and £2 respectively being paid for the corresponding pupil-teachers who pass fairly—while £5 (or £4) is to be paid for each fourth year pupil-teacher who secures a place in the First (or Second) Class at the Queen's Scholarship Examination.

For the future pupil-teachers will not, after the completion of their apprenticeship, be recognised as assistant teachers, unless they pass the Queen's Scholarship Examination; with regard, however, to the present ex-pupil-teachers, it is not stated whether their continued recognition will be in any way similarly affected. Recognition as "provisionally certificated teachers" is for the future to be restricted to "pupil-teachers who have obtained a place in the first class in the Queen's Scholarship Examination."

Assistant Teachers.—These are, as at present to consist of "persons who have passed the Queen's Scholarship Examination," of "graduates of any University in the United Kingdom," and of "women over eighteen years of age who have passed University and other examinations recognised by the Department"—to the list of which examinations several important additions are made, including the Durham University's second year examination in Arts, the Victoria University's Preliminary Examination and the College of Preceptors' Examination for the teacher's diploma. It should be observed that the Queen's Scholarship Examination is not limited to pupil-teachers, but is open to any person who will be over eighteen years of age on the following 1st of January; and that candidates who are not successful the first time are allowed one further opportunity of passing this examination. To encourage managers to provide facilities for their assistant teachers to qualify themselves for certificates, a grant of £15, or £10, is made to them for each of such teachers who, after serving for three years in that capacity, and receiving during that time special instruction under arrangements approved by the Department, obtains a place in the first, or second, division on second year's papers at the certificate examination.

Certificated Teachers.—The whole complicated system of First, Second, and Third Class certificates which has hitherto prevailed is summarily abolished, and for the future there will be "only one class of certificate;" but only those teachers who pass in the first or second division on second year's papers will be permitted to have the charge of pupil-teachers. Acting teachers will be required, like students in training colleges, to pass on first year's papers as well as on second year's—with an interval of at least one year between the two examinations. They must also obtain from the Inspector a favourable report on their teaching power before each examination. These examinations are to be held as at present at the existing training colleges each December; provision is, however, made for similar examinations being held not only as now at other places, but also at other *times*. This latter provision has probably in view the possible needs of the Day Training Colleges now contemplated—to which reference is made later. Certificated teachers who are not entitled to have the charge of pupil-teachers may be re-examined at intervals of not less than two years, with a view to qualifying themselves for that duty. The right, however, of superintending pupil-teachers may be withdrawn if the Department consider that the teacher has neglected his duty to the pupil-teachers under his charge.

Admission to a training college as a Queen's Scholar is to be limited, as at present, to those who obtain places in the first or second class in the Queen's Scholarship Examinations, and to "acting teachers" who have past the First Year's Certificate Examination. The general arrangements with regard to (residential) training colleges remain practically unaltered, except that the approval of the Department is needed to the "curriculum and general arrangements" as well as to "the premises, management and staff," and that a third year of training may, "with the consent of the Department," be allowed to any particular student, but, apparently, without any corresponding increase of grant.

Parchment certificates will, as at present, be issued after the usual period of probation; and it is now provided that "service" in a training college will be recognised for this purpose. But entries upon teachers' parchment certificates will for the future be entirely discontinued.

Day Training Colleges.—A new departure in the matter of the training of teachers is contemplated by the establishment of non-residential Training Colleges * and the admission of non-resident students into ordinary Training Colleges.† The change is to be introduced experimentally and on a limited scale ‡—not more than 200 day students being recognised at one and the same time as Queen's Scholars; and it is required that a Day Training College shall "be attached to some University or College of University rank." § Bursaries of £25 will be allowed to each male, and of £20 to each female non-resident student towards the cost of their maintenance, and a grant of £10 a year made to the Training College for their instruction and professional preparation.

Evening Schools.—The arrangements as to grants to Evening Schools remain unchanged in their general features. A "fixed grant" of 4s. will still be made on the average attendance of a school which has been open 45, and of 6s. on that of one open 61 or more times; and a grant of 2s. will be made for each "pass" in any elementary or special (*i.e.* Class or Specific) subject, provided that the scholar examined has attended the school for eight weeks and has made at least 24 attendances. Several important changes, however, are made in the detailed arrangements—which, it may be hoped, will remove some of the evils which have of late years tended to discourage evening schools. Pupils who have passed the Fifth Standard in a Public Elementary School (day or evening) need no longer be examined in elementary subjects,‖ but may be presented in not "less than two or more than four of the special subjects." As in the day schools "the Standards in which scholars are presented need not be the same for all subjects," but pupils who have not passed the Fifth Standard must be presented in some standard in each of the three elementary subjects. "Cookery" is recognised as a "special subject" for girls "presented in Standard IV. or any higher Standard" provided that, in addition to the 24 attendances required to qualify for any examination grant, the girls have attended the cookery class for 20 hours, and have spent 10 hours in cooking with their own hands.

Small Schools.—In addition to the special grant of £10 or £15 made under the provisions of Section 19 of the Elementary Educa-

---

* Recommendation 40.
† Recommendation 41.
‡ Recommendations 40, 42, and 45 (4).
§ Recommendation 42.
‖ Recommendation 142.

tion Act of 1876 to schools in districts with a population of less than 300 or 200 respectively, a further special grant of £10 may be made to any school, situated in a district in which the population is less than 500, or where the population within two miles of the school does not exceed that number, provided that "there is no other public " elementary school recognised by the Department as available for that district or that population." This additional grant, however, is not to be made unless the fees charged in the school " are suitable to the population," and the staff more ample than the minimum ordinarily required for an attendance of the like amount.* For the latter purpose the principal teacher is to be reckoned as sufficient for only 40 instead of 60 scholars, an assistant teacher for 30 instead of 50, a pupil-teacher for 20 instead of 30, and a candidate for 10 instead of 20.

Among the Recommendations of the Royal Commission to which apparently effect might have but has not been given in the Code may be enumerated, Recommendation 173 for grants in aid of the Salaries of organizing Masters and of itinerant teachers; Recommendation 152 for liberal grants to be made, as in Scotland, for advanced instruction to scholars who have passed the highest standard; Recommendation 32 for extra grants to be made to managers who extend to their pupil-teachers the advantages of central class instruction. Recommendation 79 for the encouragement of School libraries; and Recommendation 110 for the introduction of a system of physical instruction.

Recommendation 140.

PART XII.
EDITORIAL SUMMARY AND CONCLUSION.

The preceding essays have been written, not to prove the value of education, for that is a truism which not even the most reactionary member of any civilised community would in our day venture to deny; but rather to show how indispensable it is to progress, and what an advantage is enjoyed by those nations amongst whom it is the most carefully fostered.

It has been shown that in India educational institutions, although they have been established by foreign rulers and even in an alien tongue, are bringing into closer union and imparting a new national life to vast populations of varying creeds and races; that the same potent influences are breaking down the superstitions and prejudices of centuries; and are elevating not only the men of those lands, but also the women, who almost from time immemorial have been regarded as mere creatures of convenience, and amongst some oriental races are even now believed to be without a soul. And when, in the last connexion, we read the account of what education has done for the fair sex in Western lands, a narrative here recorded by one of themselves possessing wide experience and holding a high position in the literary and journalistic world, we find that although there may be some walks of life for which her physical frame and her place in Nature have unfitted her, yet in other vocations which were hitherto regarded as the exclusive privilege of Man, his helpmate Woman is displaying remarkable intelligence and activity without in any way interfering with her general usefulness in the domestic circle. There can be little doubt that this renaissance of Woman will further the spread of refinement and civilisation; and it is not hoping too much, that it may initiate a new era of chivalry shorn of its ancient coarseness, and of its more than doubtful morality.

Turning to the distinctive features in the educational systems of various countries and the effect they have produced or are producing on the national life and character, we find that in many States both of the Old and New World universally gratuitous and compulsory instruction has been long in operation, and that in those countries the lower classes have attained a higher standard of knowledge than where such a system is absent or but recently introduced. Other conditions being equal, the effect of gratuitous primary education is undoubtedly to diminish pauperism and mendicancy and to add to the national prosperity. At first sight it may appear strange that the system should not have been established in this country, but anyone who has studied the influence of our insular position in this and other matters will easily understand the cause. It is all of a piece with our backwardness in adopting easier and more scientific methods of calculating weights and values, and whilst the old-fashioned " weights and measures " are driven into the brains of the rising generation, hardly any trouble is taken to make them acquainted with the more rational systems of other countries. A glance at the latest education Code shows that only in the sixth standard the word " decimal " makes its appearance, and then care is taken to notify that " questions involving recurring decimals will not be put to girls."

The objection to gratuitous education has not arisen so much from religious prejudice or bigotry (for it is found to exist in countries where superstition and intolerance run high,) as from a desire not to interfere with existing methods and to respect " vested interests." A remarkable illustration of this tendency in our people and one that is quite germane to the question at issue is the training of the deaf and dumb in this country. It is now pretty generally, but by no means universally known that the old system of " dactylology " or finger-speaking by which the deaf were formerly taught to communicate with the world, is rapidly giving place to the new or " Oral " method, which enables persons so afflicted to *speak*, and to follow the motions of the lips in conversation, with more or less facility. But we are so far behind other countries in this reform that even intelligent writers in our journals regard the oral method as one that is just discovered, and a leader-writer in one of our principal daily papers stated recently that it had made rapid progress since its introduction into England " about eight years ago." The fact is that the oral system, which has been largely employed in Holland and elsewhere for half-a-century, was introduced into this country quite thirty years since in private families, and an able teacher of the new system was engaged by our Government and sent to fill the post of Superintendent of the Deaf and Dumb institutions of New Zealand about fifteen years ago. But a comparison of the systems existing all over the world shows that in England alone the old barbarous method (for barbarous it is, inasmuch as it keeps the deaf who are able to articulate dumb all their lives) is still largely in vogue, and is by many well-meaning persons warmly defended; whilst in some places a truly English compromise, known as the " combined system " is employed. As a matter of fact the old mode of instruction has been retained because the supply of efficient teachers of the oral method is restricted; because the teachers of the finger-system have found it easier to convince Committees of Management that the new system is imperfect than to master it themselves; and where the Committees have known better they have hesitated to dismiss the teachers and engage others more competent; and finally because many of the clergy who take an active part in the religious instruction of the deaf and dumb, besides having a dread and an abhorrence of anything emanating from the Continent, find it more convenient to impart such instruction indirectly through an interpreter than to qualify themselves for direct communication with the children. It is to be hoped that the interest which is being awakened in this phase of the Education question will lead to a more rational treatment of what are known as deaf-mutes, and we have dwelt upon it here because it explains much that is backward and imperfect in other branches of Education. We have seen, for example, that whilst in nearly every other country training schools for teachers have been founded and are managed by the State, and the attendance at them is gratuitous, here they are denominational only, however liberally they may be aided by the State; and that the scarcity of trained instructors perpetuates a system of "pupil-teachers" which is admittedly a makeshift. That the Government is beginning to awaken to its responsibility in this respect is witnessed by the extension of training facilities afforded by the New Code. The zeal which the people of the United States have thrown into this movement is seen in the "Teacher's Institutes" which have been described by our esteemed writer on American Education, and we can testify from personal observation to the great benefits which they are conferring upon the educational world of the West. Those conferences have been in existence there for many years, and no time should be lost in establishing similar institutions in Great Britain. We are surprised that the Scotch have not long since taken the initiative.

The defects of the system of "payment on results" have also been recognised and in part remedied by the New Code, and whilst it is certainly undesirable that the State should relax its vigilance, and that inefficient teaching should be permitted, there is still a "retail" look about the whole method of remunerating teachers, which is unworthy of a great people. What will after-generations say when they take up the perfected Code, and read that whilst a teacher receives a fixed grant of 12s. 6d. each, for his older pupils, he is entitled to the munificent sum of 1s. 6d. extra, if their memory has been trained, or it may be tortured, until they are capable of reciting 150 lines of Milton or Shakespeare!

To return to "free schools," however: If there be one principle upon which all thoughtful persons seem to be agreed it is that elementary education which is compulsory, should also be gratuitous, and it is no longer a question whether, but when and by whom it shall be granted. It is much to be regretted that with the means in hand the present Government has not conferred that boon upon the people. Sectarianism, as usual, stops the way, and, for the moment, the clergy having taken fright, have influenced the Government to inaction. But this cannot be of long duration; the Liberal party is pledged to free education, and if the Prime Minister was correctly reported, he told his followers at a secret conclave that his party are bound to deal with the matter; for if left untouched by the present Government and their opponents should obtain a majority, they would deal with it in such a manner that the voluntary schools would be swept away.

This was a most unfortunate mode of explaining the situation. Few, if any, wish to sweep away denominational schools, nor is it right that those who have done so much for education in the past, and whose exertions are still active in the cause, should have their zeal damped or their antagonism aroused by drastic measures. It is estimated that during the last 20 years seven and a half millions have been expended by denominationalism in providing school accommodation for children, and this alone entitles them to respect and consideration. The real question at issue is whether the State shall exercise extended control in granting extended aid, and those who are best acquainted with the views of Parliament have expressed the opinion that if a measure of moderate popular local control (and the present Government would make it as moderate as possible) were proposed in Parliament it would meet with the acquiescence of the whole of the Liberal party and of half the Conservatives. The votes of the "dissentient Liberals" would therefore count for little, on whichever side they might be recorded.

We have seen that in the most advanced of the United States of America not only is education gratuitous, but its importance to the people is so far recognised as to lead the State authorities to provide books and apparatus for the scholars, and free education for all classes of citizens. And why should free education in England be granted to one class only? Is it fair to the middle classes, especially the lower middle class, that they should not only have to educate their own children, but should be compelled to contribute to the school-rates for the benefit of those of the labouring classes? Is it not a fact that in many instances the artisan is better able to pay for the education of his children than is the clerk or tradesman of limited means? And is not the training of the mind a more vital necessity to those who have to earn their livelihood with the pen than to the artisan working with his hands? It will not be long before these questions will be considered and answered by the middle classes, and "free education" in the broadest sense will be the necessary consequence.

As to the greater advantages of Board or Secular Schools as compared with denominational schools, and the consequent disappearance of the latter, that is a problem which time alone can solve. No one, unless it be the secularists, would desire to see a "Godless" system of education, but that is very different from the association of creeds with secular instruction. Creeds and catechisms may be essential to salvation, but the comparison drawn in our first article, between the Mohammedan and the Hindoo system in the East, and the general results so far in the West, show that where the mind of the young is relieved from the strain of committing creeds and religious formularies to memory, the secular training is more efficient, and such schools prosper where the denominational institutions languish.

But important as the much debated questions of "free" and of "denominational" schools may be, there are others which appear to us of far greater moment. The first of those is the problem which perplexes the local authorities, especially in our large towns, as to how they shall deal with "waifs and strays." This was the primary object for which School Boards were established, for the first duty of the State is to diminish crime, pauperism, and mendicancy, by preparing the children of the poor to earn an honest livelihood. But the end proposed has so far been very partially accomplished. The greatest enemies of universal education are the vicious and criminal classes who will neither work themselves nor give their offspring the chance of gaining their bread by honest industry, for as it has been stated in one of the preceding articles, they train them to beg or steal, or at best allow them to earn a precarious living on the street, instead of labouring for them in their infancy and giving them the best preparation they can afford for their duties in after-life. Here, too, it must be borne in mind, that the shortcomings of the State have been atoned for by the efforts of individuals, and that in the large towns at least, the work of rescue has been mainly undertaken by philanthropic clergymen and laymen, who have not waited for the children to be "committed" before opening the door of reform, but have snatched them from the streets and brought them under civilising influences. In this respect the State has acted to a great extent as in the case of normal schools, giving support to existing institutions, but (excepting in connection with workhouses) taking no initiative. Undoubtedly in any future action the disinterested benefactors of society should be considered and encouraged, but if this country wishes to hold its place amongst the nations, prompt measures will have to be taken to rescue the crowd of poor neglected children who, from no fault of their own, swarm in the streets of our large cities. But here again comes in the convenient cry of "interference with the liberty of the subject," a cry that is too frequently raised in order to block the path of reform. "What is to be done with them?" we are asked. "If you take them away from their parents and put them into industrial institutions, you are interfering with paternal rights, diminishing the responsibility of parents, and depriving the children of their natural guardians." Natural guardians, forsooth! And do you give the children a better chance in life, by putting their parents in gaol, and leaving them to shift for themselves? Both humanity and expediency suggest that the industrial school system must be greatly extended, the streets must be watched more closely, and the work of rescue and punishment undertaken, not by private societies, but by the State and local authorities; the great staring blot upon our national character which is pointed at with scorn by the visitors to our shores, must be wiped out; and *coûte que coûte* the waifs and strays of the rising generation must be rescued from vice and crime, and trained to useful employment, not only for their own advantage, but in the interests of the whole community.

A more delicate matter, one which it is necessary to treat without reserve, but which is not always so handled, is the subject of "technical instruction." The Code just issued shows that there is every desire on the part of the State to adopt the recommendations of the Royal Commission based largely on the experiences and action of other countries. But as a matter of fact the chief opponents of technical or trade instruction are to be found in the ranks of the skilled operatives themselves. Those persons are much more anxious to confine trade-instruction to the workshop and factory than to extend it even in the schools which have been founded for their own benefit. Such men think far less of their children than of themselves, and this is how they reason: "We are at present brought into competition with the sons and friends of our employers, who are sent into the workshop where they get a little manual instruction, and are then placed in authority over us, filling the higher posts whilst we are kept in the position of day-labourers. And not that alone," they add, " but the introduction of machinery makes the career of such intruders into our fields of industry easier, for with the aid of technical knowledge they can work the machine that is supplanting our hand-labour." This last is no imaginary argument. It was recently urged in the public prints by a compositor in one of our large cities, as a reason for discountenancing technical instruction, for, he said, owing to the introduction of machines into the printing-offices which work swifter than men, " persons that have no connexion with the trade would be enabled to foist themselves upon the profession through learning the principles of the business at a technical school."

In this respect the operative reasons precisely as he does when he goes out on strike on insufficient grounds and gives up the fort to the enemy! It is quite true that gentlemen send their sons into workshops to go through a course of manual labour, not often, however, to pick up a smattering of practical work, but to fit themselves thoroughly for the control of a manufacturing concern, and of the men employed therein; and at the same time they take care that their sons shall acquire all the theoretical knowledge necessary for pursuing their avocation. But if the employer teaches his son the workman's trade is that any argument against the workman's securing for his children the knowledge which maintains the employer in his position of superiority? If the facts here stated prove anything, they show that the educated parent of the middle classes teaches his son that he must "stoop to conquer," and that he has greater forethought for his welfare than he of the artisan class has for *his* children. And again, if machinery is supplanting hand-labour owing to its greater efficiency, is that a reason for keeping his children ignorant of the nature and action of such machinery, and of the technical knowledge requisite for its proper construction, management, and repair?

The earnestness with which young men of the middle classes are directing their attention to the study of mechanics, chemistry, &c., arises mainly from the new spheres of enterprise opened up by perfected machinery and improved chemical processes, and it rests with the skilled artisans and operatives whether they will leave the field to young men who study in the colleges, or whether, by taking the control of their own schools and fitting them with the best appliances for trade-instruction, they will help their children to rise above the rank of day-labourers. Neither co-operation nor industrial partnership will avail them unless they train their children's minds as well as their hands. It is unwise of well-intentioned employers and friends of education to bandy words with, or seek to coax the artisan class into the acceptance of trade-instruction by calling it "technical education" which may mean anything or nothing. It is not a pill to be gilt, but a reform in our industrial system which should be welcomed by all intelligent workmen desirous of promoting the welfare of their children. We want and we shall have trade-instruction of two kinds ; one for children in connexion with elementary education (and the New Code looks very promising in that respect), and the other of a more advanced description, such as we find in the programme of the Manchester Technical School, and in agricultural, weaving, and other trade-schools for young persons already established in different parts of the country. Abroad such schools have long existed, and although here their extension may be delayed by the causes already assigned and by the national tardiness, it is only a question of time, and we venture to predict that not a few of those artisans who are the earliest to appreciate their utility, and are prompt to avail themselves of their advantages, will be reckoned amongst the wealthiest and most enterprising capitalists of the future.

But there are other and even graver considerations connected with the spread of education than its bearing upon the material condition of the poorer classes, or upon Woman, or commerce and the national industries. That education is an important factor in the political life of a nation goes without saying. In despotic Russia, which is constantly on the brink of a revolution, it is said that not one in twelve of the populace can either read or write, whilst, looking at the other end of the political scale, we find free Massachusetts possessing the highest degree of education in all classes of society; and Washington long since declared that knowledge is in every country the surest basis of public opinion. In this country opposition to the extension of the franchise has always been based upon the unfitness of the masses to exercise it, owing to their defective education; whilst at this very hour we are told that India is not ripe for representative Government because the mass of the people are still ignorant and uneducated. These facts and arguments are all focussed in the call of the political reformer to "Educate, educate, educate!"

And when we come to reflect upon the relations between education and religion, we find that although the circumstances may vary, the principles and policy are identical. Not even the most bigoted theologians will now affirm that it is for the advantage of religion that education should be neglected. They may differ as to its form, and some may wish to restrict the amount of certain kinds of knowledge which should be imparted, lest it should lead to inquiry into dogmas which they think should be accepted on trust; but each religious denomination has by this time arrived at the conviction that if its members be kept in ignorance of what the rest of the world knows, it means decadence and extinction for that denomination and—as in everything else—the survival of the fittest; so all are eager to profit by State endowments, although, as we have seen, all are not equally prepared to accept the conditions upon which they are granted.

And finally education treated as an abstract subject, call it what you will, "the science of education," or "comparative education," presents itself as an intensely interesting and absorbing study, for the elucidation of which the materials are being actively collected and collated by a thousand busy pens and brains. Nothing can be more fascinating than to follow the development of the intellect of peoples of varying tastes and occupations ; here of a nation enjoying peculiar physical or geographical advantages ; there of another surrounded by the grandest natural phenomena ; or again of an emigrant race, forced by political or religious exigencies to quit the soil of their ancestors, and carrying with them the impress of their past history, to wander far away and settle down in a distant land and under new and untried conditions. Here Art reigns supreme ; there Commerce rules ; and elsewhere Agriculture has ever been the national industry. How have these nations trained their youth in the past? How do they propose to train them in the future to fit them for the battle of life under the ever-changing conditions of civilisation ? All nations, especially all civilised peoples of the earth, are rapidly merging into one great human family, not any longer in the biological sense only, but in their intellectual and moral nature ; and this fusion will be undoubtedly accelerated by the extension of knowledge, the interchange of national thought and experiences, and the adoption of common methods of educating the young.

How heartily should we rejoice, if in gathering together in these pages a few of the materials for the study of "comparative education" we could feel that we have given ever so slight an impulse to the expansion of that unlimited faculty in Man which, we believe, exalts him high above all known created beings.

BIBLIOGRAPHY.

The following are the titles of a few Works and Reports which will be found useful to the reader who desires to make himself fully acquainted with the branches of education of which they treat. Most of them have been contributed by the authors of the preceding articles: for the French list we are indebted to M. Buisson, Councillor of State, Director of Primary Instruction in the Ministry of Education, Paris; and for the Reports on Swedish, Norwegian, and Danish instruction, to the respective Departments in those countries. Without instituting any comparison between the various excellent Reports on Continental education, we desire particularly to draw attention to that of Dr. Laishley, of Wellington, New Zealand, on the educational systems of several leading Continental States, which, we think, should be reprinted for the benefit of readers and students in the Mother Country. Most of the titles of Educational Journals have been extracted from the remarkable and interesting "Insertions Kalender" of Mr. Rudolf Mosse (Berlin: London Agency, 16 & 18, Victoria Street); and we have to thank many friends both at home and abroad for the assistance they have rendered to us in the compilation of what must necessarily be a very incomplete list of recent Works and Reports on Education.

ENGLAND.*
    Reports of the Education Department. 1839—1889.
    Report of the Royal Commission on Education.
    Report of the Royal Commission on Technical Instruction.
    "The Schools for the People." By George C. T. Bartley. Bell & Daldy.

SCOTLAND.
    Reports of Scotch Education Department. 1872—1889.
    Parochial Law. By Alexander Dunlop, Advocate. 1841.
    Compendium of the Laws of the Church of Scotland. 1830.
    Reports of Commission of Inquiry on Schools in Scotland. 1865—66.
    Report of Commission on Endowed Schools and Hospitals in Scotland. 1873.
    Reports of Commission on Endowed Institutions in Scotland. 1880—81.
    Report of Scottish Educational Endowment Commissioners. 1882—1889.
    Reports of Board of Education in Scotland. 1873—1878.
    The State and Education. By H. Craik. (Citizen Series) 1884.

* See also "Technical," etc.

IRELAND.
Reports of Commissioners of National Education. 1834 to 1888.
Evidence taken by Committee of House of Lords on Education in Ireland. 1837.
Evidence taken by Committee of House of Commons. 1837.
Evidence taken by Committee of House of Lords. 1854.
Report of Royal Commission on Science and Art. 1866.
Report of Royal Commission on Primary Education in Ireland (Powis). 1868-1870.
Report of Select Committee on Education, Science and Art. 1884.
Report of Royal Commission on Industrial and Reformatory Schools. 1884.
Report of Royal Commission on Education. 1887.
Report of Royal Commission on the Deaf, Dumb and Blind. 1889.

FRANCE.
Michel Bréal.—Quelques mots sur l'instruction publique en France. Paris, Hachette, in-12°.
Félix Pécaut.—Études au jour le jour sur l'éducation nationale. Paris, Hachette, in-12°.
Jules Simon.—L'École. Paris, Hachette, in-12°.
O. Gréard.—Éducation et instruction : Enseignement primaire ; enseignement secondaire, enseignement supérieur. Paris, Hachette, 4 vols. in-12°.
Anthoine.—À travers nos écoles. Paris, Hachette, in-12°.
Leysseune (P.).—Tableau général de l'enseignement primaire public et privé à ses divers degrés. Paris, Impr. Nat¹ᵉ., 1889, in-8vo.
Buisson (F.).—Dictionnaire de pédagogie et d'instruction primaire. 1ᵉʳᵉ Partie.—Encyclopédie théorique et historique de l'instruction primaire. 2ᵉ Partie.—Encyclopédie pratique de l'enseignement primaire. Paris, Hachette, 4 vol. in-8vo.
Marion (H.).—Mouvement des idées pédagogiques en France depuis 1870. Paris, Impr. Nat¹ᵉ., 1889, in-8vo.
En général, consulter la Collection des Mémoires et documents scolaires publiés par le Musée Pédagogique. 1ᵉʳᵉ et 2ᵉ Séries.

Législation Scolaire.

Pichard.—Nouveau Code de l'instruction primaire. Paris, Hachette, in-12°.
Martel (F.).—Législation et réglementation de l'enseignement primaire. (1878 à 1888). Paris, Impr. Nat¹ᵉ., 1889, in-8vo.

Education of Women.

Paul Broca.—Rapport fait au Sénat au nom de la Commission chargé d'examiner le projet de loi adopté par la Chambre des Députés sur l'enseignement secondaire des jeunes filles.
Journal Officiel, 21 Nov. 1880, 10 Dec. 1880, et 17 Dec. 1880.
Comptes Rendus des Séances du Congrès Français et International du Droit des Femmes. Dentu, 3 Place Valois, Paris.

BIBLIOGRAPHY.

FRANCE—*continued.*

Aubert, Inspecteur primaire de Lille ; et *P. Vincent*, Inspecteur Primaire de la Seine.—Législation et Administration de l'enseignement primaire, Code annoté des lois organiques. Fernand Nathan, 18 Rue de Condé.

Enseignement primaire public à Paris, 1877—1888.

Les Ecoles Maternelles ; les Ecoles élémentaires. Ville de Paris, à la direction de l'Enseignement Primaire.

Rapport adressé au Président de la République par le Ministre de l'Instruction Publique au sujet de la statistique de l'enseignement secondaire, de 1876 à 1889.

Sée, Camille.—Proposition de loi sur l'enseignement secondaire des jeunes filles, présenté à la Chambre des Députés.

Rapport de M. *Camille Sée*, présenté à la Chambre des Députés sur l'instruction secondaire des jeunes filles.

Journal Officiel du 16 Dec. 1879, du 20 Janvier, 1880, et du 21 Janvier, 1880.

GERMANY.

Monnier, Frédéric.—L'instruction populaire en Allemagne, en Suisse, &c. Paris, 1867, 8vo.

Kehr, C.—Geschichte der Methodik des deutschen Volksschulunterrichtes, 4 M. Gotha, 1877—1882, 8vo.

Kaemmel, H. J.—Geschichte des deutschen Schulwesens in Uebergange. Leipzig, 1882, 8vo.

Davis, G. B.—Report on Schools in Germany and Switzerland. Birmingham, 1879, 8vo. Houghton & Hammond.

Perry, C. J.—Reports on German Elementary Schools and Training Colleges. Rivingtons, 1887.

BELGIUM.

Discailles, E.—Histoire des concours généraux de l'enseignement. 3 tom. P. Weissenbach, Bruxelles, 1882—83, 8vo.

Monthaye, P. A.—Code de l'instruction primaire de Belgique. E. Gailliard, Bruges, 1873, 8vo. New edition, 1878.

Stasse, Alexis.—Code administratif de l'enseignement primaire en Belgique. G. Thiriat, Liège, 1881, 12°.

Barnard.—National Education, pt. ii., pp. 369 to 401.

ITALY.

Giordano, M.—Dell' istruzione pubblica in Italia. Napoli, 1882, 8vo.

Boschi, G.—La Scuola elementare. Napoli, 1882, 8vo.

Documenti sull' istruzione elementare nel Regno d'Italia. 3 vols. Florence, 1868, &c.

Statistica dell' istruzione elementare pubblica e privata in Italia. Roma, 1881.

Celesia, Emanuele.—Storia della pedagogia Italiana. 2 vols., Milano, 1872—4, 8vo.

SWITZERLAND.

Statistique sur l'instruction publique en Suisse pour l'année 1881, &c. 7 tom. Zurich. (Tom. 1—3, Statistiques des écoles primaires. Tom. 4, Écoles enfantines, écoles d'adultes, écoles professionnelles. Tom. 5, Écoles moyennes et écoles supérieures, académies, universités. Tom. 6, Tables. Tom. 7, Législation scolaire.)

Hunziker, Dr. O.—Geschichte der Schweizerischen Volksschule. F. Schulthess, Zurich, 1880—82, 8vo.

Kinkelin.—Statistik des Unterrichtswesens in der Schweiz im Jahre, 1871. 7 vols. Basel, 1874, &c., 8vo.

SWEDEN.

H. Klinghardt.—Das höhere Schulwesen Schwedens und dessen Reform in modernem Sinne. Leipzig, 1887.

Dictionnaire de Pédagogie et d'Instruction, publié sous la direction de F. Buisson. Paris, Libraire Hachette et Comp. (art. Suède).

Encyclopädie des gesammten Erziehungs- und Unterrichtswesens, herausgegeb. von K. A. Schmid. Leipzig, 1887 (art. Schweden).

Stadga angående folkundervisningen. 18 Juni, 1842.

Reglor för folkskolelärare seminarierna i riket. 1 December, 1865.

Stadga för rikets elementarläroverk. 29 Jan. 1859.

Akademi Statuter. 2 April, 1852.

NORWAY.

Lov om Almueskolevæsenet. i Kjöbstæderne, 12 Juli, 1848.

Lov om Almueskolevæsenet paa Landet. 16 Mai, 1860.

Lov om offentlige Skoler for den höiere Almuedannelse. 17 Juni, 1869.

Lov indeholdende Fundats for det Kongelige norske Fredriks Universitet i Christiania. 28 Juli, 1827.

DENMARK.

Plan for Undervisningen i Kjøbenhavns Kommunes offentlige Skoler. Schultz, Copenhagen, 1888.

Beretning om det Kjøbenhavnske Borger- og Almueskolevæsens Tilstand for Aaret 1888. Schultz, Copenhagen, 1889.

EUROPE (GENERAL).

Laishley.—Report on State Education in Great Britain, France, Switzerland, &c., &c., &c., and the U.S.A.; with a special report upon Deaf Mute Instruction.* Wellington, New Zealand, 1886.

Arnold, Matthew.—Schools and Universities on the Continent. Macmillan, London, 1868, 8vo.

* For information concerning the Oral Instruction of the Deaf, see the various works of Van Praagh, of Fitzroy Square Training College.

EUROPE (GENERAL)—*continued.*
Barnard, Henry.—National Education in Europe. Case, Tiffany & Co., Hartford, 1854, 8vo.
Klemm, L. R., Ph.D.—European Schools, or what I saw in the Schools of Germany, France, Austria and Switzerland. D. Appleton.

THE UNITED STATES.
Report to the Schools Inquiry Commissioners (Blue Book). Rev. James Fraser, 1867.
The Free School System of the United States. Francis Adams, 1875.
Cyclopædia of Education. Kiddle & Schem, New York, 1883.
Cyclopædia of Education. Sonnenschein, London, 1889.
Notes on American Schools and Training Colleges (Blue Book). Dr. J. G. Fitch, H.M.I., 1889.
Reports of the Commissioner of Education, U.S.A. Washington, 1886—1888.
Report of the Royal Commission on the Elementary Education Acts. Foreign Returns (Blue Book), 1888.
Report of the Massachusetts Board of Education. Boston, 1887—88.
Education. Monthly Magazine edited by Wm. A. Mowry. Boston 1880—1889.
City School Systems in the U.S. Dr. John D. Philbrick (Government Publication), 1885.
Rural Schools : Progress and Means of Improvement (Government Publication), 1884.

CANADA.
Report to the Schools Inquiry Commissioners (Blue Book). Rev. James Fraser, 1867.
Cyclopædia of Education. Sonnenschein, London, 1889.
Educational System of the Province of Ontario (Government Publication). Toronto, 1886.
The Schools of Greater Britain. John Russell, London, 1888.
Report of the Royal Commission on the Elementary Education Acts. Foreign Returns (Blue Book), 1888.

AUSTRALIA.
Report of the State of Public Education in Victoria. Chas. H. Pearson, Melbourne, 1878.
Report of the Minister of Public Instruction, Victoria. Melbourne, 1886—87.
Acts and Regulations of the Education Department, South Australia. Adelaide, 1885.
The Schools of Greater Britain. John Russell, London, 1888.

AUSTRALIA—*continued*.
>Impressions of Australia: Education. Dr. R. W. Dale (Article in the Contemporary Review). London, Feb. 1889.
>Report of the Royal Commission on the Elementary Education Acts. Foreign Returns (Blue Book), 1888.

INDIA.
>Report of the Indian Education Commission. Government Press, Calcutta, 1883.
>Collection of Despatches from the Home Government on the subject of Education in India, 1854 to 1868. Being Volume LXXVI. of Selections from the Records of the Government of India, Home Department.
>A Note on the State of Education in India during 1865—66, by Mr. A. M Monteith, C.S. Being Volume LIV. of Selections from the Records of the Government of India, Home Department.
>A Note on the State of Education in India during 1866—67, by Mr. A. P. Howell, C.S. Being Volume LXVII. of Selections from the Records of the Government of India, Home Department.
>Review of Education in India in 1886, with special references to the Report of the Education Commission, by Sir Alfred Croft, K.C.I.E., M.A., Director of Public Instruction, Bengal, Calcutta. Printed by the Superintendent of Government Printing. India, 1888.
>Decennial Statement of the Moral and Material Progress and Condition of India, presented to Parliament (1885) by J. S. Cotton, Esq., M.A., formerly Fellow of Queen's College, Oxford (Blue Book).
>Statement exhibiting the Moral and Material Progress and Condition of India during the years 1887—88. Twenty-fourth Number (Blue Book).

TECHNICAL AND GENERAL.
>Report of the Royal Commissioners on Technical Instruction, 1884.
>Report of the Special Committee on the Subjects and Modes of Instruction in the Board Schools (School Board for London), 1888.
>Report of the Royal Commission on the wording of the Education Acts, 1888.
>Special Report of Mr. Arnold on certain points connected with Elementary Education in Germany, France and Switzerland, 1886.
>Report of the Commissioner of Education for the year 1887-88. Washington, 1889.
>Technical Education in Europe. First Part. Industrial Education in France. By J. Schoenhof. Washington, 1888.
>*Galloway.*—Education, Scientific and Technical. Trübner, 1881.
>*Magnus.*—Industrial Education. Kegan Paul, 1888.
>*Compayré, G.*—The History of Pedagogy. Translated by W. H. Payne, M.A. Swan Sonnenschein, 1888.

BIBLIOGRAPHY. 169

PHYSICAL, MUSICAL, AND INFANT TRAINING.

Watkins, A.—Singing in Elementary Schools: a course of lectures. J. Curwen & Sons, London, 1885, 8vo.

Hoskins, A. B.—Singing in Schools. A complete course of practical teaching. Bemrose & Sons, London, 1885, 8vo.

Moore, H. R.—Music in the Kindergarten. Sonnenschein, London, 1881, 8vo.

Goldammer, H.—The Kindergarten. Williams & Norgate, London, 1882, 8vo.

Löfving, Concordia.—Physical Education, and its place in system of Education. Sonnenschein, London, 1882, 8vo.

Leny's Swedish Gymnastics for Schools. Hachette, London, 1885, 8vo.

Shirreff, Emily.—The Kindergarten. Principles of Froebel's System. Sonnenschein, London, 1883, 8vo.

Essays on the Kindergarten delivered before the Froebel Society. Sonnenschein, London, 1880, 8vo.

Philip's Music Series. Philip & Son.

(See also "Switzerland," p. 166.)

A FEW EDUCATIONAL JOURNALS.

GREAT BRITAIN AND IRELAND.

London.—The School Guardian.
　,,　　The School Board Chronicle.
　,,　　The Schoolmaster.
Edinburgh.—Educational News.
Dublin.—Irish Teachers' Journal.

GERMANY, AUSTRIA, AND SWITZERLAND.

Aachen (Aix-la-Chapelle).—Rheinisch-Westfälische Schulzeitung.
Baden-Baden.—Badische Fortbildungsschule.
Berlin.—Deutsche Schulzeitung.
　,,　　Neue Deutsche Schulzeitung.
　,,　　Preussische Schulzeitung.
　,,　　Zeitschrift für Gewerblichen Unterricht.
　,,　　Deutsche Lehrerzeitung.
Bern.—Berner Schulblatt.
Breslau.—Katholische Schulzeitung für Norddeutschland.
Budapest.—Ungarischer Schulbote.
Dresden.—Pädagogische Studien.
Elberfeld.—Der Kinderfreund.
St. Gallen.—Amtliches Schulblatt.
Hamburg.—Pädagogische Reform.
Hanover.—Han. Schulzeitung.
Innsbruck.—Tiroler Schulfreund.

Leipzig.—Sächsische Schulzeitung.
„ Allgemeine deutsche Lehrerzeitung.
(And many more excellent educational journals.)
Mannheim.—Neue Badische Schulzeitung.
Prag.—Beseda ucitelska.
Stuttgart.—Die Volksschule.
Vienna.—Die Volksschule.
„ Œsterreichischer Schulbote.
„ Die Bürger Schule.
„ Niederœsterreichische Schulzeitung.
Zurich.—Schweitzerisches Schularchiv.
„ Die Praxis der Schweiz : Volks u. Mittelschule.

OTHER CONTINENTAL CITIES AND TOWNS.

Amsterdam.—Het nieuwe Schoolblad.
Copenhagen.—Dansk Laedeforenings Medlemsblad.
Paris.—Le Journal des Instituteurs.
„ L'École des Communes.
Rome.—La Scuola elementare.
Stockholm.—Svensk Läreretidning.
Warsaw.—Swiat (The World).

UNITED STATES AND CANADA.

Boston.—Journal of Education.
Chicago.—School Herald.
Cincinnati.—Academica.
Indianopolis.—School News.
Milwaukie.—Erziehungs Blätter.
Montreal.—Educational Record.
New York.—School Journal.
„ El Educador Popular.
„ College Mercury.
Quebec.—Journal de l'Instruction Publique.
San Francisco.—Pacific School Journal.
Toronto.—Canada School Journal.

INDEX.

ABERDEEN University, 53
Act, Education, of 1870...30, 32-34
—— Educational Endowments, of 1882... 52, 53
—— Scotch Education, of 1872...49
Acts, Education, 30
—— Factory, 41, 42
—— Reformatory and Industrial Schools, 41, 42
Adam, Mr., Report on indigenous village schools of Bengal, 5
Almsgiving in India, 19, 20
Andrews, St., University, 53
Argyllshire, Scarcity of Schools in, 46
Armstrong, Lord, on education, 135
—— On manual training, 142
Arnold, Matthew, On English and Continental Schools, 134, 135
Auckland, Lord, and State Education in India, 5
Australia, Boards of Advice in, 110
—— Education in, 109-111
—— Education Department in, powers of, 109, 110
—— Pupil teacher system in, 111
—— South, Education not free in, 109
—— West, Education not free in, 109
Australian Colonies essentially democratic, 109

BACHELLERY, Madame, and her High Schools for girls, 121
Banking in India, 23
Barnard, Dr. Henry, 102
Bartlett, Rev. Miss Carrie J., 130
Belgium, School attendance not compulsory in, 78
—— Schools in, and religious instruction, 74, 75
Benares, Sanskrit College at, founded, 3
Bengal, Effects of State Education in, 10-12
—— Hindus in public offices in, 8, 9
—— Mr. Adam's Report on indigenous village schools of, 5
Bengalis, The, 11, 12, 18, 19
Blanche of Castille, 117
Boards of Advice in Australia, 110
Bombay Education Society, 4
Bonaparte decrees primary schools for boys, 120
"Book of Policy," 45
Boston, Girls' English High School at, 94

Boston, Girls' Latin High School at, 94
—— English High School at, 93
—— Latin High School at, 93
British and Foreign School Society, 26
—— Columbia, Education compulsory in, 108
—— —— Education free in, 108
Bryn Mawr University, 130
Buddhist Monasteries and education, 3
Building grants in Ireland, Difficulties regarding, 60

CALCUTTA, Hindu College, 4
—— Sanskrit College, founded, 4
—— School Society, 4
Canada, All teachers adults in, 108
—— Education in, 105-109
—— Education in, under provincial and local control, 106
—— Normal Schools in, supported by the Provincial Government, 108
—— Pupil-teacher system unknown in, 108
Carnot's scheme of National Education,'120
Chicago, Female Medical College at, 130
Code, Changes required in the, 141
—— New, for 1890...146-154
—— —— Assistant teachers, 152
—— —— Certificated Teachers, 152
—— —— Class Subjects, 148
—— —— Evening Schools, 153
—— —— Examinations of Scholars, 149
—— —— General Conditions of, 146, 147
—— —— Grants, 149, 150
—— —— Manual Instruction, 148
—— —— Military Drill, 148
—— —— Physical Exercises, 148
—— —— Pupil Teachers, 150, 151
—— —— Small Schools, 153, 154
—— —— Staff, 150
—— —— Subjects of Instruction, 147, 148
—— —— Training Colleges, 152, 153
—— Revised, introduced by Mr. Lowe, 29
—— Scotch, 50, 51
Colleges, Denominational Training, in Ireland, 70
—— Training, under Code 1890, 152, 153

INDEX.

Common School open to all classes in United States, 86
—— System in America, 83
—— Universal in United States, 84, 85
Condorcet recommends Secondary State Schools, 120
Convent Boarding-schools for Girls in France, 122
Cyr, St., Limits of age, and subjects taught at, 119
—— Racine at, 119

DALHOUSIE, Lord, and Vernacular Schools, 5, 6
—— Measures of, for development of India, 12
Deaf and Dumb Training in England, 156, 157
Denmark, Gratuitous Instruction in, 78, 79
—— Religious Instruction in Schools, 75
Deraismes, Maria, 128
Desrandes, Abbé, and his Scheme for Public Instruction, 119
Diane de Poitiers, 118
Dupanloup, M., and his articles in *Le Correspondent*, 124
Duruy, M., and the Education of Women, 124, 125

EAST INDIA COMPANY and Education, 3
Edinburgh University, 53
Education, Commercial, in England, 112–115
—— Commission of Lord Ripon, 13–18
—— Department in Australia, Powers of, 109, 110
—— Elementary, English and Continental Systems compared, 74–81
—— Elementary, in England, 26–43
—— Elementary, in England contrasted with other Countries, 31
—— Elementary, in England, First grant by Parliament in aid of, 27
—— Elementary, in Scotland, 44–45
—— English and United States' Systems of, compared, 82–104
—— Female in India, 16, 17
—— Free, in Ireland, 72, 73
—— Gratuitous, in England, 157, 158
—— in Canada, 105–109
—— in Australia, 109–111
—— Lord Armstrong on, 135
—— Modern, in India and Ancient Civilisation, 1–24

Education, National, in Ireland, 56–73
—— National, in Ireland, and its results, 57–60
—— Professor Huxley on, 135
—— State, destroys Musalman influence in India, 7, 8
—— State, Immediate effects of, in India, 7
—— State, in Bengal, Effects of, 10–12
—— State Board of, in United States, Function of, 85
—— State Boards of, in United States, 83, 84
—— Technical, in England, 80
England, Absence of physical training in schools of, 79, 80
—— Board Schools in, and religious instruction, 34, 35, 76
—— Church of England Schools and religious instruction, 76
—— Commercial Education in, 112–115
—— Deaf and dumb training in, 156, 157
—— Elementary Education in, 26–43
—— Grammar Schools in, 25, 26
—— Gratuitous education in, 78, 79, 157, 158
—— Roman Catholic Schools in, and religious instruction, 76, 77
—— School attendance compulsory in, 78
—— Training Schools in, 81
—— Technical Education in, 80
English language the medium of higher instruction in India, 6

FEMALE artists in America, 131
—— education in India, 16, 17
Foreign correspondents in England, 113
France, Convent boarding-schools for girls in, 122
—— Instruction gratuitous in, 78
—— Manual instruction in, 142
—— Manual technical instruction in Primary Schools of, 80
—— Religious instruction in schools, 75, 76
—— Salaries of teachers in, 127
—— School attendance compulsory in, 78
—— Statistics of women employed on railways, &c., 128
—— System of inspection in, 140
—— Three grades of inspectors in, 140
—— Women in, 116–128
Froebellian system in United States, 87

INDEX.

GEORGE HERIOT's Hospital, 53
Germany and gratuitous instruction. 78
—— and religious instruction, 74
—— and trade schools, 80
—— School attendance compulsory in, 77
Gladstone, Dr., statistics of, 136
Glasgow University, 53
Gordon's College, Aberdeen, 53
Grant, Municipal, in Canada. 107
Grants to schools in England, 36 38
—— under Code 1890...149, 150
Guizot, and his bill for primary instruction, 121
Gupta, Mr. Das, 16

HASTINGS, WARREN, establishes the Calcutta Madrasa, 3
Hindu, Position of, 20, 21
—— Society, moral changes at work, 20, 21
Hinduism, Modern, character of, 19
Hindus, The, in public offices, 8, 9
—— Progress of the, in industrial life, 21-23
Hutcheson's Schools, Glasgow, 53
Huxley, Professor, on Education, 135

INDIA, Almsgiving in, 19, 20
—— Ancient civilisation and modern education in, 1-24
—— Banking in, 23
—— Committee of Public Instruction, 4
—— English Language the medium of higher instruction in, 6
— English rule in, 1-3
—— Female education in, 16, 17
— Immediate effects of State Education in, 7
—— Indian National Congress, 18
—— Lord Dalhousie and Vernacular Schools, 5, 6
—— Musalman influence destroyed by State Education in, 7, 8
—— Religion in, 19
—— Secondary Schools in, 6
—— Sir Stafford Northcote's despatch, the Charter of Education in, 5
—— Standards of the pass-examination in Universities of, 15, 16
—— Statistics of School Attendance in, 6, 7
—— Statistics of Universities in, 15
—— Vernacular Schools the foundation of Public Instruction, 5
Inspection, System of, in France, 140

Inspectors in France, 140
Inverness-shire, Scarcity of schools in, 46
Ireland, Agricultural Schools in, 71, 72
—— Building Grants in, difficulties regarding, 60
—— Compulsory School Attendance in, 72
—— Denominational Training Colleges in, 70
—— Free Education in, 72, 73
—— Model Schools in, 71
—— Monitorial System in, 69
—— National Education in, 56-73
—— National Education in, and its results, 57-60
—— Organisers of Schools appointed, 69
—— Pay of Teachers in, 63, 64
—— Protestant Charter Schools established, 56
—— Protestant Diocesan Schools established, 56
—— Queen's Scholars in, 69, 70
—— Results-Fees, Scale of, 67, 68
—— Results System in, 66
—— School Books in, difficulties regarding, 60
—— School Books in, supply of, 70, 71
—— School Inspection, 62, 63
—— School Management in, 61, 62
—— Training of Teachers in, 69, 70
Italy, Attendance compulsory in Schools, 78
—— Instruction gratuitous, 78
—— Religious instruction in Schools, 75

JEWS, Female education advanced in France by the, 125

KANSAS gives municipal rights to women, 129
Kildare Place Society, 57
Kindergarten, Advanced, 142, 143
—— Mr. Ricks' exercises for, 143
—— System in United States, 87

LAKANEL's scheme of national education, 120
Lancaster, Joseph, 26
Lancastrian Society, 26
Lexington, First State Normal School established at. 101
Limonnier, Madame, 122, 123
London Chamber of Commerce and Commercial Education, 114

INDEX.

Louis Philippe, No primary State instruction for girls under, 121
Lyceums, Girls', 126

MACAULAY, Lord, Minute of 1835, 4
Maintenon, Madame de, founds St. Cyr, 119
Manitoba, Education compulsory in, 108
—— Education free in, 108
Manual training, 159-161
—— —— Advantage of, 141
—— —— in France, 142
—— —— Lord Armstrong on, 142
—— —— Objectors to, 142
Maráthás, The, 10, 11, 18, 19
Mayo, Lord, and his de-centralisation scheme of Finance, 12, 13
Mecklenburg-Schwerin, Helena, Princess of, 121
Medici, Catherine de, 118
Monitorial System in Ireland, 69
Montreal, Education not free in, 108
—— Schools in, 106
Mosques and education, 3
Musulman influence in India destroyed by State education. 7, 8

NATIONAL Society, 26
New Brunswick, Education not compulsory in, 108
—— Schools in, unsectarian, 107
Newcastle's, Duke of, Commission, Report of, 29
New South Wales, Education not free in, 109
New Zealand, Education free in, 109
Northcote's, Sir Stafford, despatch, the Charter of Education in India, 5
Norway, Attendance compulsory in schools, 77, 78
—— Instruction gratuitous, 78
—— Religious instruction in schools, 75
Nova Scotia, Education compulsory in, 108
—— Education free in, 108

ONTARIO, Education compulsory in, 108
—— Education free in, 107

PARIS, Females in Medical schools of, 126
—— the heaven of the Primary schoolmistress, 128

Paris, Technical Schools for girls in, 122
Payment on results, and Technical Education, 133-145
—— Evils of, 36-38
Philadelphia, High School for Girls at, 101
—— Women's Guilds in, 129
Prince Edward Island, Education compulsory in, 108
—— Education free in, 108
Public Instruction. Committee of, in India. 4
Pupil-Teacher system introduced in England. 28
Pupil-teachers under Code. 1890, 150, 151

QUEBEC, Education not compulsory in, 108
—— Education not free in, 108
Queensland, Education free in, 109
Queen's scholars in Ireland, 69, 70
—— scholarships, 39, 40
Quinet, Edgar, 121

RACINE at St. Cyr. 119
Religion in India. 19
Religious instruction in Belgian Schools, 74, 75
—— in Board Schools in England, 34, 35, 76
—— in Church of England Schools, 76
—— in Danish Schools, 75
—— in French Schools, 75, 76
—— in German Schools, 74
—— in Italian Schools, 75
—— in Norwegian Schools, 75
—— in Roman Catholic Schools in England, 76, 77
—— in Swedish Schools, 75
—— in Swiss Schools, 74
Ricks', Mr., exercises for advanced Kindergarten, 143
Ripon, Lord, Education Commission of, 13-18

SCHOOL Attendance Committees, 41
—— Attendance in Belgium not compulsory, 78
—— Attendance compulsory in England, 78
—— Attendance compulsory in France, 78
—— Attendance compulsory in Germany, 77

INDEX.

School Attendance compulsory in Ireland, 72
— Attendance compulsory in Italy, 78
— Attendance compulsory in Norway, 77, 78
— Attendance compulsory in Sweden, 77
— Attendance compulsory in Switzerland, 78
— Attendance compulsory in the United States, 96
— Attendance in India, statistics of, 6, 7
— Boards in England, 33-35
— Boards, City, in United States, 84
— Books in Ireland, difficulties regarding, 60
— Books in Ireland, supply of, 70, 71
— Common, in America, 83
— Common, in United States, instruction confined to secular subjects, 97
— Common, in United States, open to all classes, 86
— High, in United States, rule as to admission, 90
— High, in United States, special studies of, 92
— High, in United States and in England, contrasted, 92
— Inspection in Ireland, 62, 63
— Management in Ireland, 61-62
— Teachers in Ireland, pay of, 63, 64
— Teachers in Ireland, training of, 69-70
— Teachers in United States, training of, 99-102
Schools, Agricultural, in Ireland, 71, 72
— Belgian, and religious instruction, 74, 75
— Board, in England, cost of, 35
— Burgh, in Scotland, 47
— Burgh, in Scotland, defects of, 48, 49
— Church of England, and religious instruction, 76
— Danish, and religious instruction, 75
— Day Industrial, in England, 42
— Elementary, in Ontario, free, 107
— English, absence of physical training in, 79, 80
— in England, grants to, 36-38
— English Board, and religious instruction, 34, 35, 76

Schools, English and Continental, Matthew Arnold on, 134, 135
— Evening, under Code, 1890...153
— French, and religious instruction, 75, 76
— German, and religious instruction, 74
— Grammar, in England, 25, 26
— Grammar, in Scotland, 45
— Grammar, in United States, 87, 88
— High, in Ontario, free, 107
— High, in United States, 88-95
— Higher, in Scotland, 51, 52
— Indigenous, in the Punjab, 13
— Indigenous, the basis of the Dept. of Public Instruction in Lower Provinces of India, 13
— Italian, and religious instruction, 75
— Model, in Ireland, 71
— Model, in Ontario, free, 107
— Normal, in United States, 100
— Norwegian, and religious instruction, 75
— Parish, in Scotland, 45-49
— Primary, in United States, 87, 88
— Protestant Charter established in Ireland, 56
— Protestant Diocesan, established in Ireland, 56
— Question of free, 145
— Roman Catholic, in England, and religious instruction, 76, 77
— Secondary in India, 6
— Secondary State, recommended by Condorcet, 120
— Small, under Code, 1890...153, 154
— Swedish, and religious instruction, 75
— Swiss, and religious instruction, 74
— Technical, for girls in Paris, 122
— Trade, in Germany, 80
— Training, in England, 81
— Truants, in England, 43
— Voluntary, and payment by results, 139
Science teaching in schools, 143
— Importance of, 135
Scotland, and free education, 55
— Burgh Schools in, 47
— Burgh Schools in, defects of, 48, 49
— Elementary education in, 44-55
— Grammar Schools in, 45

Scotland, Gratuitous instruction in, 79
—— Higher Schools in, 51, 52
—— Parish Schools in, 45–49
—— Schools Inquiry Commission of 1864...48, 49
—— Universities of, 53, 54
Sée, Camille, 125
Sévigné, Madame de, 118
Society for Promoting Christian Knowledge, 26
State Board of Education in United States, function of, 85
Sweden, Instruction gratuitous in, 78
—— Religious instruction in schools, 75
—— School attendance compulsory in, 77
Switzerland, Instruction gratuitous in, 78
—— Religious instruction in schools, 74
—— School attendance compulsory in, 78

TALLEYRAND, and his scheme for public instruction, 119
Tasmania, Education not free in, 109
Teachers' Institute in United States, 101, 102
—— Salaries of, in France, 127
Technical and Secondary Education, Association for Promotion of, 137
—— Instruction, 133–145, 159–161
—— Instruction, Royal Commission on, 1881...133
—— Schools for girls in Paris, 122
Toronto, University of, education almost gratuitous at, 108
Training Colleges in Ontario free, 107

UNITED STATES, Absence of physical training in schools of, 79
—— and compulsory school attendance, 96
—— and English systems of education compared, 82–104
—— and religious school instruction, 98
—— City School Boards in, 84
—— Common Schools, instruction confined to secular subjects, 97
—— Common School in, open to all classes, 86

United States, Common School system in, 83
—— Common School universal in, 84, 85
—— Each State responsible for the education of its population, 83
—— Free books and stationery movement in, 96
—— Froebellian system in, 87
—— Grammar Schools in, 87, 88
—— High Schools in, 88–95
—— High Schools in, rule as to admission, 90
—— High School in, special studies of, 92
—— High School in, and in England contrasted, 92
—— Instruction gratuitous in, 95
—— Kindergarten system in, 87
—— Normal Schools in, 100
—— Primary Schools in, 87, 88
—— State Boards of Education in, 83, 84
—— State Board of Education, function of, 85
—— Teachers' Institute in, 101, 102
—— Training of Teachers in, 99–102
Universities in India, standards of the pass-examination, 15, 16
—— Statistics of, 15

VERNACULAR Schools in India the foundation of Public Instruction, 5
Victoria, Education free in, 109

WAHÁBÍ State Trials, 9
Watson's College, Edinburgh, 53
Women, and the French Revolution, 119
—— Education and status of, 116–132
—— Employed in Journalism, 131
—— Guilds in Philadelphia, 129
—— in France, 116–128
—— Medical College at Chicago, 130
—— Municipal rights in Kansas, 129
—— Statistics of employment of, in France, 128
—— Suffrage in United States, 129
Women's Christian Temperance Union, 129
Wyoming, Territory of, Woman's Suffrage in, 129

YOLANDE, Queen of Sicily, 117
Young's, Lord, Scotch Education Act of 1872...49

FINIS.

BRADBURY, AGNEW, & CO., PRINTERS, WHITEFRIARS.

www.ingramcontent.com/pod-product-compliance
Lightning Source LLC
Chambersburg PA
CBHW020248170426
43202CB00008B/283